The History of Our United States

Fourth Edition

A Beka Book® Pensacola, FL 32523-9100
an affiliate of PENSACOLA CHRISTIAN COLLEGE®

A Beka Book®
History and Geography Series in Christian Perspective

K *Social Studies K*
Grade 1 *My America and My World*
2 *Our America*
3 *Our American Heritage*
4 **The History of Our United States**
5 *Old World History and Geography*
6 *New World History and Geography*

(Support materials and Grades 7–12 materials also available.)

The History of Our United States
Fourth Edition

Staff Credits
Author: Judy Hull Moore
Edition Editor: Christina Kelley
Contributors: Joshua Birx, Denis McBride, Tracy Glockle
Designer: Stan Shimmin
Illustrators: Paul DeLuna, Becca Huber

Copyright © mmviii, mcmxcviii, mcmxc, mcmlxxxi Pensacola Christian College
All rights reserved. Printed in U.S.A. 2010 C10

No part of this publication may be reproduced or transmitted in any form or by any means, electronic or mechanical, including photocopy, recording, or any information storage and retrieval system, or by license from any collective or licensing body, without permission in writing from the publisher.

A Beka Book, a Christian textbook ministry affiliated with Pensacola Christian College, is designed to meet the need for Christian textbooks and teaching aids. The purpose of this publishing ministry is to help Christian schools reach children and young people for the Lord and train them in the Christian way of life.

Cataloging Data

Moore, Judy H. (Judy Hull)
        The history of our United States/Judy Hull Moore.—4th edition. Pensacola, Fla.: A Beka Book, 2008.
        iv, 292 p. : ill. ; 28 cm. (A Beka Book history and geography program in Christian perspective)
        Includes Index
        Includes a geography mastery section
        1. United States—History—Study and teaching (Elementary) 2. Geography—Study and teaching (Elementary)
        Library of Congress: E178.1 .B45 H5 2008
Dewey System: 973

Contents

INTRODUCTION:
One Nation Under God

I Pledge Allegiance

I pledge allegiance to the flag of the United States of America and to the Republic for which it stands, one nation under God, indivisible, with liberty and justice for all.

Every school morning, students all over our land rise, face the flag of the United States and with hand over heart, pledge allegiance to the flag. A **pledge** is <u>a promise to do something</u>. **Allegiance** means <u>devotion or loyalty</u>. When you repeat the Pledge, you are promising to be faithful and loyal to your country, the United States of America. You are also saying, "I believe that the flag stands for my country. I believe in a republic where the people choose those who govern them. I believe that our Union of fifty states is united, not divided. I believe that God wants liberty and justice for all people."

This year as you study the history of our United States, you will learn why we promise to be faithful and loyal to our country. You will learn how God has blessed America because of the principles (truths) for which America stands. You will learn to love these wonderful truths that our Declaration of Independence proclaims:

Principles of American Government

1. God has given all men the right to life, liberty, and the pursuit of happiness.

2. It is the job of governments to make sure that these rights are not taken away from the people.

3. The government should not be so powerful that it could take away from the people these God-given rights of life, liberty, and the pursuit of happiness.

One Nation under God

In the beginning, God told men to spread out over the whole earth. He wants people to live and work together as separate **nations.**

People want to do their best when they are serving their nation. In time of war, people even die for their nation. By being willing to die for a noble cause, they show how very different people are from animals. They value not just life, but a noble life. <u>Next to our love of God and family, nothing should be more dear to us than the love and respect we have for our nation</u>.

<u>Each nation has its own government</u>. This way it is easier for people to keep governments in control and serving the purposes for which God set up governments.

Each nation has a language that all the people speak. People cannot live well together in a nation unless they speak a common language. It needs to be a language with rules that everyone knows and follows. This is why we study English grammar in school—so we can learn the rules of our language in order to work with the people in our nation. People come to love their own language very much, and their common language helps them to become attached to their neighbors who speak the same language.

This book is the story of one nation, our nation, the United States of America. You will learn how America came to be a nation, who its famous people have been, and what important events have taken place in America. You will learn some of America's great **documents** (writings), and you will learn how the truths of the Bible made America the greatest nation on the face of the earth. This year you will learn how America became "one nation under God, indivisible, with liberty and justice for all."

All through history men have struggled for freedom and justice and the right to govern themselves. In many countries people have never seen these wonderful ideas come true for them. But the government of America was founded on the wonderful principles that all men are created equal and are equally deserving of liberty and justice. The people who founded our country, our Founding Fathers, said that these truths were so obvious and clear that everyone who heard them would naturally believe and understand them. This is why they said, in the Declaration of Independence, that all men are created equal.

All Men Are Created Equal

Our Founding Fathers believed that God has created us all. Because God has created us all, we are all of equal value to God, they said. All men belong to God, not to any other man or any government. Everyone is not as strong or smart or talented as everyone else. But everyone belongs to God, and everyone is equally responsible to God to

In CONGRESS, July 4, 1776.

A DECLARATION

By the REPRESENTATIVES of the

UNITED STATES OF AMERICA,

In GENERAL CONGRESS ASSEMBLED.

do his duty. No man or government has a right to selfishly take away the rights that God has given to all men equally.

> We hold these truths to be self-evident
> [open and obvious],
> that all men are created equal;
> that they are endowed by their Creator
> with certain unalienable rights;
> that among these are
> life,
> liberty, and
> the pursuit of happiness.

Life, Liberty, and the Pursuit of Happiness

Our Founding Fathers believed that God has given all men the right to **life** and **liberty.** Liberty is **freedom.** It is not freedom to do whatever you want to do, though. We are not free to hurt other people or steal from them. If we were free to do that, we would be taking away *their* freedom. Our country has laws to protect the freedoms of *all* people.

Our Founding Fathers believed that all men should be free to work hard and earn a living for themselves and their families. This is what they called the right to the **pursuit of happiness.**

The Land of the Free

America is often called the Land of the Free. Americans have freedoms that people in many other countries do not have. We should thank God for our freedoms and pray that they will never be taken away from us.

In America we have **freedom of speech**— we do not have to be afraid to say what we believe. We also have **freedom of the press**—we can print things in books and newspapers for everyone to read and think about. We have **freedom of assembly**—we can freely meet together in churches and other meetings.

The most wonderful freedom in America is **freedom of religion.** Parents in America are free to take their children to any church they want to. Americans are free to read the Bible for themselves and openly worship God the way they think is right. Americans are free to preach the gospel throughout our land. America is a nation in which people are free to spread Christianity as well as other religions. We should especially thank God for our freedom of religion and pray that no one will ever take it away from us.

As you study American history this year, you will meet many people who came to America to be free. You will learn about people who were even willing to die to make our country free. And you will learn about people all over our land who have used their freedoms to make new homes, study, write, teach, invent things, build cities, preach the gospel, and serve the people of our United States. You will learn of many things that *you* can do to be a good citizen of the United States of America.

Comprehension Check

1. What are you promising when you pledge allegiance to the flag?

2. What are some of the great American documents? (See pages 250–257.)

3. What is liberty?

4. Do we have freedom to do whatever we want to do? Why not?

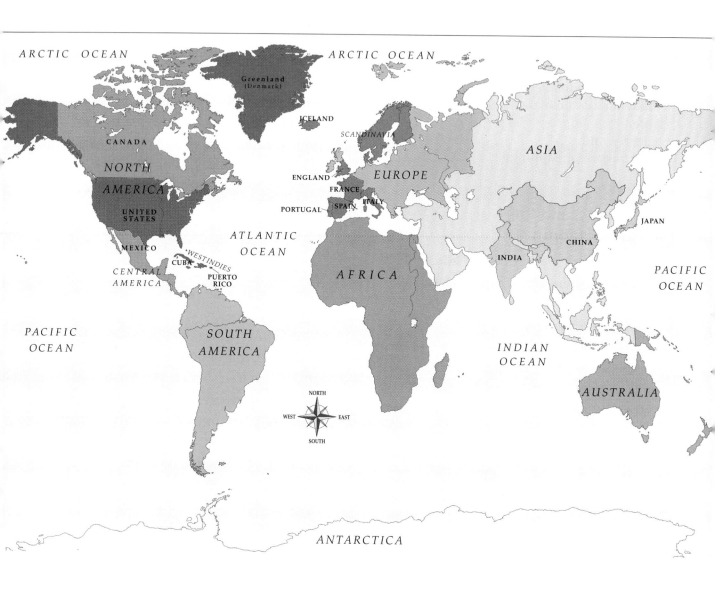

TIME LINE OF IMPORTANT DATES

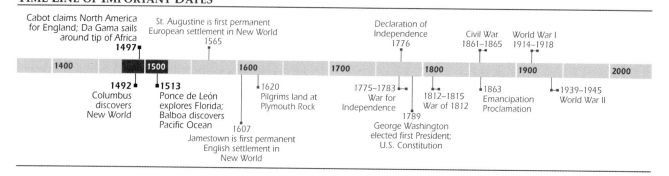

Cabot claims North America for England; Da Gama sails around tip of Africa
1497

St. Augustine is first permanent European settlement in New World
1565

Declaration of Independence
1776

Civil War 1861–1865

World War I 1914–1918

| 1400 | | 1500 | | 1600 | | 1700 | | 1800 | | 1900 | | 2000 |

1492
Columbus discovers New World

1513
Ponce de León explores Florida; Balboa discovers Pacific Ocean

1620
Pilgrims land at Plymouth Rock

1775–1783
War for Independence

1812–1815
War of 1812

1863
Emancipation Proclamation

1939–1945
World War II

1607
Jamestown is first permanent English settlement in New World

1789
George Washington elected first President; U.S. Constitution

The Years of Discovery

Europe:
Where the New World Began

Today the United States of America is one of the largest, wealthiest, and most powerful nations on earth. But for hundreds of years most people in the world did not even know there was an America! The only people who lived in America were Native Americans or Indians. Cities, roads, farms, factories, schools, or churches like we have today did not exist.

History is the story of what has happened in the life of a country or people. The history of America as we know it actually began in Europe [yŏor′əp]. Europe is a **continent,** a large mass of land. There are seven continents on the earth: **Europe, Africa, Asia, Australia, North America** (where the United States is), **South America,** and **Antarctica.** Although Europe is one of the smallest continents, it was responsible for the settlement of America. Brave men from Europe set sail over 500 years ago and found two new continents that came to be known as **North America** and **South America.** Many Europeans came to settle the new lands. **England, France, Spain,** and **Portugal** were the four European countries most responsible for the settlement of America.

See if you can find all seven continents on the world map, p. 4. Did you notice that about three fourths of the earth's surface is covered with water? **Geographers,** people who study the earth call the largest bodies of water **oceans.** There are four oceans: the **Atlantic** (the most heavily-traveled ocean), the **Pacific** (the largest ocean), the **Indian** (the warmest ocean), and the **Arctic** (the coldest and the smallest ocean).

Five hundred years ago, Europeans did not have accurate maps like the maps in this book. They did not know how many continents and oceans are on the earth. Many people *thought* they knew what the earth looked like, but they could only guess. Some people made maps. Many ancient maps do not look anything like the true surface of the earth because they were based on incorrect information.

Columbus Discovers America

One man who thought he knew what the earth's surface looked like was **Christopher Columbus.** Columbus was an Italian from Genoa, **Italy,** who had spent much of his life as a sailor. He had read every book he could find about **geography,** the study of the earth's surface.

Marco Polo was a merchant who had traveled *east* to Cathay **(China)** and had visited the **Khan** [kän′: the ruler of China]. After seeing the great wealth of China, Marco Polo returned to Europe and wrote about the wonders he had seen. Some Europeans did not believe Polo's amazing stories. Others, however, were eager to visit Asia and get some wealth for themselves. Christopher Columbus read and believed Marco Polo's story and devised a plan to sail to **Asia.** He wanted to visit the lands of China and Cipango [sĭ·păng′gō: **Japan**].

Columbus thought that if he sailed *west* from Europe he would eventually come to Asia. If you look again at the map on p. 4, you can easily see what was wrong with his plan: Columbus did not know that when you travel west *two* continents and *two* oceans lie between Europe and Asia. He did not even know the Pacific Ocean existed.

Ferdinand and **Isabella,** the king and queen of Spain, gave Columbus part of the funds that he needed. Columbus prepared three ships—the *Niña* [nē′nyə], the *Pinta*

Christopher Columbus wanted a short route to Asia but instead discovered a New World.

[pēn′tə], and the *Santa Maria* [săn′tə mə·rē′ə]—for the unusual journey.

Finding the ships was not as hard as finding the men to sail the ships. The fearful and superstitious sailors did not want to go with Columbus into an ocean that no one had crossed before. Some of the more uneducated sailors thought that the earth was flat. They were sure that Columbus would fall over the edge of the earth if he sailed too far. Even those who knew the earth was round were afraid that the unknown sea was too big to cross. They were afraid that the men would die of starvation and thirst before they reached Asia. There were also stories about sea monsters that ate ships that wandered too far into unknown waters.

Finally, Columbus found a crew brave enough to go with him and began his first voyage in August 1492. As the three ships disappeared over the horizon, no one was sure if Columbus or his crew would ever be seen again.

New Words
1. **continent**—a large mass of land
2. **oceans**—the largest bodies of water
3. **history**—the story of what has happened in the life of a country or people
4. **geography**—the study of the surface of the earth
5. **Old World**—name given to Europe after America was discovered
6. **New World**—name given to America

New Names
7. **Christopher Columbus**—Italian sailor who discovered America in 1492
8. **Marco Polo**—Italian merchant who visited China and described its riches to Europe
9. *Niña, Pinta, Santa Maria*—the three ships used on Columbus's first voyage
10. **Ferdinand and Isabella**—king and queen of Spain who financed Columbus's voyages
11. **Indians**—name Columbus gave to the people of the New World because he thought he was in India
12. **Vikings**—sea-going Scandinavian people

The *Niña*, *Pinta*, and *Santa Maria*

After two months of sailing west into unknown waters Columbus's crew began to get nervous. There had been no sign of land since they left Europe. No other crew had ever sailed so far away from land. The men grew angry and rebellious. They wanted to turn around and head back to Spain, but Columbus persuaded them to sail on for three more days. On the evening of the second day, land was sighted.

Columbus landed on the island of **San Salvador** on October 12, 1492. Because Columbus thought he had reached **India,** a part of Asia, he referred to the people on the island as **Indians.** Even though Columbus was thousands of miles away from India, the name he gave to the Native Americans remains to this day, and the islands he reached are now called the **West Indies.**

Columbus was interested in the Native Americans, but he was more interested in gold. He asked the Indians where they had gotten the little gold ornaments that almost all of them wore. One place the Indians mentioned was **Cuba.** We know that Cuba is a large island south of Florida, but to Columbus—who thought he was near Asia—the word *Cuba* was the Native Americans' way of saying *Cipango* (Japan).

Columbus landed on the island of San Salvador October 12, 1492.

13. **Leif Ericson**—Viking who was the first European to visit America
14. **John Cabot**—explorer who claimed North America for England in 1497
15. **Amerigo Vespucci**—explorer who was the first to call America a New World
16. **Vasco da Gama**—Portuguese explorer who was the first to sail around the tip of Africa
17. **Vasco de Balboa**—Spanish explorer who claimed the Pacific Ocean for Spain and named it the Great South Sea
18. **Ponce de León**—first European to explore the land that is now the United States; explored and named Florida

New Places
19. **San Salvador**—island in the West Indies where Columbus first landed
20. **Vinland**—Vikings' name for America

New Dates
21. **1000**—Viking explorers visit North America
22. **1492**—Columbus, seeking a route to Asia, discovers America
23. **1497**—Cabot claims North America for England; da Gama sails around the tip of Africa

Columbus visited several islands in the West Indies as he continued his search for gold. On this first journey, Columbus never actually landed on the coast of North or South America.

Columbus lost one ship, the *Santa Maria,* when it hit a reef and sank. With the two remaining ships, Columbus headed back to Spain. Despite furious storms along the way, both ships returned safely to Spain.

Christopher Columbus had accomplished a magnificent feat. His bravery and his skill as a navigator had allowed him to explore new lands and new seas. Columbus became an instant hero. The king and queen gave him a royal welcome. Everyone all over Europe praised Columbus for his bravery and waited eagerly to see what he had brought back from his journey.

Columbus brought back strange plants, brightly colored birds, carvings, and other interesting items. He even brought back several Native Americans. But he brought back very little gold. In truth, Columbus's first journey was a disappointment.

Columbus made three more journeys to America. On each one he showed his superior talents as a navigator. Such was his skill that, using only crude maps and instruments, he could always land at the exact point where he landed on his first journey. He was such a good navigator that he could sail around the waters of the New World as though it were his own back yard. But as years passed, people forgot about the excitement they felt when Columbus returned from his first journey. They lost interest in his later journeys. In 1506 Columbus died, a lonely and forgotten man.

Columbus himself never realized that he had discovered a new world. He always insisted that he had really reached Asia. Columbus also thought that he was claiming new lands for the Catholic Church. He wanted the gold he found there to be used by Spain to conquer the world for that church. But God's plans are not always the same as man's plans.

Columbus was a great man because he showed others the way to do something that was supposedly impossible—sail across the unknown ocean. Other explorers quickly realized what Columbus had found.

Soon after Columbus's early voyages other men sailed west. Columbus led the way for the settlement of the New World, part of which was to become the United States of America. Columbus's daring deeds started a chain of events that would lead to a new country with freedom for all.

Christopher Columbus was not actually the first person to discover America, though his discovery was the one that counts. No one realized in 1492 that Europeans had visited America almost 500 years before Columbus.

The **Vikings,** a group of people from **Scandinavia** (a part of northern Europe), were always short of two things: land and food.

To get food, the Vikings raided countries around them bringing fear to many people. When a Viking ship neared their shores, people knew that the Vikings had come to steal food and possessions.

As the Vikings' population grew, they looked desperately for more lands to settle. This search for land caused the Vikings to make three interesting discoveries. First they found **Iceland,** a small island between Europe and America. Next they found **Greenland,** the largest island in the world. The Vikings established settlements on both of these islands. Then about the year A.D. 1000,

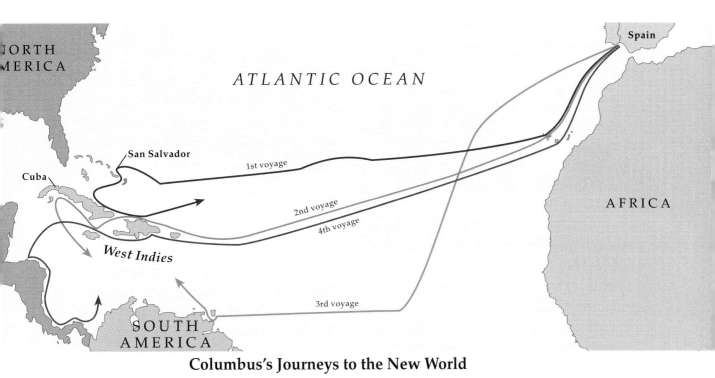

Columbus's Journeys to the New World

a storm blew off course a Viking ship that was traveling from Scandinavia to Greenland. When the ship finally arrived in Greenland, the crew told of a strange land they had seen to the west. A Viking named **Leif Ericson** [lēf ĕr'ĭk·sən] decided to see the new land for himself. <u>Leif Ericson and his crew became the first Europeans to visit America</u>. They probably landed somewhere in **Canada,** although no one is sure exactly where they landed. <u>Leif Ericson named the new land</u> **Vinland** because of all the grape vines the Vikings found there.

After other Vikings went to Vinland and failed to establish a settlement there, the Vikings lost interest in Vinland. Europe had to wait 500 years for the next "discovery" of America.

Why is Columbus more famous than the Vikings? The Vikings kept their discovery a secret; they wanted all the food and land for themselves.

Columbus eagerly shared the news with Europe. His voyages led to the settlement of America by Europeans. Columbus's discovery made a difference in history; the Vikings' discovery did not. The Vikings' discovery of America was a well-kept secret that was almost completely forgotten by history.

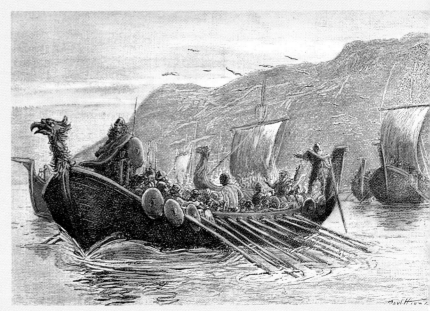

Viking explorers landed on the North American continent 500 years before Columbus reached the New World.

According to an old story, Columbus was having dinner with some rich men not long after he returned from his first voyage. The men, who were jealous of all the attention that Columbus was getting, began to belittle Columbus's achievement by saying that anyone could have done what Columbus did. Columbus picked up an egg and asked the men if they could balance the egg on its end. Each man tried and failed. "It's impossible!" they said. Then Columbus tapped the egg on the table, breaking the shell slightly. When he set the egg on the table, it did not topple over. Columbus looked at the men. "See?" he said. "Even something impossible is easy to do— once someone shows you how."

"It's impossible!"

Comprehension Check 1A

1. What do we call the story of what has happened in the life of a country or people?
2. Who discovered America? When?
3. What was he trying to find?
4. What three ships did he use on his first voyage?
5. Why did he have a difficult time finding sailors willing to make the voyage with him?

North America Is Claimed for England

Excitement was in the air. News had just reached England that Christopher Columbus's voyage had been successful. Everyone believed what Christopher Columbus himself believed—that he had reached the Far East.

John Cabot, an English mapmaker, liked to sail on the Mediterranean Sea and trade goods. Like everyone else, he was eager to find a sea route to the Indies in order to trade goods for more spices. "If Columbus had sailed farther north, he would have found an even shorter route to the Indies," thought Cabot. "If only I could try it myself!"

King Henry VII of England gave Cabot permission. With a crew of only 18 men, Cabot set sail. No one knows for sure where he landed, but it was most likely in a part of what is now Canada. Thinking that he, too, had reached the lands of the Far East, he claimed the land for England. This was <u>the first trip an English ship had made to North America</u>. The year was 1497.

John Cabot's claim would give England the right to begin English colonies in America, though many years would pass before any colonies were established. At the time when the English colonies were started, the Bible was being read and preached all over England. Englishmen were working hard for self-rule and for the right to worship God as they thought the Bible teaches. The English people who would finally come to America would bring with them biblical ideas that would be used to make our country a land of freedom.

America Gets Its Name

After news of Columbus's discovery spread, other sea captains lost their fear of sailing across the Atlantic Ocean. They were eager to make their own discoveries. One such explorer, an Italian named **Amerigo Vespucci** [ä′mä·rē′gō vĕs·poo′chē], claimed that he had crossed the Atlantic Ocean four times between 1497 and 1500. He wrote a letter saying, "I have found a new world." Like Columbus, he had reached South America, but unlike Columbus, he realized that this could not possibly be part of the Indies.

Although Columbus really found the New World before Vespucci, Vespucci was the first person to call it the "New World." To Europeans, the land Columbus discovered and the land Vespucci discovered were two different places! From that time on, Europeans spoke of the land Amerigo Vespucci had found as the **New World.**

In 1507, a German mapmaker did not know what name to give the New World. After reading Vespucci's letters, the mapmaker decided to name the New World "America" to honor the man he thought had discovered it—Amerigo Vespucci.

At first the name "America" meant only South America. With the passing years, as other explorers found out that there were two continents, the name "America" meant both North and South America. Within 30 years, the **Old World** (Europe) realized that Columbus, not Vespucci, had discovered the **New World** (America). However, the name "America" remained.

The people of the Old World still believed they could find a faster sea route to the rich Indies from America. To find this route, men tried to get around America. They tried to find a river through America. Little by little, they began to realize the enormous size of the New World. Columbus's discovery was leading to greater discoveries in the history of America.

In 1507, a map like this was the first to use the name "America" for the New World. America lies near the center of this map; as you can see, the mapmaker had very little idea of what America actually looked like.

1. What explorer claimed North America for England in 1497?

2. What explorer first called America a "New World"?

3. What name was used to refer to Europe once the New World was discovered?

Did Anyone Ever Really Find a Sea Route to the Indies?

Before Columbus ever sailed, sea captains from **Portugal** talked about reaching India by sailing around Africa. Even after Columbus claimed he had reached the Indies in 1492, the Portuguese sea captains went ahead with their plans to sail around Africa.

On July 8, 1497, four Portuguese ships, commanded by **Vasco da Gama** [väs′kō dä gä′mä], sailed south in the Atlantic Ocean, below the tip of Africa, and then north to India.

When Vasco da Gama returned to Portugal, his ships carried the spices and goods from India. Da Gama's discovery gave Europe a much faster and cheaper way to get the spices and goods it had longed for.

Vasco da Gama made a great discovery for Europe by finding a way to <u>sail around Africa to get to India</u>. Although Europe did not realize it yet, Christopher Columbus had also made a great discovery for Europe by discovering America. While Portugal interested itself in developing a good trade with the Indies, Spain interested itself in the New World.

A New Ocean Is Found

Many Spanish explorers sailed to the New World to find as much gold and wealth as they could. One of these explorers was **Vasco de Balboa** [väs′kō dä băl·bō′ə]. Balboa treated the Spanish men who worked for him fairly. He also treated the Native Americans with kindness and soon won their friendship. The Indians began to tell Balboa wonderful things about their land. They told Balboa that there was another sea to the west.

Taking both Spaniards and Native Americans, Balboa set out to find the sea. It was not an easy journey. The men had to cut their way through thick jungles and fight sickness and danger in the Central American land we now call Panama.

Balboa claimed the Pacific Ocean and the land for the king of Spain.

After days of hard work, the Indians pointed to a steep hill from which the ocean could be seen. Hurriedly, Balboa climbed the hill and saw only a part of the tremendous body of water that would one day be called the **Pacific Ocean.** Balboa named it the Great South Sea.

It took Balboa and his men four more days of walking to reach the shore of the ocean they had seen from that hill. Stepping into the waves of the beautiful blue ocean, Balboa claimed the ocean and the land for the king of Spain.

Juan Ponce de León Explores Florida

By now, you must be wondering when an explorer would ever explore land that is now a part of the United States. As far as we know, the first European to reach what is now the United States was a Spanish explorer, **Juan Ponce de León** [hwän päns′ dā lā·ôn′].

After Ponce de León sailed with Christopher Columbus on his second voyage to America, De León was eager to explore for himself the many islands he saw in the New World. Ponce de León led Spanish soldiers against unfriendly Indians in America, and later became the governor of **Puerto Rico,** an island that he had conquered in the West Indies.

One day he heard a Native American say that on the island of Bimini there was a special spring or fountain of water. The Indian's story went on to say that if anyone

Ponce de León explored Florida but never found the Fountain of Youth.

drank from this fountain, he would become young again. In 1513, Ponce de León led Spanish explorers to search for the Fountain of Youth, as it came to be called. He found a land that was bright with many wonderful new kinds of flowers. He thought it was an island, but it was really a **peninsula,** a body of land with water on three sides. He named it **"Florida,"** the Spanish name for flowers.

Ponce de León explored Florida's coast, but did not find what he was searching for—a Fountain of Youth. He did find many unfriendly Indians who fought against him. Ponce de León decided to return to Puerto Rico.

Several years later, Ponce de León planned to begin a settlement in Florida. This time, he took about 200 men, tools, seeds, and other supplies. However, the Native Americans in Florida fought fiercely and most of De León's men were killed. Ponce de León himself was wounded by an arrow. The men who survived took Ponce de León to the nearby island of **Cuba,** where he died. He never knew the greatness of the land he had found.

Florida and the West Indies

★ ★ ★ ★ Chapter 1 Checkup ★ ★ ★ ★

Answer the questions on notebook paper.

1. What is a continent?
2. What are the seven continents?
3. What is history?
4. What is the study of the surface of the earth called?
5. What continent is responsible for the settlement of America?
6. What are the four oceans?
7. What was Columbus searching for when he found America?
8. Who told Europeans about his journey to China?
9. Name Columbus' three ships.
10. What happened on October 12, 1492?
11. Where did Columbus land?
12. What did Columbus call the people he met in America?
13. What group from Scandinavia were the first Europeans to visit America?
14. When did the Vikings land in America?
15. What did the Vikings call America?
16. What did John Cabot claim for England in 1497?
17. What did the name *America* first stand for?
18. What Portuguese explorer first sailed around Africa to get to Asia?
19. Who was the first Spaniard to reach the Pacific Ocean?
20. What did he name the Pacific?
21. What explorer wanted to find the Fountain of Youth?
22. What land did he explore?

Early Exploration

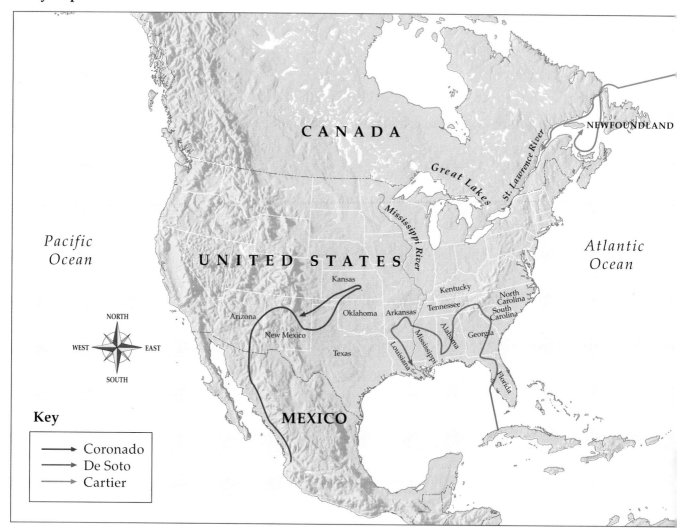

Pacific
Ocean

CANADA

Great Lakes

St. Lawrence River

NEWFOUNDLAND

UNITED STATES

Mississippi River

Atlantic
Ocean

Kansas

Kentucky

North
Carolina

Arizona

Oklahoma

Arkansas

Tennessee

South
Carolina

New Mexico

Mississippi

Alabama

Georgia

Texas

Louisiana

Florida

NORTH

WEST   EAST

SOUTH

MEXICO

Key

→ Coronado
→ De Soto
→ Cartier

TIME LINE OF IMPORTANT DATES

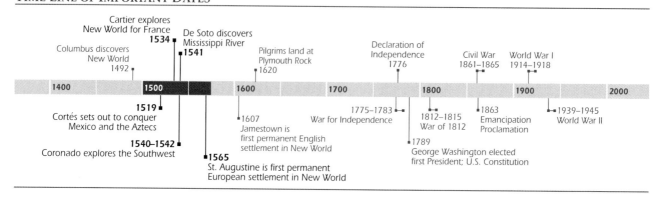

Cartier explores
New World for France
1534

De Soto discovers
Mississippi River
1541

Columbus discovers
New World
1492

Pilgrims land at
Plymouth Rock
1620

Declaration of
Independence
1776

Civil War
1861–1865

World War I
1914–1918

| 1400 | | 1500 | | 1600 | | 1700 | | 1800 | | 1900 | | 2000 |

1519

Cortés sets out to conquer
Mexico and the Aztecs

1607
Jamestown is
first permanent English
settlement in New World

1775–1783
War for Independence

1812–1815
War of 1812

1863
Emancipation
Proclamation

1939–1945
World War II

1540–1542
Coronado explores the Southwest

1789
George Washington elected
first President; U.S. Constitution

1565
St. Augustine is first permanent
European settlement in New World

Chapter 2

The Years of Exploration

Spain: The Conquest of Mexico

As we have seen, one man's discovery led to explorations by others. Now we will study the Spanish explorations of Mexico, which soon led to other explorations in the land that is now the United States.

The Aztecs

The **Aztecs** were <u>Indians in Mexico</u> who had built a large and beautiful city. **Montezuma** [mŏn′tĭ·zōō′mə] was the <u>Aztecs' ruler</u>. The Aztecs were so rich and powerful that other Native Americans hundreds of miles away from them had heard of their wealth. Then Spanish explorers heard stories of the Aztecs' wealth from other Indians.

When Cortés and his soldiers reached the Aztec capital, Montezuma greeted them with gifts of silver and gold.

Hernando Cortés

In 1519, the Spanish explorer **Hernando Cortés** [hər·năn′dō kôr·tĕz′] <u>set out to conquer Mexico</u>, or <u>to win it by force</u>. With him, he took a fleet of ships, and many soldiers, cannons, and horses. When Cortés's ships arrived in Mexico, he gave orders that all ships but one be sunk.

The crews watched as one by one, each ship sank below the waves. The one ship that was left was sent back to Spain to give a report to the king.

With the ships gone, every man knew there was no chance to turn back. Cortés reminded his men of great wealth yet to be found. And so, they marched forward with their cannons and horses.

When the Spaniards reached the beautiful Aztec city, Montezuma himself greeted them with gifts of silver and gold. The Spaniards and the Indians were amazed with each other. The Indians had never seen white men, cannons, or horses before. They felt sure that the Spaniards were white gods come to visit them. The Spaniards had never before seen a pagan religion which included such cruel religious practices and such a wealth of gold and silver!

The Aztecs were very generous with their gifts of silver and gold, but Cortés was not satisfied. He felt he must have all of the Aztecs' wealth. After years of fighting in which many died, <u>Cortés and his men conquered Mexico</u>. Mexico then became a Spanish colony.

Ship after ship loaded with gold and silver left for Spain. In the next few years, Mexico and other Spanish colonies made Spain the wealthiest country in the world.

The king of Spain was very happy; because of Cortés, Spain was rich. How happy was Cortés? You may be surprised to know that he died a poor, lonely man. People became jealous of Cortés. His friends became his enemies. Too late, Cortés realized that gold cannot buy happiness.

People in Spain began to hear how cruelly the soldiers were handling the Indians of Mexico. Catholic priests came from Spain and set up missions to teach the Native Americans Catholic beliefs. Often the priests genuinely loved the Indians and treated them well, but sometimes the priests were just as cruel to the Indians as the soldiers were.

France: Cartier Explores the New World

Spain was not the only country interested in what the New World might have to offer. Gold, silver, and furs were powerful riches that drew England and France to explore the New World, too.

But more than finding gold and silver, <u>the French and English hoped to find a sea route through America</u> that would lead to even greater riches of the Indies.

If you look on a map of America, you will see that there is no waterway through America. Of course, in the 1500s, no one had a true map of America. There was only one way for explorers to find out the size of this new land—explore it!

In 1534, a Frenchman named **Jacques Cartier** [zhäk kär·tyā′] set sail hoping to <u>find a waterway through North America to the Pacific Ocean</u>. Then he planned to sail on to China. If Cartier could find such a route, he would gain wealth for the king of France.

Cartier sailed around the island of Newfoundland. Then he discovered the mouth of a great river that later was named the St. Lawrence River. Cartier explored this river hoping to find a waterway to the Pacific. On the banks of this river, Cartier landed and set up a wooden cross that had these words written upon it: "Long live the king of France." In doing this, he claimed this part of North America for France.

Many Indians watched as Cartier claimed the land for France. They probably did not

New Names

1. **Aztecs**—Indian tribe that lived in Mexico
2. **Montezuma**—ruler of the Aztecs
3. **Hernado Cortés**—Spanish explorer who conquered the Aztecs
4. **Jacques Cartier**—French explorer who hoped to find a waterway through North America to the Pacific Ocean
5. **Francisco de Coronado**—Spanish explorer who explored throughout the Southwest and discovered the Grand Canyon
6. **Hernando de Soto**—Spanish explorer who discovered the Mississippi River
7. **"sea dogs"**—English sea captains who raided Spanish boats
8. **Sir Francis Drake**—the most famous "sea dog"

understand what he was saying, but they trusted him. Unlike many Spanish explorers, French explorers were friendly to the Indians. Cartier wanted the valuable furs that the Indians had, but he did not take them. Instead, he traded colorful coats, caps, beads, knives, and other goods for the furs. Because the Indians had no other way to get such goods, they were eager to trade with their new friends.

Cartier was delighted to have furs to take back to France, but he did not find what he had set out to find—a water route through North America to Asia.

However, Cartier did three important things for France:
1. He opened the way for a valuable fur trade between the French and the Indians.
2. He made a lasting and valuable friendship between the French and the Indians.
3. Above all, Cartier's explorations gave France a claim to part of the New World.

Comprehension Check 2A

1. Where did the Aztecs live?
2. Who was the leader of the Aztecs?
3. What Spanish soldier conquered the Aztecs?
4. Who explored North America for France?

Spain: Coronado's Search for the Seven Cities of Cibola

The year was 1540. Eager to get rid of the Spanish explorers, the Indians in Mexico kept telling them stories of golden cities far from the Indian villages of clay. Perhaps the Indians did this in hopes that the Spanish would wander far away and never bother them again. The Spanish explorers became excited whenever they heard Indian stories of the **Seven Cities of Cibola.**

"These cities in the country of Cibola are rich in gold and silver," the Native Americans told the Spanish. "Even the walls of their cities are made of gold."

The Spanish believed these stories and decided to search for this gold, too. **Francisco de Coronado** [frän·sēs′kō dā kŏr·ō·nä′dō] was chosen to lead 300 Spaniards, as well as several hundred captive Indians, in search of the cities.

In his search for the Seven Cities of Cibola, Coronado and his men explored much of what is now the southwestern United States. He marched his men through **Arizona,** where they discovered the beautiful Grand Canyon. But there were no riches there. Coronado and his men marched on through New Mexico, Texas, Oklahoma, and Kansas. They saw

9. **Samuel de Champlain**—French explorer who founded Quebec

New Places
10. **Seven Cities of Cibola**—fabled cities which Coronado searched for, but never found
11. **Arizona**—area where Coronado discovered the Grand Canyon

12. **Mississippi River**—greatest American river, discovered by De Soto
13. **St. Augustine**—first permanent European settlement in the United States; the first lasting Spanish settlement in the New World
14. **New France**—name first given to Canada
15. **Quebec**—first successful French settlement in the New World

Coronado and his men never found the Seven Cities of Cibola, but they were the first Europeans to see the Grand Canyon.

clay pueblos [pwĕb′lōz: Indian villages] that glowed like gold in the beautiful sunrise and sunset, but they found no gold.

Finally, Coronado realized that he had been tricked by the Indians. Coronado returned to Mexico in 1542. Only 100 of the 300 soldiers he started with returned with him. The trip had been long and hard. Many men had died. Some had been killed by Indians. Some had left Coronado to explore for themselves.

Coronado was brokenhearted. He and his men had marched over 3,000 miles. He had his heart set on finding cities of gold. Instead, he found cities of clay.

Spain: De Soto Discovers the Mississippi

Hernando de Soto [hər·năn′dō dē sō′tō] was already a very rich Spanish explorer. But after hearing false stories that Florida was a "land of gold," he decided to search for that gold, too. The true stories of fierce Indians that had killed Ponce de León did not bother De Soto. He planned to conquer the Indians of Florida.

De Soto and 600 soldiers sailed to Florida. Through land that was one day to become Florida, Georgia, South Carolina,

North Carolina, and Tennessee, De Soto led his men. Many Native Americans fought fiercely; they did not welcome strangers who came to steal from them.

Though many of his soldiers were being killed by Indians and many more became sick, De Soto would not give up his search for gold. Down through the land that would become Alabama and across Mississippi, De Soto marched his men.

In May 1541, <u>De Soto and his men discovered a great river</u>. The Indians called it "the Father of Waters." Later it would become a great highway for boats and would be named the **Mississippi River.** The Mississippi would then become the most valuable river in the United States. But De Soto did not know that.

He did know that the wide river forced him and his men to spend several weeks building boats. They finally crossed the Mississippi River and continued to search through what is now Arkansas and Louisiana. But for all his trouble, De Soto found no gold.

De Soto became sick with a fever and died. Fearing that the Indians would attack if they knew the Spanish leader was dead, the soldiers buried De Soto in the Missis-

De Soto and his men discovered the great Mississippi River.

sippi River. The remaining soldiers built their own boats, sailed down the Mississippi River, and then continued on until they found safety at a Spanish settlement in Mexico.

Comprehension Check 2B

1. Who searched for the Seven Cities of Cibola?

2. What natural wonder did he discover on his journey?

3. What did De Soto discover on his journey to search for gold?

4. Why were the discoveries of the Grand Canyon and the Mississippi River **not** especially exciting to the Spanish explorers?

England: "Drake the Dragon"

Spain had become very wealthy from the explorations of the New World. Her wealth made her a world power. Soon other countries noticed Spain's wealth and power. "Why should Spain have all the New World's riches?" they asked themselves.

Pirates began to sail where only Spanish ships had sailed before. At that time, **Queen Elizabeth I** ruled England. She encouraged English sea captains to make surprise attacks on Spanish boats. These English sea captains who raided Spanish boats were called **"sea dogs."**

The most famous "sea dog" was **Sir Francis Drake.** The queen sent Drake to capture the goods on Spanish ships. After he had taken the goods on board his ship, he often sank the Spanish ship. Then Drake would bring back the Spanish gold, silver, and other treasures to the English queen.

To the Spanish, Drake became the most feared pirate of the time. He was so successful in raiding Spanish ships that the Spanish nicknamed him "Drake the Dragon."

Slowly but surely, Spain lost its great wealth and power. Sir Francis Drake helped England to become more powerful, both on the sea and in the New World.

Queen Elizabeth knighted Francis Drake because he helped England fight against Spain.

France: The First French Settlement in the New World

The 16th century had passed. The 17th had begun. Although "Drake the Dragon" had weakened Spain's power, Spain was the only country that had a settlement in America. That <u>first permanent European settlement in North America</u> was **St. Augustine,** Florida.

The French had discovered that the beautiful animal furs of North America could be sold for high prices in France. Wealthy Frenchmen were willing to pay high prices for beaver hats. Others enjoyed coats made from animal skins. Many Indians were eager to trade their furs with the Frenchmen, who treated them as friends.

In 1603, **Samuel de Champlain** [shăm·plān'] arrived in Canada. At that time in history, <u>the French called Canada **"New France."**</u> Champlain and his men explored and traded with the Indians. The French then sailed home with a valuable cargo of furs.

The king of France became interested in starting a settlement in North America. He knew that trading furs with the Indians would be a valuable business. He decided that Frenchmen must be sent to live in the New World.

In 1608, Champlain returned to New France (Canada). This time, he also explored New England's coastline, making good maps along the way. He discovered beautiful

One of St. Augustine's old homes

Lake Champlain in what are now the states of New York and Vermont. Then he returned to New France, where he helped to build **Quebec** [kwĭ·bĕk'], <u>the first successful French settlement in the New World</u>.

<u>Three powerful countries now claimed land in the New World: England, Spain, and France</u>. Soon you will see how England gained more and more land that is now the United States of America, and you will learn about a sea battle that made England one of the most powerful countries in the world. Because the English people at the time America was settled read and preached the Bible, our country was to become a land of freedom and liberty.

Castillo de San Marcos is a fort that was built by the Spanish to defend St. Augustine.

Answer the questions on notebook paper.

1. What great Indian tribe lived in what is now Mexico?
2. Who was Montezuma?
3. What Spanish soldier conquered the Aztecs?
4. What was Cartier searching for?
5. What three important things did Cartier do for France?
6. What legendary place did the Indians describe to the greedy Spaniards?
7. Who searched for the cities?
8. What area did he explore?
9. What natural wonder did Coronado discover on his journey?
10. Who discovered the Mississippi River?
11. What was he really searching for?
12. What queen permitted English pirates to attack Spanish ships?
13. What were the English pirates called?
14. Who was the most famous "sea dog"?
15. What was Canada first called?
16. What was the first successful French settlement in America?
17. Who helped found it?
18. What was the first permanent European settlement in America?
19. Name the three powerful countries with claims in the New World during the years of discovery.

American Indian Dwellings

Wichita Indian lodges

A lodge made of earth and wood

Indian cliff dwellings

A pueblo dwelling

The First Americans

A Sioux tepee

A hogan

The Differences in American Indians

When Columbus discovered America, he mistakenly called the people who lived there "Indians" because he thought he was near India. Even today descendants of these Native Americans are called Indians.

The original Americans had never called themselves "Indians" before Columbus came. Although each tribe had a name for its own group, as far as we know, no tribe had a name for all the Native Americans combined. Each tribe thought of itself as a separate nation and was different from the others in many ways.

Native American Homes

Many people today have the mistaken idea that all Native Americans lived in **tepees,** tents made by stretching animal skins over poles. Actually, few Indians lived in tepees. Pictured are homes of six different groups of Indians, and there were many more.

Transportation

How did Indians travel? Before European explorers came, Native Americans had no horses or oxen, so they had no need for wagons. For most tribes, water was the best way to travel. Therefore, American Indians built many different kinds of boats. Some traveled in birch bark canoes or canoes that were dug out of a tree trunk. Others made **bullboats** by <u>stretching buffalo skins over a round frame</u>.

Indian Games

Native Americans of all ages loved games. Indian children played much the same as children do today. Little girls often played with dolls made from corn husks and other dried plants. Boys were given toy bows and arrows with blunt points. With these, they could pretend to be mighty hunters bringing home deer or buffalo for their family's meat.

Of course, there were always games of skill such as fishing, swimming, target practice, and canoe and foot races. These games provided the children with fun and gave them practice for the day when they would need these skills.

But children were not the only ones who enjoyed games. Both men and women enjoyed sports. Have you ever played the game "Which hand is it in?" in which you tightly close both fists? Inside one fist is an object. The other player then tries to guess which hand holds the object. Nearly all Indians liked to play this game in some form. The most popular way was with moccasins. An object was placed inside each of several moccasins, but only one object was marked. Each Indian tried to guess which moccasin contained the marked object.

Indians traveling in birch bark canoes

For those Indians who lived in the North, there were winter sports. One popular winter game was **snowsnake.** First, a track was made by dragging a log through the snow. Then long sticks were found and made smooth, and one end was carved to look like a snake's head. Each player would try to slide his snowsnake farther than anyone else. When one snowsnake stopped, it was stuck upright in the snow to mark that player's place. Then the next person would try to send his snowsnake even farther.

The Indians' Way of Life Changes

Before Europeans began exploring America, many Native American tribes took care of all their own needs. Because many Indians did not trade with other tribes, European explorers often thought these tribes were very poor.

Indians were isolated from the gospel and had never seen the Scriptures. Each tribe made its own religion. Some worshiped idols; some worshiped the sun and moon.

New Words
1. **tepee**—tent made by stretching animal skins over poles
2. **bullboat**—boat made by stretching buffalo skins over a round frame
3. **syllabary**—the Cherokee alphabet

New Names
4. **Indians**—name Columbus gave to the people of the New World because he thought he was in India; often called American Indians or Native Americans
5. **John Eliot**—missionary who translated the Bible into the language of the Massachusetts Indians

An Indian encampment

When white men began to explore and settle America, the Indians' way of life slowly changed. They began to trade furs and food for strong iron pots and shiny copper kettles. Making pottery and baskets was no longer necessary for some Indians. They began buying cloth to make clothes instead of using animal skins. Colorful beads replaced the bones and shells used to make Indian jewelry. Guns and knives began to replace arrows.

As white men built more homes and killed more game animals, there was less meat for Indians to eat. Some Indians who had been hunters became farmers in order to have enough food to eat.

With the white men came horses, oxen, and cattle. The horse especially changed the Indians' way of living.

Even the Indians' ways of building homes changed. In the 1800s, some Native Americans built log cabins.

The Indians' way of life changed when white men came to America. Here, Indians are displaying furs they brought to trade with the Europeans.

Comprehension Check 3A

1. Who gave Indians their name?

2. Why did he call them *Indians?*

3. Which Indian dwelling was made by stretching animal skins over poles?

6. **Roger Williams**—missionary who made friends with the Indians by treating them fairly

7. **David Brainerd**—young missionary who gave his life to take the gospel to the Indians

8. **John Wesley**—famous preacher from England who preached to the Indians

9. **Sequoya**—Cherokee who developed the only known Indian alphabet of his time

10. **Jim Thorpe**—Native American who, in 1950, was voted the greatest athlete of the 20th century.

Missionaries to the Native Americans

The biggest change of all came when the Indians heard about the one true God. The very first Americans did not have the Bible until European settlers came to the New World. Because they did not have the Bible telling them about the one true God, they often offered prayers and sacrifices to the "god of the sky," the "god of the forest," the "god of the river," and many other false gods.

Then, white men came from Europe bringing the Bible with them. Some Europeans simply forced the Indians to be baptized without knowing anything about how to be saved. Some Indians did come to understand the truths of the Bible, however. A few white men loved the Indians and wanted to see them accept Christ.

John Eliot

One such man was **John Eliot,** who came to America in 1631. While he was preaching in the Massachusetts colony, Eliot learned the language of the Massachusetts Indians and began to translate the Bible into their tongue. It took him nearly thirty years of patient work to do this, and all that time he was preaching and teaching as well. His Bible was one of the first books printed in America, and many of his "praying Indians," as his followers were called, learned to read it.

Eliot was a simple and very generous man. Once, when his small church gave him his salary, they tied the money up in a handkerchief with several knots so Mr. Eliot would not give it all away before he got home. Eliot met a poor family and tried to give them some money, but he could not untie the knots. That did not stop John

Eliot from helping people in need. He gave the family the handkerchief, with all the money in it!

Eliot also showed his kindness by speaking up when people tried to sell Native Americans as slaves. Eliot's kindness and Bible teaching kept many Indians from fighting against the English during times of Indian wars.

Roger Williams

Roger Williams, whom you will read more about later, was another missionary to the Indians. Roger Williams left a large colony in 1636 to set up his own colony. Usually Indians would kill a white man who lived by himself, because white men often stole Indians' land. But this man was different.

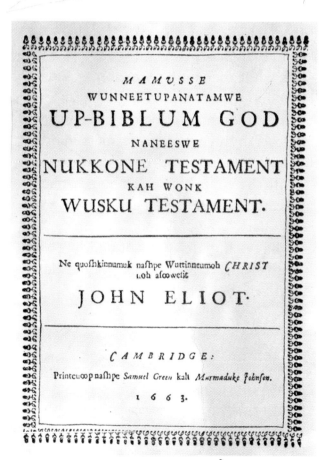

A page from John Eliot's Indian Bible

Roger Williams soon <u>became the Indians' friend because he was willing to treat them fairly</u>. He bought land from them instead of merely taking it. More important, he truly loved them. He saw that Indians were men just like himself, that they were sinners like all men, and that they needed to be saved. For many years he taught Indians the Bible and witnessed to them about Christ.

David Brainerd

David Brainerd [brā′nərd] also wanted the Indians to know more about Christ. Brainerd was a brilliant Bible scholar who lived in the early 1700s and could have become the pastor of a large church. Instead he left the comforts and security of his home to spend his life preaching to Native Americans in the wilderness. He knew that winning lost souls to Christ was more important than living in comfort.

<u>His hard work and the poor conditions where he lived caused him to die when he was only twenty-nine</u>. Many people felt that David Brainerd had thrown his life away, but some knew that he had given his life to bring the message of salvation to Indians whom he loved.

John Wesley

John Wesley also brought the good news of salvation to Native Americans. Wesley was <u>one of the most famous English preachers of his day</u>. When he came to America in 1735, he went out among the Indians and preached to them.

God's Word is far more valuable than anything else Europeans brought to America. Europeans who truly preached the Bible to Indian tribes did more good than kettles, horses, and farming methods could ever do. Influenced by the Bible, Indians, like other Americans, would later have the opportunity to enjoy freedom and liberty and play their role in building the country.

Comprehension Check 3B

1. What caused the greatest change in the Indians' way of life?

2. Which missionary to the Indians translated the Bible into their language?

3. Which young missionary gave his life to take the gospel to the Native Americans?

John Wesley preached to the Indians when he came to America from England.

Sequoya developed the syllabary, or Cherokee alphabet.

Sequoya

California's tall sequoia trees are named after a famous Cherokee Indian, **Sequoya** [sĭ·kwoi′ə], who lived in North Carolina.

After twelve years of hard work, he created the only known Indian alphabet of his time. Other Native American tribes had only spoken languages. If they did write, they wrote in pictures. Sequoya created eighty-six symbols. Each symbol stood for a sound in the Cherokee language. After the Cherokee alphabet or **syllabary** [sĭl′ə-bĕr′ē] was completed, the Cherokee Indians quickly learned how to read and write in their own language. The New Testament was translated. And soon, the Cherokees were printing their own newspaper!

The Indian athlete Jim Thorpe was one of the greatest sportsmen of all time.

Jim Thorpe

Some people would say **Jim Thorpe** (1888–1953), a Native American from Oklahoma, was the greatest athlete that ever lived.

Jim Thorpe was the great-great-grandson of the Indian chief Black Hawk. His incredible abilities in several different sports amazed his coaches. Jim was a talented baseball pitcher; he set world records in track and field; and he played football so well that his school was soon beating the best college teams in the nation.

Jim competed in the 1912 Olympics and brought home two gold medals. After college Jim played professional baseball and professional football for many years.

In 1950 sports writers were asked to name the greatest athlete of the century. They named Jim Thorpe. Everyone across America agreed with the sports writers: Jim Thorpe, an Indian who had learned to love sports by racing his brothers across Oklahoma fields, was the greatest athlete the world had seen in years.

Something Worth Finding Out

How many Indian tribes can you name? If you studied the names of states, towns, lakes, and rivers in our country, you would find many names of Indian tribes. Following is a list of places that were named for Indian tribes. If the tribe's name is a state, put an *S* beside it. If it is a town or a city, put a *T* beside it. If it is a river, put an *R* beside it. If it is a lake, put an *L*. You may have to look in an encyclopedia or a dictionary. (Some of the names have two answers.)

_____ Illinois	_____ Susquehanna	_____ Massachusetts
_____ Wichita	_____ Omaha	_____ Cheyenne
_____ Huron	_____ Kansas	_____ Erie
_____ Delaware	_____ Iowa	

★ ★ ★ ★ Chapter 3 Checkup ★ ★ ★ ★

Answer the questions on notebook paper.

1. What did Columbus call the people who lived in America? Why?
2. What is a tepee?
3. Name at least four different types of homes in which Indians lived.
4. What is a bullboat?
5. Did the Indians enjoy playing games?
6. What game did many Northern Indians play?
7. What animal changed the Indian's way of living?
8. What caused the greatest change in the Indian's way of life?
9. Name four missionaries who took the gospel to the Native Americans.
10. Who developed the Cherokee alphabet? What was the alphabet called?
11. What Indian was named the greatest athlete of the 20th century in 1950?

Early Settlement

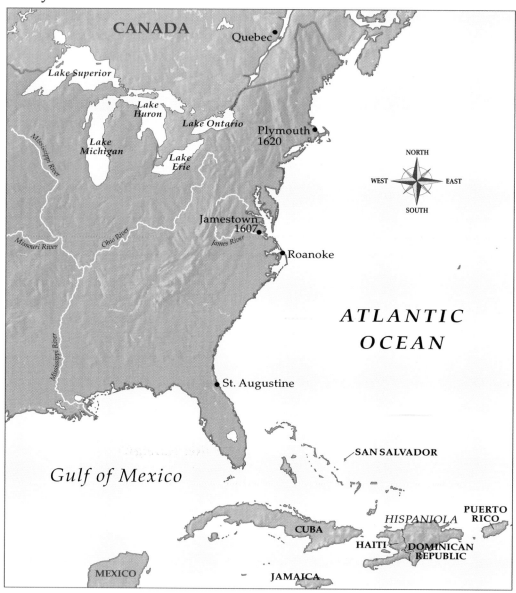

CANADA
Quebec

Lake Superior

Lake Huron

Lake Ontario

Lake Michigan

Lake Erie

Mississippi River

Plymouth 1620

NORTH
WEST — EAST
SOUTH

Missouri River   Ohio River

Jamestown 1607

James River

Roanoke

ATLANTIC OCEAN

St. Augustine

SAN SALVADOR

Gulf of Mexico

PUERTO RICO

HISPANIOLA

CUBA

HAITI   DOMINICAN REPUBLIC

MEXICO

JAMAICA

TIME LINE OF IMPORTANT DATES

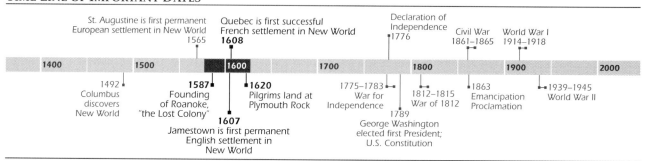

St. Augustine is first permanent
European settlement in New World
1565

Quebec is first successful
French settlement in New World
1608

Declaration of
Independence
1776

Civil War
1861–1865

World War I
1914–1918

| 1400 | 1500 | 1600 | 1700 | 1800 | 1900 | 2000 |

1492
Columbus
discovers
New World

1587
Founding
of Roanoke,
"the Lost Colony"

1620
Pilgrims land at
Plymouth Rock

1775–1783
War for
Independence

1812–1815
War of 1812

1863
Emancipation
Proclamation

1939–1945
World War II

1789
George Washington
elected first President;
U.S. Constitution

1607
Jamestown is first permanent
English settlement in
New World

The English Come to America

Planting a Colony

The year was 1585, and the English people were ready to begin a very difficult task. They were going to plant a colony in the **wilderness,** <u>a wild, empty land that has not been settled</u>. America was that wilderness. Of course there were many Native Americans living in America. Some stayed in one area and farmed while many others traveled from place to place. But for the most part, America was still a wilderness—a wild, unsettled land.

England and the Bible

Nearly one hundred years had passed since 1497, when John Cabot claimed North America for England. By this time, an important change had taken place in England—all the people in England were free to read the Bible for themselves. This freedom had an important effect on the kind of people who came to America from England and the kind of government they set up.

The Lost Colony

Queen Elizabeth I was the powerful ruler of England in 1585. She was proud of England and wanted all Englishmen to be proud, too. A successful English colony in the New World would boost her people's pride.

The Pilgrims were the most famous group of English settlers to come to America.

Walter Raleigh [rô′lē] was a good friend of the queen. When he <u>asked for permission to begin a colony</u>, Queen Elizabeth gave it to him without hesitation. But the queen told him that he himself could not go to America—he had to choose someone else to go!

How strange it seems that the man who was to plan the first English colony in America never went to America himself! The queen had very good reasons. England was having trouble with Spain. If a war broke out, she knew she could trust Raleigh's judgment to help England.

Raleigh sent two sea captains to find a good place in America for an English colony. When they returned, they reported finding an island called **Roanoke** [rō′ə·nōk] that would be a good place to begin a colony.

Queen Elizabeth was as delighted as Raleigh. For his excellent plans, the queen added a title to his name. From now on, he would be called Sir Walter Raleigh. The land the sea captains explored was also given a name. This <u>part of the New World belonging to England</u> would be called **Virginia,** after Elizabeth, the "Virgin Queen."

Raleigh sent about one hundred men and five ships to begin a colony on Roanoke Island. However, these men were more interested in becoming rich and returning to England than they were in beginning a colony and living in the New World. They probably did not realize how dangerous the American wilderness was, and how much work it would take to live there. Because they were more interested in searching for gold than in planting gardens, they soon ran out of food. Trying to force the Indians to give them food only made more trouble. Tired and hungry, the men returned to Eng-

Queen Elizabeth I was a powerful ruler of England during the 1500s.

Sir Walter Raleigh planned the first colony in America, but he never went to America himself.

land. The colony had failed. Would Raleigh try again?

Starting a colony in the wild lands of America was a dangerous task, but he would try again. Raleigh made plans for another colony. In 1587 another group of colonists—brave men, women, and children—sailed for Roanoke Island. Raleigh reasoned that families would be more interested in building houses, planting gardens, and settling down than single men who desired only wealth and adventure.

The colonists arrived safely at Roanoke and began repairing houses that the first

New Words

1. **wilderness**—wild, empty land that has not been settled
2. **merchants**—businessmen
3. **charter**—an official permit to start settlements
4. **Common House**—combination house, fort, and church
5. **self-government**—when a group of people makes plans to govern or rule themselves
6. **treaty**—a written promise or agreement

New Names

7. **Queen Elizabeth I**—powerful queen of England
8. **Sir Walter Raleigh**—Englishman who tried to start the colony of Roanoke in America
9. **Virginia Dare**—first English child born in America

10. **King James I**—English king who wanted to have a successful colony in America
11. **London Company**—group of merchants who paid for the founding of Jamestown
12. ***Susan Constant, Godspeed, Discovery***—three ships which brought the Jamestown settlers to America
13. **Captain John Smith**—leader of the Jamestown colony who said, "He that does not work shall not eat."
14. **Separatists**—Englishmen who wanted to separate from the Church of England
15. ***Mayflower***—ship that brought the Pilgrims to America
16. **Strangers**—people on board the *Mayflower* who were not Separatists

colonists had left. A little girl was born and named **Virginia Dare.** She was the <u>first English child born in America</u>.

Soon afterward, John White, the governor of the colony, decided to return to England for supplies that the colony badly needed.

John White sailed back to England, but unfortunately, he found England ready to go to war with Spain. The queen gave orders that every English ship was to be used to fight Spain. Even Sir Walter Raleigh could not get a ship to help John White. In 1588 England won the war with Spain in what is called the **defeat of the Spanish Armada.** England was becoming the most powerful country in the world.

Three years had passed before John White could return to Roanoke. When he returned, there was no one to greet him. It seemed as if everyone had vanished! <u>Carved on a tree was the word</u> **Croatoan** [krō′ə·tō′ən], the name of another island where friendly Indians lived. No trace of them could be found.

What happened to the colony at Roanoke? No one knows. The <u>first English</u>

The only clue left behind by the settlers of Roanoke was the word *Croatoan* carved on a tree.

<u>colony in America had failed</u>. John White returned to England. Sir Walter Raleigh sent several ships in search of the colonists, but the settlers were never found. Today <u>Roanoke is known as "The Lost Colony."</u> It has become a great mystery to all who study history, and it shows us what a dangerous task the English had ahead of them in settling the New World.

Comprehension Check 4A

1. What was Sir Walter Raleigh's colony in America called?

2. Who was the first English child born in America?

3. What happened to Roanoke?

17. **Pilgrims**—name given to the Separatists and Strangers who traveled together on the *Mayflower*

18. **Mayflower Compact**—the first written agreement for self-government in America

19. **John Carver**—first governor of Plymouth

20. **Elder Brewster**—the Pilgrims' minister

21. **Captain Miles Standish**—soldier chosen by the Pilgrims to guide them in dealing with the Indians and in building a settlement

22. **Samoset, Squanto, Massasoit**—friendly Indians who helped the Plymouth settlers

23. **William Bradford**—governor of Plymouth for nearly thirty-six years

24. *Of Plymouth Plantation*—a history of Plymouth written by William Bradford

New Places

25. **Roanoke**—early English colony in America that disappeared; called "The Lost Colony"

26. **Virginia**—name given to England's land in America

27. **Jamestown**—England's first permanent settlement in the New World

28. **Chesapeake Bay**—bay on which Jamestown was built

29. **Massachusetts**—area where the Pilgrims settled

30. **Plymouth**—settlement founded by the Pilgrims in 1620

New Dates

31. 1588—England defeats the Spanish Armada

32. 1607—Jamestown is founded

33. 1620—Plymouth is founded

Jamestown:
The First Lasting English Colony

Twenty years had passed since England had tried and failed to begin a colony at Roanoke. Queen Elizabeth I was dead. **King James I,** England's new ruler, wanted to have a successful English colony in the New World.

By beginning a colony, King James hoped to

1. **find a sea passage through America to the riches of the Indies;**
2. **find gold, silver, and valuable minerals;**
3. **find the people of the Lost Colony of Roanoke; and**
4. **teach the Indians Christianity.**

The London Company

A group of **merchants,** or businessmen, made a plan to begin a new colony in Virginia. Each businessman would pay part of the cost of sending ships of colonists to the New World. The colonists would repay these merchants by sending back furs, lumber, and, perhaps, gold and silver from the New World. Of course, if a colonist happened to find a sea passage to the Indies, the merchants would be rich. This group of merchants called themselves the **London Company.** King James was delighted with their plans.

The London Company obtained a **charter,** an official permit to start settlements in America. Then it busied itself with buying supplies and finding ships and colonists.

To make this voyage to Virginia, 101 men and 4 boys were chosen. What kind of men would you have chosen to begin a new colony? Let's see what was needed. A new colony in a wilderness would need hardworking men to clear the land and farmers to farm the land for food to eat. It would need carpenters to build houses and a fort for protection against unfriendly Indians. Since one of King James's purposes was to teach the Indians Christianity, missionaries would be needed. And a new colony would need men of good character who were willing to do whatever work needed to be done.

Those are the kinds of men a successful colony would need, but unfortunately the London Company did not choose such men. Half of the men that were chosen were wealthy men who could afford to have servants do most of their work for them. They were not used to doing manual labor themselves. Wealthy men arc often hard workers, but these wealthy men were lazy.

Why, then, would such men come to the New World to begin a colony? The London Company was eager to send people to Virginia. They, who had never been to the New World, spread stories around that in Virginia, gold nuggets lay on the beaches, just waiting to be picked up. They said that food was plentiful. However, they did not say anything about the unfriendly Indians.

Is it any wonder then that these wealthy gentlemen pictured themselves strolling along the beaches, picking up gold nuggets? These men were thinking only of becoming even richer and then returning to England. They had no thoughts of building a colony. This laziness would cause them some real problems.

The Founding of Jamestown

In April of **1607,** three small wooden ships, the *Susan Constant,* the *Godspeed,* and the *Discovery,* sailed into the **Chesapeake Bay.** From the mouth of the Chesapeake Bay, they sailed into a river. They named it the **James River,** in honor of their king.

Jamestown was the first permanent English colony in America.

It was springtime. Sweet clover blossomed in fields. Wildflowers gave a colorful appearance and sweet perfume to the fields and green forests.

The men on board the ships thought they must make a quick settlement and begin to explore Virginia. Instead of taking time to search out the land and plan wisely for the future, they quickly decided on a place to settle. They did not realize that the peninsula they chose was hunting grounds for a tribe of Native Americans. This alone would mean trouble, but it was not the only danger.

The land was swampy. In the summer, sickness would spread from the mosquitoes that lived in the swamp, an area where the ground is wet and spongy and where the land cannot be farmed. The colonists would have trouble finding fresh drinking water. But their thoughts of the future were thoughts only of finding gold. Again, in honor of their king, the new settlement was named **Jamestown.**

Spring does not last forever. Soon it became too late to plant gardens. The summer heat dried up the water supply. Mosquitoes swarmed in from the

John Smith saved the Jamestown colony by making everyone do a fair share of the work.

swamps, bringing fever and sickness with them. Before the summer was over, half of the colonists had died.

Winter was coming. Because few gardens had been planted, there was little food to see the colonists through. Yet, even though they faced starvation, only a few colonists would work.

A Hard Worker

Fortunately for Jamestown, at least one colonist was a hard worker. His name was **Captain John Smith.** With his help, huts were built to house the colonists. He managed to trade with nearby Indians for food to help the colonists through the winter.

In 1608, Captain Smith took control of Jamestown. He knew that unless every colonist, including the gentlemen, worked hard, they would starve again that winter. Wisely, he made a new rule: "He that does not work shall not eat."

At first the gentlemen did not believe him, but when dinnertime came and they were refused food, the men knew Smith meant business. Grumbling, they picked up their tools and began working. How much better it would have been if they could have made themselves work!

Life was still not easy that second winter in Jamestown. The London Company had sent several hundred new colonists to Jamestown, but sent very little food to feed them. Pocahontas, an Indian princess, was a great help to the Jamestown settlers. She even saved John Smith's life when her father threatened to kill him.

The Starving Time

Jamestown faced failure again when Captain Smith was badly burned in an accident. He had to return to England where he could be helped. With their leader gone, the gentlemen again refused to work. The winter of **1609–1610** was so bad that the colonists called it **"the starving time."**

When Captain Smith left, Jamestown had 500 colonists. In the spring, only about 60 were still alive. The few who did not die were weak from hunger and sickness. What was there to do, but to make plans to return to England? This colony seemed doomed to failure, too!

With all the strength they had, the remaining colonists packed their few belongings on boats and began sailing back. Suddenly, they saw a sail of a ship. The London Company was sending more colonists, more supplies, and more food! The sixty colonists turned their boats around and sailed back to Jamestown.

Progress at Last

Jamestown would not fail. When the colonists saw that there was no gold there, they began to look for other ways of making a living. Slowly and painfully <u>Jamestown became the first permanent English colony in America</u>.

In 1619, ninety women arrived in Jamestown. Now that the colonists had families to take care of, they were eager to build stronger houses and to earn a living to provide for the needs of their families. <u>Tobacco became the most important money-making crop</u>. At one time, colonists even grew tobacco in the streets of Jamestown. Money made from selling tobacco, as harmful as it is, may have saved Jamestown from failing.

King James I had hoped to accomplish four things by beginning an English colony in America, but

1. no sea passage through America to the Indies was found;
2. no gold or silver was found;
3. no one from the Lost Colony of Roanoke was found; and
4. the Indians were taught very little about Christianity.

Yet Jamestown was successful in becoming the first lasting English settlement. Because of it, other English people would have the courage to come to America and begin other colonies.

As these and later other men found out, America's greatest wealth was not in gold or silver, but in the happiness of building their own homes and working in freedom in a wonderful new land.

Comprehension Check 4B

1. What king reopened England's efforts to establish a colony in America?
2. What group of merchants or businessmen agreed to finance the founding of a colony?
3. What was England's first permanent settlement in the New World? When was it founded?
4. What leader of Jamestown demanded that men work for their food?

The Pilgrims: Lovers of Religious Freedom

We have seen that most of the men who first settled Jamestown were lovers of gold. They became successful only when a man strong enough to make them work became their leader. They did not have the strength of character to govern (rule) themselves. Now we will study the real heroes of America's beginning: the **Pilgrims.**

The Pilgrims were able to govern themselves because they loved religious freedom and strove for the glory of God. Their love for God and freedom came from their understanding of the Bible and from their English heritage.

There was a lack of freedom in England at this time, even though the English were a freedom-loving people. James I was still the king of England. He said that he was head of the church as well as the head of the government. Because the king forced everyone to attend his church, the **Church of England,** the English people were not free to worship as many thought they should.

The **Separatists** <u>wanted to separate from the Church of England</u> because they believed that it was not being true to the Bible. Because the Separatists wanted to preach and do what the Bible really teaches, these brave people held secret meetings to study the Bible. When the king heard of these meetings, he sent men to spy on the Separatists. When the Separatists were caught, they were often put in jail for their beliefs.

The Move to Holland

The Separatists wanted to form their own churches. But they could not do this in England. They loved England, but they loved God and religious freedom more. When they heard that in Holland there was freedom of worship, they <u>gave up their homes in England and moved to Holland</u>.

However, the Separatists were not happy in Holland. In England, they had been farmers. In Holland, they had no money to buy farms, and they had to work in factories. They missed being among English people. With time, their children were beginning to speak Dutch. They were forgetting the English ways that their parents wanted them to remember. More importantly, the children were starting to copy their Dutch friends and do things that the Bible says not to do.

The Separatists had heard of the settlement in Jamestown. Perhaps the king of England would allow them to make their own settlement in America. There they could build an English colony and yet worship in their own way. Their dream was to build their own churches in their own land so they could have freedom of worship. They asked permission from King James to found a colony in America, where they would remain loyal subjects of King James but be able to worship God in their own churches. King James gave them permission to go to America.

The Pilgrims searched for religious freedom and found it in America.

Aboard the Mayflower

In September of **1620,** a group of Separatists boarded a little ship known as the *Mayflower.* On board were 102 passengers. Not every passenger was a Separatist. Many were <u>people who wanted a chance to work in the New World, and others went for adventure</u>. The Separatists called these people **Strangers.**

Most of the Strangers were content with the Church of England. The Separatists did not try to force the Strangers to believe as they did, though they probably witnessed to them about God's truth in the Bible. The Separatists were not at all like King James. They believed that they should have the freedom to worship God as they thought best, and they were willing for other people to have the same freedom.

The Separatists and the Strangers were two groups of people with different beliefs. Yet both were wanderers to the New World. <u>Together, they became known as the</u> **Pilgrims.**

The group on board the *Mayflower* in 1620 reminds us of what the United States of America would be like over 150 years later. There were different kinds of people aboard with different ideas, different backgrounds, different goals, and different beliefs. But all were lovers of freedom—not just for themselves, but for others as well. They followed the words of Jesus, Who said, "Therefore all things whatsoever ye would that men should do to you, do ye even so to them" (Matthew 7:12). They knew that if they were to have freedom for themselves they must let others have freedom, too.

There were probably some arguments during the sixty-five days that it took the *Mayflower* to cross the storm-tossed Atlantic Ocean, but because the Separatists and Strangers respected each other and had good character they were able to work things out.

It is the American way for different kinds of people to get along together in one country because they respect the rights of others. This little ship, the *Mayflower,* was a picture of what America was to become.

Surprising News

When land was finally sighted, the *Mayflower*'s captain, Christopher Jones, had some surprising news for the Pilgrims. He had planned to sail the *Mayflower* closer to Jamestown, but storms had blown the ship far off its course.

"We are off the coast of **Massachusetts,**" Captain Jones told the Pilgrims. "You had planned to settle on land owned by the London Company, but you are too far north. If you settle here, you will have no government."

Planning a Government

A few men on board said that when they got off this ship they would be free to do

The *Mayflower* brought the Pilgrims to America.

whatever they wanted, and no-body could tell them what to do. The wise Pilgrims knew that this is not true freedom. They knew that if people are left to do anything they want, bad people will take away the freedom and safety of other people.

In order to protect themselves and others, and in order to protect their right to worship God the way they felt was best, the Pilgrims knew that they must set up a government. They wanted a government by laws rather than a government by men only. That way a bad man could not come in and take away their freedoms. They wanted to set up the best kind of laws that would help them to govern themselves.

The Pilgrim leaders met together in the cabin of the *Mayflower.* Here they wrote what is known as the **Mayflower Compact.** It is an important part of American history, because it is the first written agreement for self-government in America. The Mayflower Compact says many things that the Declaration of Independence and the Constitution of the United States would say later.

The Jamestown colonists were not self-governing; they had a governor given to them by England.

The Pilgrims chose their own governor, **John Carver.** They made their own plans for their own government. This is what is meant by **self-government.** It takes people who are able to control themselves to make self-government work. This is the kind of people that God wants us to be. This is the kind of people the Pilgrims were.

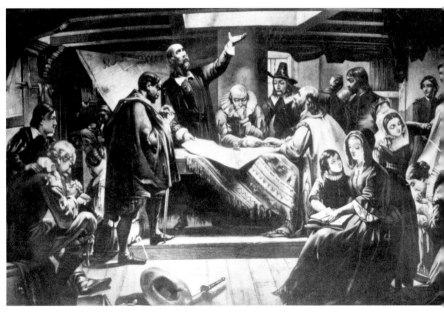

The Mayflower Compact declared Pilgrims free to govern themselves.

In the Mayflower Compact, the Pilgrims promised to make just laws. Here is what they wrote:

In the name of God, Amen. We whose names are underwritten, the loyal subjects of our dread sovereign Lord, King James, by the grace of God, of Great Britain, France, and Ireland king, defender of the faith, etc. Having undertaken, for the glory of God, and advancement of the Christian faith, and honour of our king and country, a voyage to plant the first colony in the Northern parts of Virginia, do by these presents solemnly and mutually in the presence of God, and one of another, covenant and combine ourselves together into a civil body politic, for our better ordering and preservation and furtherance of the ends aforesaid; and by virtue hereof to enact, constitute, and frame such just and equal laws, ordinances, acts, constitutions, and offices, from time to time, as shall be thought most meet and convenient for the general good of the colony, unto which we promise all due submission and obedience.

The Pilgrims read the agreement. Then the Mayflower Compact was signed. Later on, the Pilgrims would make laws. Each man who signed the Mayflower Compact was promising to obey those laws when they were made.

The Mayflower Compact was signed on Saturday, November 21, 1620. The Pilgrims spent the next day, Sunday, as they always did—praying and listening to the preaching of their <u>minister</u>, **Elder Brewster.** Then on Monday the men left the *Mayflower* and went ashore to find a good place for the group to settle.

The Pilgrims knew that it is important to have laws. They knew that the Bible says, "For all have sinned, and come short of the glory of God" (Romans 3:23). We need laws to protect us from those who would do wrong. We need a government to make laws and punish those who break the law.

Settling in Plymouth

How different were the attitudes of the Pilgrims compared to those of the Jamestown settlers! The men of Jamestown had been eager to settle anywhere, but the Pilgrims knew they must search for a place where they had

1. **a good supply of drinking water,**
2. **a good harbor for ships to sail into, and**
3. **a place free from unfriendly Indians.**

The Pilgrims realized the importance of listening to their captain. Even before they left England, the Pilgrims realized they would need <u>a soldier to guide them in dealing with the Indians and in building a settlement</u>. For this job, they hired **Captain Miles Standish,** a very wise and brave man. Captain Standish was not a Separatist him-

self, but he did much to protect these people, and they were thankful for his wise guidance. They obeyed him and respected his authority.

For several weeks, Captain Standish led a group of men exploring the area where the *Mayflower* landed. At last they found a place that filled all their requirements. The men sailed the *Mayflower* to this new area, called **Plymouth.** It was now December.

New England winters are cold and snowy. The Pilgrims' food supply was limited, but they would have to wait until spring to plant crops. Even wild animals take shelter from the cold, so there were few deer or wild turkeys to be found by hunters.

Just before Christmas, the men began chopping down trees in the snow to build what they called a **Common House.** It would be <u>a house, fort, and church</u> to all the Pilgrims that winter.

Many of the Pilgrims became sick that winter. At one time, only seven were strong enough to be up taking care of the sick. By spring, half of the Pilgrims had died. Yet there was no thought of giving up or complaining about being sick and cold and hungry. They were confident that God would help them.

Comprehension Check 4C

1. What boat brought the Pilgrims to America?

2. What was the name of the Pilgrims' colony? When was it founded?

3. Who was the first governor of the Pilgrims' colony? The minister?

4. Whom did the Pilgrims choose as a soldier to protect them?

5. Why did the Pilgrims have a thankful spirit and determine to continue on even during the hard times that first winter?

Making Friends with the Indians

Imagine the Pilgrims' surprise when one day a Native American walked into their settlement and said, "Welcome, Englishmen!" This friendly Indian's name was **Samoset.**

Are you surprised that an Indian knew how to speak English? The Pilgrims were not the first Englishmen to visit New England. Captain John Smith (the same person who had helped Jamestown) had explored and made a map of New England. In fact, the Pilgrims were using John Smith's map. The Indians had met and traded with Englishmen and even learned a few words of English. Thus, Samoset greeted the Pilgrims in English.

Samoset left and brought back **Squanto** [skwŏn′tō], an Indian who had been to England and who spoke English well. He also brought **Chief Massasoit** [măs′ə·soit′] and other Indians.

Chief Massasoit came to make peace with the Pilgrims. Together, Massasoit and the Pilgrims made a **treaty,** a written promise or agreement. They promised to help each other. They promised never to fight. The promises they made were never broken as long as Chief Massasoit lived.

Afterward, the Indians returned to their home, but Squanto chose to stay with the Pilgrims. The Pilgrims soon realized that God had sent Squanto to them. Without Squanto's help the Pilgrims might not have survived.

Although Chief Massasoit's tribe was friendly, there were other tribes that were unfriendly. Yet through the courage of Captain Standish and the help of Chief Massasoit, the Pilgrims had little to fear.

Hard Times

In April 1621, the *Mayflower* sailed back to England. The Pilgrims, who had already suffered so much in this new land, must have been tempted to give up and leave. But not one of them asked to go back to England. After the *Mayflower* had sailed away, Governor Carver became ill and died, and **William Bradford** was elected to take his place. Governor Bradford was such a good leader that the people elected him again and again, and during the next 36 years he was head of the colony nearly all the time. He wrote a book, *Of Plymouth Plantation*, that tells us much of what we know about the Pilgrims.

Squanto became a great favorite of the Pilgrims. He played with the children, taught the boys to trap animals, taught the settlers the best time to plant corn, and told them to put a fat fish in each hill to fertilize the growing grain.

Once the crops were all planted, the Pilgrims finished building their homes, made peace with nine Indian chiefs, and traded with the Indians for furs. Although they lacked many of the comforts they had known in England and Holland, the Pilgrims did not complain. Instead they thanked God for what they did have—food, shelter, and safety.

The First Thanksgiving

The Pilgrims were grateful for God's mercy during this first hard year. After the crops were harvested, they set aside a special time for giving thanks and feasting. Men went out to hunt deer and turkeys.

Chief Massasoit promised to help the Plymouth settlers.

Pilgrims and Indians joined together to thank God for His blessings.

Plymouth Grows

In November of that year, a ship arrived from England. It brought newcomers who would be staying. The Pilgrims were glad to see old friends and hear news from England, but they were disappointed to hear that the newcomers had brought no food for the winter. Without a second thought, the Pilgrims would share their homes and their food with the new settlers. Because of the unexpected extra people they had to feed, there would be less food than they had thought. There would be many times when they might wish that they had more to eat. But there would be no starving time during their second cold New England winter.

These brave people, the Pilgrims, who had such a deep faith in God, were the true heroes of our country's beginnings. We remember them for their courage, for their love of religious freedom, for their establishment of self-government, and for their faith in God and thankfulness to Him. They set up a free government in the New World—a government in which the leaders were selected by the people and in which people could vote no matter what religion they were.

Pumpkins, corn, and beans were cooked. Nuts were gathered from the woods.

Chief Massasoit and ninety of his men came to join the feast. That first time of Thanksgiving lasted three days. The Indians listened as the Bible was read and prayers of thanksgiving were raised to God. It was a special time to thank God, but the Pilgrims thanked God at all times, whether they had plenty of food or not.

Everyone had fun that first Thanksgiving. The Indians ran races with the Pilgrims. Captain Standish showed how his men could march. Then everyone ate and ate and ate! It was with happy hearts and full stomachs that everyone returned home.

★ ★ ★ ★ Chapter 4 Checkup ★ ★ ★ ★

Answer the questions on notebook paper.

1. What is a wilderness?
2. To whom did Queen Elizabeth give permission to start a colony in America?
3. What was the name given to England's land in America?
4. What English colony is known as "The Lost Colony"?
5. What event caused England to win the war against Spain?

6. What were King James I's four goals for beginning a colony in America?

7. What was the London Company?

8. What is a charter?

9. What kind of men were needed to establish a colony in America?

10. Name the three ships which brought the men to Virginia.

11. On what river was Jamestown built?

12. Why was the land where Jamestown was built important to the Native Americans?

13. On what bay was Jamestown built?

14. What is a swamp?

15. What was John Smiths' rule for the colonists of Jamestown?

16. What did the Jamestown colonists call the terrible winter of 1609–1610?

17. When did the first women arrive in Jamestown?

18. What became Jamestown's main "money crop"?

19. Were King James I's four goals for Jamestown met?

20. What religious group wanted to separate from the Church of England?

21. Where did the Separatists go before coming to America?

22. What boat brought the Separatists to America?

23. What were the people who were *not* Separatists on board the *Mayflower* called?

24. What name was given to the Separatists and Strangers who traveled together on the *Mayflower*?

25. What document was the first written agreement for self-government in America?

26. What was the name of the Pilgrim's colony?

27. Who was the first governor of Plymouth?

28. Who was the minister in Plymouth?

29. Who helped the Pilgrims in dealing with the Indians and building their settlement?

30. What governor of Plymouth wrote *Of Plymouth Plantation*?

The New England Colonies

NORTH
WEST   EAST
SOUTH

CANADA

New Hampshire

New York

Boston ● Massachusetts
● Plymouth

Providence ●
Hartford ● Rhode Island

Connecticut

Pennsylvania

New Jersey

Delaware

Maryland

Ohio River

Appalachian Mountains

Virginia

Atlantic Ocean

North Carolina

South Carolina

Georgia

Key
New England Colonies
Middle Colonies
Southern Colonies

SPANISH FLORIDA
● St. Augustine

The New England Colonies

Settling the North

America's population grew very slowly. For many years America remained a vast land dotted here and there with tiny villages. But as time went by, more and more people from England and other countries in Europe journeyed to America, hoping to find a better life. You have learned of **Jamestown,** the first lasting settlement in Virginia, which was started in **1607.** You have also learned of **Plymouth,** which was settled in **1620** in Massachusetts. <u>By 1735 there were thirteen colonies in America</u>.

The **thirteen original colonies** were Virginia, Massachusetts, Rhode Island, New Hampshire, New York, Connecticut, Maryland, Delaware, New Jersey, Pennsylvania, North Carolina, South Carolina, and Georgia. We often divide the colonies into three regions: the **New England Colonies,** the **Middle Colonies,** and the **Southern Colonies.** In this chapter you will learn how the colonies in New England were founded. The **New England Colonies** are <u>Massachusetts, Rhode Island, Connecticut, and New Hampshire</u>.

Massachusetts Bay Colony

As you have read, Plymouth was one of the first colonies in America. The Pilgrims of Plymouth were happy in their new land, even though life there was very hard. The Separatists loved the religious freedom they found in Plymouth. They knew that they could worship God in the way they believed was right.

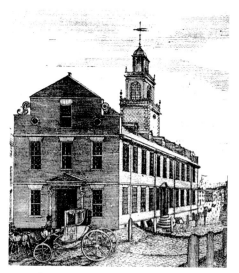

Boston has preserved many of its historical buildings. Left is a picture of the Boston state house early in the colonial period; at the right is a more recent photograph of the same building. The surroundings have changed, but the building itself has changed little over the last 300 years.

The Puritans

Back in England, there was another group that was unhappy with the Church of England. The **Puritans** wanted to "purify" or to remove all the things that they thought were bad from the Church of England. The Puritans wanted to *belong* to the Church of England, but they wanted to *change* it. Of course, the king of England would not permit this. He wanted everyone to believe and worship as he did. Anyone who disobeyed was thrown into jail.

Because of their unhappiness, the Puritans began to think about going to America. "If the Separatists can build a colony in the New World, so can we," they said.

Sailing to America

In the spring of 1630, eleven ships with nearly 1,000 men, women, and children on board sailed to New England. Later that same year, more ships followed until there were 2,000 Puritans in the New World. They called their colony the **Massachusetts Bay Colony.** The biggest town in that colony was **Boston.** Later, Plymouth would become a part of the colony, and the colony would be called simply **Massachusetts.**

Many Puritans were wealthier than their neighbors in Plymouth. Massachusetts quickly became a prosperous center of trade and commerce. Boston grew to be one of the most important cities in America.

New Names

1. **Puritans**—people who wanted to purify the Church of England
2. **John Winthrop**—governor of Massachusetts
3. **Obadiah Holmes**—man who was beaten with a whip in Massachusetts for preaching the gospel
4. **Roger Williams**—man who founded Rhode Island
5. **Dr. John Clarke**—minister who went to England to get a charter for Rhode Island
6. *Jonathon*—English ship that brought the first settlers to New Hampshire
7. **John Mason**—man who gave New Hampshire its name
8. **Thomas Hooker**—preacher who built Hartford, the first major settlement in Connecticut
9. **Fundamental Orders of Connecticut**—document that established Connecticut's system of government; provided a good pattern for the Constitution of the United States

Governor John Winthrop

The Puritans are remembered today for their trust in God, their willingness to work hard, their high standards, their strict discipline, and their belief that everyone should have a good education. <u>One of their most famous leaders</u> was **Governor John Winthrop,** who was elected governor twelve times. Another leader praised Governor Winthrop for his "piety, liberality, wisdom, and gravity." The Indians recognized Winthrop's good character, too. They called him "Single Tongue" because he was a truthful man.

John Winthrop, governor of Massachusetts, was an honest and generous leader.

Governor Winthrop was a generous man. The first winter in Boston was very cold, and some people could not get enough fuel. One man was caught stealing wood from Governor Winthrop's yard. The Puritans considered stealing almost as bad as murder, and if the man had been brought to trial, he might have been put to death. When Governor Winthrop was told about the thief, he cried, "I'll put a stop to that!" Then he turned to the thief and said,

"Friend, I fear that you have not wood enough for this winter. Help yourself from my pile whenever you choose."

"Didn't I tell you I would put a stop to it?" the governor said to the man who had reported the theft. "Find him stealing if you can!"

Like the Plymouth colonists, the Puritans were threatened with starvation long before their ships could return from England with provisions. Governor Winthrop generously gave people food from his own storehouse. He actually gave the last flour he had in his house to a poor man who came to beg. But the good governor did not suffer because of his generosity, for that very day the returning ships sailed into port, bringing plenty of provisions for all.

Massachusetts Grows

During the next 10 years, more than twenty thousand English-speaking people came over to New England. There, in time, they formed 50 villages, connected by roads and bridges. A governor was elected to rule over the Massachusetts colony, and each

---

New Places

10. **New England Colonies**—Massachusetts, Rhode Island, Connecticut, New Hampshire
11. **Massachusetts Bay Colony**—colony founded by the Puritans in 1630
12. **Boston**—largest town in the Massachusetts Bay Colony
13. **Providence**—first settlement in Rhode Island
14. **Rhode Island**—first colony to offer complete religious freedom; founded by Roger Williams

15. **Quinnehtukqut**—Indian word from which Connecticut gets its name; means "on or beside the long tidal river"
16. **Hartford**—first major settlement in Connecticut; built by Thomas Hooker

New Dates

17. **1630**—Massachusetts Bay Colony founded
18. **1639**—Fundamental Orders of Connecticut written

town ruled itself. But the people also sent representatives to the General Court, or Assembly, where public matters were discussed and laws were made to benefit the whole colony.

Freedom for Some

There were many good things about the Puritan colony of Massachusetts, and there were many good people there. Some people, however, were unhappy because there was religious freedom in Massachusetts for the Puritans, but not for anyone else! That sounds strange, because the Puritans had come to Massachusetts *seeking* religious freedom. They were so firm in their beliefs, however, that once they had control of the colony they expected everyone to worship God exactly as they did. Once they got away from the king of England, they started acting like him!

What the Puritans did was not unusual for their times. Almost every country in Europe had a state church, and very few people thought of separating religion and government. Because religion and government were ruled by the same people, the only people in Massachusetts who could vote were the Puritans. Puritans were the only people in the Massachusetts colony with religious and political freedom.

Problems for Others

Christians in Massachusetts who did not belong to a Puritan church could not start their own church. The Puritan leaders said, "You must come to our church, even if you don't belong to our church. You must pay money to our church, and you must obey the laws made by our church. And you cannot vote unless you are a member of our church." The Puritans knew it was right to attend church. But they seemed to believe that by forcing people to go to their church, they could make everyone become Christians.

Obadiah Holmes came to Massachusetts in 1638. Because he was a Baptist, he did not worship God exactly the way the other Puritans did. He moved away from Massachusetts so he could have religious liberty, but one day he went back with his pastor and another man to visit a very old, blind man who was also a Baptist. They had a church service in the man's house and preached, baptized, and held communion. The Puritan church leaders did not like this, and they sent two policemen to arrest the three strangers. The three men were tried in Boston and Obadiah Holmes was beaten with a whip for his preaching. This incident is just one sad thing that happened because of the lack of religious freedom in the Massachusetts Colony.

The Puritans were intelligent people, however, and they eventually learned that everyone ought to have religious freedom, for if everyone doesn't, then no one will for long. The Puritans of Massachusetts came to learn what the Pilgrims already knew— when one man's freedom is taken away, everyone's freedom is threatened.

The Pilgrims were not the only people who saw this truth about religious freedom very early. A Puritan named Roger Williams, whom you have already met as a missionary to the Indians, saw it, too. Roger Williams and preachers like Obadiah Holmes have gone down in history as champions in the cause of liberty for all.

Comprehension Check 5A

1. What are the New England Colonies?
2. Which religious group wanted to purify the Church of England?
3. What was the name of the first colony that religious group founded?
4. What governor of that first colony was known for his honesty, fairness, and generosity?

Rhode Island

Roger Williams was a Puritan preacher in Massachusetts. He did much to bring about religious freedom in America. Because Williams believed in salvation by faith alone, he knew that no person could ever be forced to become a Christian. He told his neighbors that it is wrong to punish people for not believing exactly as they themselves believe, since punishment can never make a person believe on Jesus in his heart.

Roger Williams's teaching upset some Massachusetts leaders. The leaders told Williams that he must either change his ways or leave Massachusetts.

Williams's ideas about the Native Americans also upset some people. He traded with them fairly and never tried to cheat them. After the trading was finished, he would tell them about God.

At times, the Massachusetts settlers were unfair to the Indians. The settlers believed that since the Native Americans were not Christians, it would be all right to take away the Indians' land. Roger Williams asked the Puritan leaders, "How do you expect the Indians to become Christians when you, as Christians, do not treat them fairly? The Indians should be paid for their land."

The Puritan leaders became very angry. They ordered a ship to take Roger Williams back to England. Learning of their plans, Williams escaped into the wilderness. It was wintertime and he became very sick. Friendly Indians found him and took care of him until spring.

In the spring he moved farther on. Williams bought some land from the Indians, which he called **Providence,** for he believed God had directed him there.

Freedom of Religion

Soon other people from the Massachusetts Bay Colony joined Williams and three cities besides Providence were settled. More and more settlers wanted to come to Roger Williams's colony, for it offered something very special—complete religious freedom. The people of Providence could worship as they chose.

Roger Williams escaped Massachusetts and founded his own colony. Friendly Indians took care of Williams during the harsh winter.

Rhode Island Becomes a Colony

As the colony grew larger, Roger Williams decided that it should have a government and that it should become an official British colony. So the colony of **Rhode Island** came into being.

Many people who had been persecuted for their beliefs helped Roger Williams set up Rhode Island. These people decided that Providence, the largest city in the colony, and the three other cities should band together and form one large government for the common good of Rhode Island. Years later, the thirteen colonies would do very much the same thing when they banded together to form the United States of America.

Rhode Island Gets a Charter

Next, the people of Rhode Island needed to get a charter or "plan" for the colony to follow. When the king approved the charter, the colony had a legal right to exist. Rhode Island's charter was far different from other charters. Here is the most important part of Rhode Island's charter:

> No person within the said Colony, at any time hereafter, shall be in any wise molested, punished, disquieted, or called in question, for any differences in opinions in matters of religion, and do not actually disturb the civil peace of our said Colony.

The charter was saying that Rhode Island's government could not bother a man whose religious beliefs were different from others, as long as that man did not disturb the peace. The charter went on to say:

> All may, at all times hereafter, freely and fully have and enjoy their own judgments and consciences, in matters of religious concernments . . . not using this liberty to licentiousness and profaneness, nor to the civil injury or outward disturbance of others.

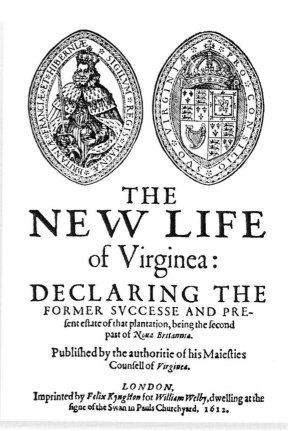

THE
NEW LIFE
of Virginea:
DECLARING THE
FORMER SVCCESSE AND PRE-
sent estate of that plantation, being the second
part of *Nova Britannia*.

Published by the authoritie of his Maiesties
Counsell of *Virginea*.

LONDON,
Imprinted by *Felix Kyngston* for *William Welby*, dwelling at the
signe of the Swan in Pauls Churchyard. 1612.

Documents such as this urged new settlers to come to the American colonies.

In other words, <u>Rhode Islanders could worship God however they chose</u>. The government was not to get involved in religion—church and state were separate. Of course, this did not mean that people could do whatever they chose to do. Those who did wrong things to others would be punished by the law.

The people of Rhode Island believed strongly in religious freedom. <u>They sent a minister,</u> **Dr. John Clarke,** <u>to England to get the charter</u>. Even though he had to stay in England for twelve years, he did not come home until he had the charter! With the charter from England, they were assured that they were legally a colony and that they had religious freedom.

Freedom for All

Because of Roger Williams and a small group of brave men, Rhode Island was the first colony to offer complete religious freedom. Because of its religious freedom, Rhode Island had political freedom, too. When Roger Williams began his colony, he could have forced everyone to do what he wanted. But he loved religious freedom and wanted everyone to be free to accept Christ by faith alone. He knew that God's truth about spiritual matters can stand alone, without being forced by a government. Roger Williams's little colony of Rhode Island offered religious freedom and political freedom—the two important freedoms that all Americans would someday know. George Washington, our first President, said of Rhode Island:

> While the Baptists have always defended the principles of religious liberty, they have never violated them. They have had but one opportunity of forming a system of civil government, and they so formed it as to create an era in the history of civilization. In the Little Baptist State of Rhode Island was the experiment first attempted of leaving religion wholly to herself, unprotected and unsustained by the civil arm. The principles which were here first planted have taken root in other lands, and have borne abundant fruit.

Comprehension Check 5B

1. What colony did Roger Williams establish?
2. What was the largest city in Roger Williams's colony?
3. What did this colony's charter guarantee?

New Hampshire

In 1623, an English ship named the *Jonathon* sailed near the coast of what is now New Hampshire. The few men who were on board came to the New World because they were hired to fish and cut down trees for lumber. They did not consider themselves colonists, for a company had hired them to do this. The fish and lumber were to be taken back and sold in England.

Since these men needed a place to live while they worked in the New World, they built a settlement. Small settlements such as this one, scattered here and there, gave new settlers a place to live. These settlements began to grow.

A few years later, the land was given to **John Mason,** who was an early English explorer of New England. He named the land given to him in the New World **New Hampshire,** after Hampshire County, where he had lived in England.

Meanwhile, some Puritans had settled in New Hampshire. In the early 1640s, the Puritans made New Hampshire a part of Massachusetts. However, the king of England later decided to make New Hampshire a separate colony once again.

Connecticut

One day some Native Americans appeared in Plymouth. They came to the colony to invite the white men to come and live on their land. "Our land is rich," the Indians said. "Beaver live in our woods. Our woods are thick with trees. The white man could trap furs and cut lumber for a living."

The Indians went on to say why they wanted the white men to come. "A fierce tribe lives on each side of our tribe. We are peaceful. Our enemies are afraid of the white man's guns. If you come, we will all live in peace."

In 1630 one man from Plymouth went into the area and built a trading post on a river. He reported that the Indians were telling the truth—the area was a good place to live. Soon other settlers were flocking to the area. The white men called the area Connecticut, their version of an Indian word, **Quinnehtukqut** [kwĭ′nĕ′tŭ·kŭt], meaning "on or beside the long tidal river."

The most famous settler was **Thomas Hooker,** a Puritan preacher from the Massachusetts Bay Colony. He and about 100 of his church members built **Hartford,** the first major settlement in Connecticut. Hartford and several smaller towns joined together to form the colony of Connecticut.

In 1638 Thomas Hooker preached an important sermon. In the sermon Hooker stated that the people should control the government rather than the government ruling the people. He said that people should have the right to elect the officials who run the government. In 1639 Connecticut put these ideas into the **Fundamental Orders of Connecticut,** the document that established Connecticut's system of government. Later, the Fundamental Orders would provide a good pattern for the Constitution of the United States.

Thomas Hooker took his people to Connecticut and built a new colony there.

Answer the questions on notebook paper.

1. How many colonies were there in America by 1735?
2. Name the New England colonies.
3. What did the Puritans want to do with the Church of England?
4. Which colony did the Puritans settle in 1630?
5. What became the largest city in Massachusetts?
6. Who was John Winthrop?
    What was he known for?
7. What man was beaten with a whip for preaching in Massachusetts?
8. Who left Massachusetts and settled Providence?
9. Whom did Rhode Island send to England to get a charter?
10. Why did the Native Americans like Roger Williams?
11. Which was the first colony to offer complete religious freedom?
12. What was the largest city in the colony of Rhode Island?
13. What did Rhode Island's charter guarantee?
14. What President referred to Rhode Island as the "Little Baptist State of Rhode Island"?
15. Which ship brought the first settlers to New Hampshire?
16. Who obtained New Hampshire and gave it its name?
17. New Hampshire was forced to become a part of what colony for several years?
18. What was the Indian name for Connecticut?
19. Which preacher built the city of Hartford?
20. Which plan of government was based upon a sermon by Thomas Hooker?
21. The Fundamental Orders of Connecticut later served as a pattern for what important document?

The Middle and Southern Colonies

NORTH
WEST EAST
SOUTH

CANADA

New
Hampshire

Massachusetts

New
York

Rhode Island

Connecticut

New York

Pennsylvania

Philadelphia

New
Jersey

Ohio River

Baltimore

Delaware

Maryland

Williamsburg

Virginia

Atlantic

Ocean

North Carolina

Appalachian Mountains

South
Carolina

Georgia

Charles Town

Savannah

Key

New England Colonies
Middle Colonies
Southern Colonies

SPANISH FLORIDA

St. Augustine

The Middle and Southern Colonies

Settling Farther South

While the New England colonies were being settled in the north, other colonies were being started along the rest of the Atlantic coast. They were the **Middle Colonies:** New York, Delaware, New Jersey, and Pennsylvania, and the **Southern Colonies:** Virginia, Maryland, North Carolina, South Carolina, and Georgia.

New York

New York was an unusual colony, because three countries claimed to own it at the same time.

The Dutch sent Henry Hudson to find a shortcut to Asia.

The **Dutch** are people who live in **The Netherlands** (also called **Holland**). In 1609, the Dutch sent a man named **Henry Hudson** to find a shortcut to Asia. Instead, Hudson found an area containing friendly Indians and plenty of beaver. Since beaver skins were very valuable, the Dutch quickly claimed the area that Hudson explored. This area is now the southern part of New York.

However, during the same year (1609), a Frenchman named **Samuel de Champlain** sailed down from Quebec and explored what is now the northern part of New York. So France became the second country to claim New York.

You will remember that in 1497 John Cabot claimed all of North America for England. Since New York is a part of North America, England also claimed New York.

Even though three countries claimed New York, only one began to build settlements there. The Dutch built a small village there that they called Fort Orange. Later the Dutch bought Manhattan Island from the Indians and built a village there. The Dutch called this city **New Amsterdam,** since Amsterdam was the capital of The Netherlands. The Dutch named the whole colony **New Netherland.**

New Netherland had rich farm land. Men were getting wealthy from beaver furs. New Amsterdam had one of the best harbors in America. Now England decided it was time to take control of what she claimed was hers. English ships sailed into the harbor, and soldiers told the people that England was going to take control of New Netherland.

The brave and fearless **Peter Stuyvesant** [stī′vĭ·sənt], the governor of the colony, at first refused to surrender to the British. But the British promised to treat the Dutch fairly, and the Dutch saw that they could never defeat the British. The Dutch people refused to fight. Brokenhearted, the governor surrendered.

The British did indeed treat the Dutch fairly. The Dutch were allowed to keep their farms, and most of them stayed on after the British took over. But the British changed a few names—New Amsterdam became **New York City,** and New Netherland was called **New York.**

The British now owned another colony in America. Eventually, England would control all thirteen American colonies.

Even though he wanted to fight, Peter Stuyvesant was finally forced to surrender New Amsterdam to the British.

Delaware

The Dutch were also the first to begin a settlement in Delaware, but there was much trouble between the settlers and the Indians. The settlement failed.

Then **Sweden** became interested in beginning a colony in the New World. However, it seems as though the people of Sweden were content to stay in Sweden. In 1638,

New Words

1. **admiral**—a chief commander in the navy
2. **indigo**—a valuable blue dye
3. **plantations**—large farms found throughout the Southern Colonies

New Names

4. **Dutch**—people who live in The Netherlands; claimed the southern part of New York
5. **Henry Hudson**—Dutch explorer sent to find a shortcut to Asia; found New York instead
6. **Samuel de Champlain**—man who explored northern New York and claimed it for France
7. **Peter Stuyvesant**—Dutch governor of New Netherland who finally surrendered to the British

8. **Sir George Carteret and Lord John Berkeley**—men who gave New Jersey its name
9. **Quakers**—religious group that settled in Pennsylvania
10. **William Penn**—founder of Pennsylvania who carefully planned the city of Philadelphia
11. **George Calvert (Lord Baltimore)**—man who had the idea of settling Maryland as a refuge for Roman Catholics
12. **James Oglethorpe**—man who founded the colony of Georgia for prisoners and poor people from England
13. **George Whitefield**—preacher who established the first orphanage in America

only about fifty settlers arrived on the two ships that Sweden sent to Delaware. They may have been few in number, but theirs was <u>the first successful settlement in Delaware</u>.

The Swedes were peaceful farmers and hard workers. So were the Indians who lived around them. Though the Indians did not get along with the Dutch, they became friends with the Swedes.

Nevertheless, the Swedes believed in protecting themselves. They built a fort that they named **"Fort Christina"** to honor Sweden's young queen. (<u>Today this area is the city of Wilmington, Delaware</u>.) They named their settlement **New Sweden.**

New Sweden never grew large. The country of Sweden was having its own problems and could not help the colony. As a result, <u>the Dutch took over all of New Sweden</u> in 1655 but kept it for only ten years before <u>the English took it away from them</u>.

This old church was built by Swedish settlers in Wilmington, Delaware, originally called Fort Christina.

New Jersey

Across the Hudson River from New York is **New Jersey.** At one time, the Dutch claimed New Jersey as part of New Netherland as they once did Delaware.

New Places

14. **Middle Colonies**—New York, Delaware, New Jersey, Pennsylvania
15. **Southern Colonies**—Virginia, Maryland, North Carolina, South Carolina, Georgia
16. **The Netherlands**—country in Europe, also called Holland
17. **New Amsterdam**—Dutch name for New York City
18. **New Netherland**—Dutch name for New York
19. **Fort Christina**—Swedish settlement that became Wilmington, Delaware
20. **New Sweden**—settlement that became the colony of Delaware
21. **Chester**—first settlement in Pennsylvania
22. **Philadelphia**—city in Pennsylvania carefully designed by William Penn; means "city of brotherly love"
23. **St. Mary's**—first settlement in Maryland
24. **Carolana**—name given to the area of land that became North and South Carolina
25. **Charles Town**—first settlement in Carolana
26. **Savannah**—first settlement in Georgia

New Dates

27. **1609**—Henry Hudson sails to America for the Dutch
28. **1681**—Quakers begin their settlement of Pennsylvania

The Dutch settled New Netherland (New York) in 1624. However, they did very little to send settlers across the river to settle New Jersey. So a few Swedish settlers from Delaware began to wander into New Jersey. This action angered the Dutch, who forced the Swedes to leave. Then in 1660 the Dutch began the first permanent settlement in New Jersey.

Now it was England's turn to be angry. New Netherland was in the middle of English colonies. England considered the Dutch a threat to English colonies. The English claimed the Dutch were living on land that belonged to England.

You will remember that in 1664, English warships sailed to New Amsterdam. Without even a shot, the English took over New Amsterdam. No longer did the Dutch rule in any colony of the New World.

The king's brother, the duke of York, received not only New Netherland, but also the land that would become New Jersey. The duke of York in turn gave New Jersey to two of his friends, **Sir George Carteret** and **Lord John Berkeley.** These are the men that gave New Jersey its name. They offered to sell land at low prices to colonists. They also offered any colonist freedom of religion. These offers brought many colonists seeking religious freedom to New Jersey, and a number of Presbyterians and Baptists who would become famous at the time of our Declaration of Independence lived there.

A Quaker meeting

Comprehension Check 6A

1. What colony was claimed by three countries?
2. Why did England have a claim on New York?
3. Which colony was named by Sir George Carteret and Lord John Berkeley?
4. What fort did the Swedish people build to protect themselves?

Pennsylvania

In 1643, Swedish settlers wandering from Delaware began the first settlement in Pennsylvania. The small settlement was later named **Chester.**

However, the settlement for which we most remember Pennsylvania began in 1681. For the story of this settlement, we must first go back to England. You will remember that England did not offer freedom of religion at that time. For this reason, many Separatists, Puritans, and Catholics had settled in the New World. However, there was one group of people whose beliefs seemed so strange to others that they were not even welcome in the new American colonies! This group was called **Quakers** or Friends.

Quaker Beliefs

Let's look at some of the beliefs that made Quakers so unpopular.

- The Quakers did not believe that one person could be more important than another. Therefore, they would not show more respect for one person than another. They would not take off their hat to show respect for someone. Neither would they bow before anyone, not even the king of England.

- The Quakers did not believe in any kind of fighting. Therefore, they would not fight to protect themselves or their country, even in time of war.

As you can see, the Quakers' beliefs were quite different from those of other groups who lived at that time. Although the Quakers were a very peaceful group of people, no other groups welcomed them. In England, they were arrested for their beliefs. Those Quakers who did go to the colonies were often beaten and treated worse than they had been in England.

William Penn

A young man named **William Penn** became curious about the Quakers' beliefs. Wanting to find out more about these people, he attended their meetings. William Penn liked what he heard. It was not long before he became a Quaker, too.

William Penn's father was an **admiral** in the British navy and a good friend of the king of England. You can imagine how angry he was when his son William said that he had become a Quaker. William's father had hoped that William would become an important officer in the British navy as he himself had done, but William would not because of the Quaker belief that fighting is wrong. Penn's father was well liked by the king, but William, being a Quaker, would not show respect for the king. Penn's father was also a very wealthy man, but because of his Quaker beliefs, William did not feel that wealth was important.

Try as he did, William Penn's father could not change his son's mind. After his father died, Penn remembered that the king had borrowed a large sum of money from his father and had never paid it back. Penn knew that the king would never give him, a Quaker, the money. But perhaps the king would give him land in America to begin a colony for the Quakers.

The king was pleased with Penn's idea. Not only could he easily repay the debt by giving Penn land in faraway America, but he would also rid England of the troublesome Quakers.

A New Colony: Pennsylvania

The king named the new colony **Pennsylvania,** which means "Penn's Woods." In 1681, William Penn sent a group of settlers to choose a good place to build a town. The next year, Penn brought a group of colonists to Pennsylvania.

Penn himself went to the Native Americans and asked them to sell land to him.

William Penn, founder of Pennsylvania

land, peaceful neighbors, good government, and freedom of religion. Settlers came from many different European countries seeking the peace and freedoms that Pennsylvania had to offer. Before long, Pennsylvania became a very important colony.

Comprehension Check 6B

1. Who founded Pennsylvania?
2. Pennsylvania was founded to be a refuge for what religious group?
3. What was the main settlement in Pennsylvania, personally designed by William Penn?

His conscience told him it was wrong to take land from the Indians. The Indians agreed to sell land to their new white friend. Then William Penn told the Indians that Quakers did not believe in fighting. They would never carry guns or knives to hurt the Indians. In return, the Indians promised peace to the white men. As a result, Quaker children played with Indian children. The Indians paid the Quakers neighborly visits. There was no fear of Indian wars for many years.

"The City of Brotherly Love"

Penn began making plans for a beautiful city with gardens and trees between houses, and straight, wide roads leading through the town. The name Penn chose for his city was **Philadelphia,** which means "the city of brotherly love."

People of all faiths would be welcome in Pennsylvania. Penn believed that no one should be forced to believe the Quakers' beliefs.

Pennsylvania had much to offer new colonists. It had good farm

Virginia

England had a difficult time establishing colonies in Virginia. The first colony at Roanoke mysteriously disappeared. The second colony at Jamestown nearly failed. Then the

Philadelphia was the largest and most important city in the Middle Colonies.

settlers began to raise crops, using some of the knowledge they had gained from the Native Americans. Finally, England had a permanent colony in Virginia.

Soon, Virginia needed to set up a better government. The colonists decided to elect **representatives,** men chosen by the people to make decisions for them. This group of representatives was called the **House of Burgesses.** On July 30, 1619, the representatives met for the first time in the choir loft of a Jamestown church. Their job was to help the governor make decisions about taxes, laws, and other issues. Virginia's new government would set the example for the future government of the nation.

Maryland

In England, the Catholics, like the Separatists and Puritans before them, could not worship as they pleased. They were forced to attend the Church of England.

George Calvert (whose title was Lord Baltimore) was a Catholic man who worked as a secretary to the king. He did his work well and became the king's friend. Realizing how unhappy his Catholic friends were, he asked the king for land in America where he could begin his own colony.

"Who could you take there?" asked the king.

"I want to take those who are Catholics, yet I would take anyone who claims to be a Christian, as long as he is willing to work together with the rest," replied Lord Baltimore. "The people of the Maryland colony will be free to build and go to a Christian church of their choice."

The king granted him his wish. While plans were still being made for the new colony, Lord Baltimore died. His son, **Cecil Calvert,** became the second Lord Baltimore. He continued his father's plans for Maryland. Because he had much work to do in England, Cecil Calvert could not go to Maryland. Instead, he chose to send his brother, Leonard Calvert, who was to become the first governor of Maryland.

Two small ships named the *Ark* and the *Dove* set sail from England. On board the ships were about 200 passengers who were coming to the New World for religious freedom.

In 1634, the *Ark* and the *Dove* sailed up the Chesapeake Bay. The colonists and the governor bought land from friendly Indians who were planning to move anyway. The Indians were delighted with the hoes, axes, hatchets, and knives they received. These tools were far better than the ones they had for planting seed, building, and chopping trees.

The new colonists named the first settlement in Maryland **St. Mary's.** These colonists had many blessings to be thankful for. They had arrived in early spring. So they busied themselves with planting gardens. Friendly Indians taught them how to plant corn. The rivers were full of crabs, oysters, and fish. The forests had plenty of deer and other animals. The colonists would not go hungry.

The Indians whom they had bought their land from left their huts for the colonists to live in until they had time to build their own houses.

The founding of Maryland is important because it showed that <u>in America Catholics would be able to worship freely</u>. Letting people worship in their own way is an important part of religious freedom.

The Carolinas

Many years had passed since Sir Walter Raleigh had tried and failed to begin a colony on Roanoke Island off the coast of what is now North Carolina. As time went on, both North and South Carolina became known as one large piece of land called **Carolana.**

By 1650 Virginia had many colonists. Some of the Virginia colonists began to wander down into what is now North Carolina. So the <u>first settlers of North Carolina came from Virginia</u>, not from across the ocean.

Meanwhile, in 1663, King Charles II of England was asked a favor by eight of his favorite workers. They wanted land to begin a colony in America. Willingly, King Charles gave them the land known as **Carolana.**

The Settlement of Charles Town

These eight men became the owners of Carolana. They could make their own laws for the settlers to obey. Their main interest was making money from their new colony. In 1670 the little village of **Charles Town** was built. Then Charles Town (which became the city of Charleston, South Carolina) was moved to a better location. The better location had a good harbor from which English ships could sail in and out.

Ships brought settlers from Europe and goods that the settlers could buy. As a result, Charles Town, South Carolina, grew rapidly. It was <u>South Carolina's first permanent settlement</u>.

Problems Arise

The eight rulers of Carolana did not set up a good government for their settlers. There were many quarrels about the laws.

Charles Town in 1672

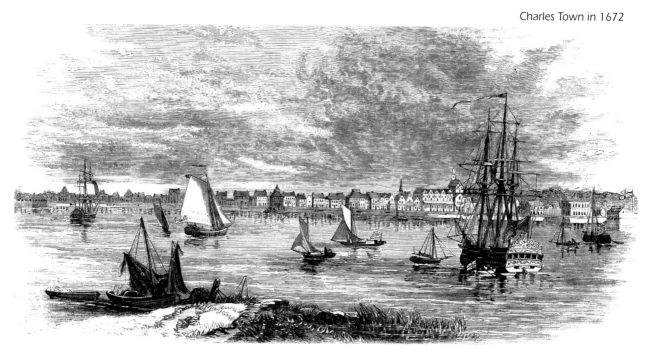

A Southern plantation

They took land unfairly from the Indians. Angered, the Indians fought against the settlers. After many years, the owners sold their land back to the king of England.

The Carolinas

The king then divided the land into two colonies, North Carolina and South Carolina. Then he appointed two men to be governors of the two colonies.

South Carolina grew quickly. The colonists found that rice, cotton, and the **indigo** plant (used to make <u>a valuable blue dye</u> also called indigo) grew very well there. Soon many <u>large farms</u> called **plantations** were built to grow large fields of these valuable crops. All three crops required much work to grow and harvest. Since there were not enough white settlers to work in the fields, the plantation owners began buying slaves from Africa to do their work.

North Carolina did not grow as quickly as South Carolina. The people who settled North Carolina were mostly poor and lived simple, hard-working lives. Many built log cabins on small farms. Most planted and worked their own fields. Because of this, there were fewer slaves in North Carolina.

When the king gave Carolana to his eight friends, the boundaries of Carolana stretched from the Atlantic Ocean all the way across to the Pacific Ocean! At that time, no one had any way to know the size of America. The great size of our land was to be discovered by explorers and pioneers in the years ahead.

"all the way across to the Pacific Ocean"

Comprehension Check 6C

1. What did Virginia call their representatives?
2. What colony was intended to be a refuge for Catholics?
3. What were North and South Carolina called when they were both one colony?
4. What was the name of the valuable blue dye produced in South Carolina?
5. What were the large farms in the Southern Colonies called?

Georgia: England's Last Colony

England, 1732

The people of London, England, were excited. Over a hundred years had passed since England had begun its first successful colony in the New World. Since then eleven other colonies had struggled to success.

Now, news was spreading that England was about to begin its thirteenth colony

James Oglethorpe, founder of Georgia

for a reason completely different from the other colonies. The thought of it made many people in England willing to donate food, supplies, and money to send the new colonists on their way.

At that time, there were many poor people in England who were willing to work, but who could not find jobs. <u>If a person was too poor to pay his bills, he was placed in prison</u>. Of course, he could do nothing to pay back his bill once he was in jail. Unless he was fortunate enough to know someone who was willing to pay his bill for him, he would spend the rest of his life in prison.

In the 1700s, England's prisons were crowded with poor people. Prisons in those days were dark, dirty, cold, and wet. Diseases spread quickly, and many prisoners died. The jailers, whose job it was to look after the prisoners, would often beat their prisoners and rob them of what little they did have, even their food. Many prisoners starved to death. Indeed, English prisons were dreadful and hopeless places.

James Oglethorpe

James Oglethorpe, a member of the English government, studied the problems of the poor people. Through his help, many were released from prison. Yet they faced the struggle of finding jobs.

"If only these people could go to America!" thought James Oglethorpe. "There would be plenty of work for them to do there."

However, there was one problem with that idea. How could these poor people earn enough money to pay their way on a ship to America?

The king of England heard Oglethorpe's idea, and he liked it.

"The land below South Carolina is unsettled," thought the king. "Spain has a colony in Florida. If England does not settle the land between Florida and South Carolina, Spain will!"

The king made some decisions. "I will appoint twenty-one men who will work without pay. They will choose the people who will go to the new colony. They will plan a set of laws for the new colony to follow, and they will govern the new colony."

The English government gave this group of men $50,000 to use in sending the colonists to the New World. When the people of England heard, many donated food and supplies for the colonists. Churches gave money.

A New Colony: Georgia

The <u>new colony</u> would be named **Georgia,** in honor of King George II. James

Oglethorpe went with the 114 colonists who were chosen to go on the first ship sent to Georgia. He became a great friend to the colonists. On board the ship, he visited the sick and helped the colonists in whatever way he could.

In February 1733, Oglethorpe and his colonists arrived in Georgia, and Oglethorpe became the first governor. In many ways, he was a wise, brave, and kind governor. He made lasting friendships with the Indians from whom he bought the land. In exchange for his gifts, the Indians presented him with a buffalo robe lined with eagle feathers, saying: "The eagle signifies swiftness, and the buffalo strength. The English are swift as a bird to fly over the vast seas, and as strong as a beast before their enemies. The eagle's feathers are soft, and signify love; the buffalo's skin is warm, and means protection: therefore, love and protect our families."

James Oglethorpe planned and directed the building of the first settlement in Georgia, which was named **Savannah.** When Spain tried to destroy the new colony, Oglethorpe successfully led the colonists to victory. Without his aid, Georgia would probably have been destroyed. Often, he used his own money to see that the needs of the colonists were met.

The Georgia colonists tried to grow olive trees and breed silkworms, but these attempts failed. Soon rice became an important crop in the colony, and the first fine cotton was raised there with seed brought from India. Oglethorpe, wanting to give his colony a good start, said that neither rum nor slaves should be allowed there. He and John Wesley, who was in Georgia at that time preaching to the colonists and the Indians, both tried to persuade the colonists that they would be far better off if they did their own work and stayed sober. The people

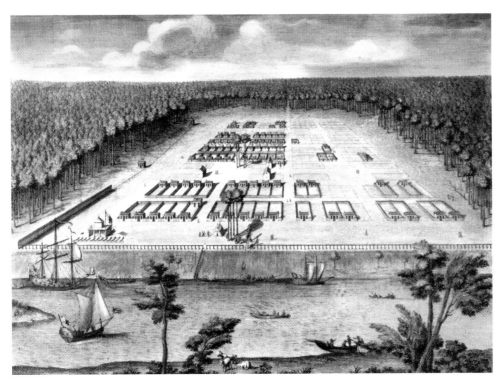

Savannah was the first settlement in Georgia.

listened for a while, but later they decided that they wanted both rum and slavery in their colony.

George Whitefield, the great preacher of colonial America, came from England to visit the Georgia colony in 1738, where he started the first orphanage in America near Savannah.

Oglethorpe gave up Georgia to the king in 1752 and went back to England. He was always interested in the settlement he had founded, and since he lived to be very old, he saw it join the other colonies in 1776 to become a part of the United States of America.

Many People: One Land

We have seen how each of the thirteen original colonies was founded. It took 125 years in all for the colonies to be formed. That may seem like a long time—but it takes time for a new nation to get started in a wilderness. Such an important event does not happen often in history!

Many different kinds of people were in America now. There were people of all different religions—Separatists, Puritans, Quakers, Baptists, Lutherans, Mennonites, Episcopalians, Catholics, and others. These people were learning to get along with each other and were developing the important ideas of freedom of religion and separation of church and state. These ideas were new to most of the world, and they would help to make America the kind of country where the Bible could be preached freely and have a great influence on the lives of the people.

Many people came to America looking for a chance to work hard and do their best at jobs of their choice. This is an important part of the American way of life.

Most of the original settlers were English, but America soon became home for people from Germany, Holland, France, Ireland, Switzerland, Scotland, and other countries as well. All of these different kinds of people would learn to respect each other and look upon themselves as one people—Americans.

★ ★ ★ ★ **Chapter 6 Checkup** ★ ★ ★ ★

Answer the questions on notebook paper.

1. Name the Middle Colonies.
2. List the Southern Colonies.
3. What explorer was hired to explore New York for the Dutch?
4. What three countries claimed New York?
5. Who explored northern New York for France?
6. What man claimed all of North America for England?

7. What did the Dutch call New York City?

8. What fiery Dutch governor did not want to surrender to the British?

9. Who settled Delaware?

10. What was Delaware originally called?

11. Who settled New Jersey?

12. Who gave New Jersey its name?

13. What colony was founded by William Penn?

14. What was the first settlement in that colony?

15. What important city in Pennsylvania did William Penn personally design?

16. What does Philadelphia mean?

17. Which colony had a group of representatives called the House of Burgesses?

18. What colony was founded as a refuge for Catholics?

19. Whose idea was it to begin the colony of Maryland?

20. What two ships brought the first settlers to Maryland?

21. What was the first settlement in Maryland?

22. What was the first settlement in Carolana?

23. What is indigo?

24. What is a plantation?

25. What kind of people settled Georgia?

26. Who founded Georgia?

27. What was the first settlement in Georgia?

28. What famous preacher went to Georgia to start America's first orphanage?

Homes from the New England and Middle Colonies

A Picture of Colonial Life

A Different Way of Life

Life in colonial America was quite different from life in America today. Yet the way people lived back then influenced the way we live now.

Homes

The first crude cabins built by the colonists were not very pleasant to live in. Because the colonists had come to America to stay, they wanted to build permanent homes. Soon larger, nicer houses began to dot the American countryside, and the one-room cabins began to disappear.

Building a new house was quite a task. Fortunately, the colonist did not have to do it all by himself. When a new house had to be built, all the men in the village would gather for a **"house-raising."** With the help of his neighbors, the colonist would clear his land of trees. Then the <u>men would cut the trees into lumber and build the new home</u>. A colonist would even have to build all of his own furniture unless he had brought a few pieces over from Europe.

Most of the time the settlers built houses that were copies of their homes in Europe. A few designs, however, were American.

A colonial kitchen

This instrument, a froe, was used to split logs to make lumber. Then colonists would use the lumber to build such things as tables, benches, and chairs.

These were two kinds of clothes that colonial Americans wore.

Inside, colonial houses were simple. There were one or two large beds, a table (usually with benches, not chairs), and perhaps a few other pieces of furniture. The bowls and plates—even spoons and forks—were carved out of wood. Candles gave light to the cabin, and a huge **fireplace** was <u>used for both cooking and heating</u>.

As you can see, colonists did not enjoy the luxuries we have today. But for almost every colonist, life in America was far better than life in Europe. And the colonists were willing to work hard to make life in America even better.

During the day, most men in the colonies were busy farming or hunting. Colonial wives were also *very* busy. One of their most important jobs was making clothes for the family. Using a spinning wheel, the wife would spin sheep's wool into yarn. Then she would use a loom to make <u>a rough, gray material</u> called **homespun** from the yarn. The homespun was useful for making shirts, dresses, and pants. Deerskin would also be available for making clothes if the husband was a good hunter. The richer colonists avoided wearing homespun clothes; they bought the latest fashions from Europe instead.

New Words

1. **house-raising**—a time when all the neighbors got together to help a new settler build his house
2. **homespun**—rough, gray material made by early colonists
3. **town criers**—men who were paid by the town to wander about the streets and call out the latest news
4. **circuit-riding preachers**—men who traveled on horseback throughout the South, preaching the Bible
5. **dame school**—a school taught in a colonial home; where many colonial children started their education
6. **hornbook**—one sheet containing the alphabet and the Lord's prayer attached to a wood paddle and protected by a thin sheet of cow's horn

At night, colonial families usually gathered around the fireplace, perhaps to work on some project, such as making candles, stitching a quilt together, or cooking molasses candy. Since there was no radio or television, families would spend their time talking about the latest news—new settlers in the area, trouble with the Indians, rumors about war with England, the latest happenings in Europe. Some colonial towns had newspapers, but most colonists got the news from town criers. **Town criers** were <u>men who were paid by the city to wander about the streets and call out the latest news</u> as loudly as they could. The colonists also heard the news in their churches on Sundays.

In most homes the Bible was read aloud every night. Other books, such as *Pilgrim's Progress* and John Foxe's *Book of Martyrs*, were also widely read; but <u>the Bible was the most important book for most colonists</u>.

Churches

Most settlers came to America so that they could worship God freely. In America, once freedom of religion was allowed, no one had to worship secretly. Large public houses of worship were built throughout the colonies. The early church buildings were also used for town meetings, where matters of government were discussed. Thus the ideas of political freedom and religious freedom took root in America's church buildings.

New England was a land filled with churches. At first, most were Puritan churches

The *Boston News-Letter*, which began in 1704, was America's first newspaper. Newspapers replaced town criers in America's cities.

7. **old-field schools**—small schools started by parents in the Southern Colonies

New Names

8. *New England Primer*—American schoolbook which was used by millions of children for over 150 years
9. **Harvard**—first college in America

10. **Christopher Dock**—German Mennonite schoolteacher who greatly influenced education in America

New Dates

11. **1636**—Harvard, America's first college is started
12. **1647**—New England passes a law ordering cities to build schools for children

A simple, sturdy New England church

because the founders and early settlers of New England were Puritans from England. <u>The first settlers of New England built churches that</u>, like their homes, <u>were plain and simple</u>. They were well built, however, and some of them are still used today.

As more and more people came to New England, changes took place. Larger and more decorative Congregational (Puritan) churches were built. Other religious groups—Baptists, Methodists, Quakers, Jews, and many others—built meeting houses in New England. By the end of the colonial period (1776), New England had changed from a land dominated by Puritans to a place where people of many faiths could live and worship. For a long time, however, all the people in some New England colonies had to pay taxes to the Congregational church whether they belonged to it or not.

The settlers who built their homes in the Middle Colonies represented many different religions, and the Middle Colonies quickly became known as a land of religious freedom. Many <u>Quakers came to the Middle Colonies</u> to escape the persecution they had faced in England. Other groups

Churches gradually became larger and more elaborate.

who came there included <u>Mennonites, Presbyterians, Baptists, Anglicans, and Dutch Reformed</u>. In the Middle Colonies, these groups were free to worship God in the way they thought was right.

<u>Because the Southern colonists planted large farms that separated Southern families from each other, the Southern Colonies had fewer churches</u> than other colonies. Families would have to travel miles each Sunday just to meet together. Therefore, traveling preachers, rather than churches, brought religion to the Southern colonists. Sometimes an Anglican (Church of England) priest would travel around to the farms and perform an Anglican service for the many Southerners who belonged to the Church of England. Later, men called **circuit-riding preachers** <u>traveled on horseback throughout the South preaching the Bible</u>, and great revivals broke out.

This meetinghouse in Pennsylvania is an example of churches built in the Middle Colonies.

A typical colonial church service

Most colonial children got their first schooling in a dame school.

Going to church was the most important part of the week in colonial America. Little if any work was done on Sunday; the Sabbath was a special time that all the people honored. Different churches worshiped in different ways, but the services usually included singing, Bible reading, and a long sermon. In fact, most of the services lasted over two hours—some longer than three!

Such long services were bound to cause people to snooze; but a man strolling through the congregation made sure that everyone stayed awake—he had a pole with which he poked anyone who had closed eyes!

Comprehension Check 7A

1. What two uses did the fireplace provide for colonial homes?
2. What was the rough, gray material made by colonial women?
3. Why was news given by town criers or in church during colonial days?
4. What was the most important book in colonial homes?

Schools

Almost every colonist believed that children in America needed a good education. The colonists built schools that would give their children what they needed.

Many children began their education in a **dame school.** A lady would agree to teach children in her home. She taught the children reading, writing, and basic arithmetic. The children had no nice classrooms, and there were very few schoolbooks.

Most children used a hornbook to learn their alphabet. A **hornbook** was a paddle-shaped board to which was

A hornbook

Harvard University, opened in 1636, was the first college in America. It was created to train ministers.

attached one sheet containing the alphabet and the Lord's Prayer. The book was called a hornbook because a thin sheet of transparent cow's horn covered the paper to protect it.

After a child had memorized the hornbook, he could begin reading in the *New England Primer,* the most widely used textbook in all of colonial America. This book had lists of words, prayers, poems about Bible stories, and short stories about doing right which gave religious instruction as well as training in reading. For over 150 years millions of American children learned to read from the *New England Primer.* After that, they would read the Bible, and almost all of them also read *Pilgrim's Progress.*

After staying in a dame school for a year or two, the boys might go on to get more education. Girls usually stayed home and learned to bake, cook, and sew, and to make yarn and cloth and candles and soap so they could care for their families when they were older.

Because American colonists wanted to make sure that their children got a good education, they passed laws ordering cities to build schools and provide education for the public. People knew that learning about God meant reading the Bible, and reading the Bible meant learning to read.

The first public schools in America were built by the Puritans in New England. As early as 1647 New England had passed a law ordering cities to build schools for children. Many schools opened their doors to eager children throughout New England. New England even opened the first college in America—**Harvard,** which was started in 1636 to train ministers to preach the gospel. When Harvard College was started, its leaders said:

Let every student be plainly instructed, and earnestly pressed to consider well, the main end of his life and studies is, to know

God and Jesus Christ which is eternal life (John 17:3) and therefore lay Christ in the bottom, as the only foundation of all sound knowledge and learning.

The Middle Colonies had fewer schools than the New England Colonies. Farms were larger here and people lived farther apart than in New England. Schools were so far apart that many children could not walk the distance. Even so, when there was a school, children had to walk as far as two to four miles one way to reach the one-room schoolhouse. Those who lived farther away were taught by their parents or were not taught at all.

Schools in the Middle Colonies usually had just one room with roughly made benches. Almost always, these children were taught by strict men teachers. Sometimes a minister of a church would be the teacher of a school. He would hold his school in the church.

In colonial days, paper was much too expensive for students to use. Pieces of birch bark were stripped from trees and used in place of paper. A piece of lead or coal was used as a pencil. Books were not very plentiful. Usually the school had only one copy of each book it used. Each student waited his turn to use the book.

For a long time, there were not many schools in the South. Wealthy farmers lived in huge homes far apart from each other; they could afford tutors to come to their homes and teach their children privately. Of course the poor people could not afford to build schools.

Eventually, parents in some areas of the South started to get together to hire a teacher for their children. The teacher and students would meet in a shabby building in an old field, in what was called an **old-field school.** A boy named George Washington attended this kind of school. One year, he had to ride on horseback every day to his old-field school, which was ten miles from home. Another year, he rowed a boat across the river every day, even when it was storming, to get to school.

Comprehension Check 7B

1. What was a hornbook?
2. For how long did American school children use the *New England Primer*?
3. What was America's first college?

Industry

America offered Europeans the promise of a better life. Europeans who came to America found that the promise was true. Not only could they worship God freely and give their children a good education, but they could also work and enjoy the fruit of their labors. People who had lived in poverty in Europe came to America and grew wealthy.

For the first part of its history, America's chief industry was farming. One of the first things that most colonists did in America was to plant a garden. After the Indians showed them how to plant corn, the colonists planted large farms, and corn became a chief food crop. Colonists ate corn at every meal. They even ate popcorn with milk and sugar as a breakfast food!

New England farmers had to work hard, for the rough New England soil was rocky and hilly. The colonists in the Middle Colo-

A plantation was like a miniature city. Rivers were often the only "roads" between plantations. This is Mt. Vernon with the Potomac River at the top of the picture.

nies found farming much easier. But the Southern farmers were the most prosperous of all. The soil was rich, and the weather was warm. Anything that the farmers planted grew. <u>Cotton</u> proved to be a good crop. Unfortunately, <u>tobacco</u> became popular in Europe, and many farmers in the South planted it.

The large Southern plantations resembled a miniature city. Everything the farmer needed was right on his farm. The plantations were so large that sometimes there were no roads between them. The people would travel down a river to reach the next plantation!

Gradually, some colonists left farming and began to manufacture goods. The goods were mostly everyday necessities. Such things as cloth, pots and pans, molasses, and other goods were produced and sold in America. <u>People in New England made fishing a major industry</u>.

People in Europe were not interested in most of America's products. For example, no one wanted to buy plain American cloth

(homespun). <u>Most goods sent to Europe were raw materials</u>. Europeans purchased <u>indigo</u>, a blue dye common in America but precious in Europe. They bought <u>lumber</u> from the vast forests of America. They bought American <u>iron, tobacco, and furs</u>, including beaver furs to make hats and other articles. The trade ships carrying these things to Europe would bring back the goods that the colonists wanted to buy. One of the most popular items was European cloth. Clothes from Europe were much nicer than American clothes and were valued highly in the colonies. America needed Europe's manufactured goods, because there were still not very many factories in America.

Still, there were a few American products that were valued in Europe. The colonists' simple, durable furniture appealed to the Europeans. For example, <u>Benjamin Franklin attached rockers to a slat-back chair to produce the classic American rocking chair</u>, which then became extremely popular throughout Europe.

America's silversmiths also manufactured goods that came up to European standards. These fine craftsmen turned lumps of silver into fine pieces of art—tea services and dinnerware that graced the tables of many wealthy people. <u>One of the best silversmiths in America was named Paul</u> <u>Revere</u>. Revere loved his silver, but he also loved freedom as all American colonists did. His love of freedom was to make him famous during the War for Independence that ended the colonial age.

Paul Revere was one of the greatest colonial silversmiths.

Iron, an important American product, was produced at factories such as this one, which was built in Massachusetts in the 1640s.

Christopher Dock was a German **Mennonite** schoolteacher in Pennsylvania. Today, he is remembered as a man who made many changes in the way school was taught.

Christopher Dock was the first teacher to use a chalkboard. Today, almost every classroom has a chalkboard in it.

In many colonial schools, a student might be whipped for not knowing the answer to a question. But Christopher Dock said that if the student was working hard and paying attention, there was no reason to spank him if he did not know an answer. Students who misbehaved were a different matter; Dock punished children who lied, cheated, or swore. He felt that a teacher should help "train up a child in the way he should go."

Christopher Dock wrote the first school manual ever published in this country. He hoped that other teachers would read about his methods so that those teachers could improve their own schools.

Christopher Dock's sincere desire to help young people lasted through his long life. He cared so much for his students that he prayed

Christopher Dock prayed for his students by name every day.

for each one of them by name every day. In fact, it was while he was praying for his students that Christopher Dock died in 1771 at his Pennsylvania schoolhouse.

★ ★ ★ ★ Chapter 7 Checkup ★ ★ ★ ★

Answer questions on notebook paper.

1. What is a "house raising"?
2. What did the colonists use for both cooking and heating?
3. What two jobs did most colonial men spend their days doing?

4. What was one of the most important jobs of a colonial housewife?

5. What is homespun?

6. Since colonial villages often had no newspaper, where did colonists get the latest news?

7. Name the most important book in colonial homes.

8. List three terms that describe New England church buildings in colonial days.

9. Name two of the religious groups that settled in the Middle Colonies.

10. Why were there so few churches in the Southern Colonies?

    Who preached to Southern families?

11. Where did most colonial children begin their education?

12. What was a wooden paddle with an attached alphabet and Lord's Prayer called?

13. What textbook was used by millions of children for over 150 years?

14. What section of the country had more schools than any other, and even passed laws requiring towns to build schools?

15. What was the purpose of Harvard, America's first college?

16. What type of school was common in the South?

17. What was the first thing most colonists did when they came to America?

18. What was the chief food crop in the colonies?

    What two crops earned money for Southern farmers?

19. What became a major industry in New England?

20. Which American products sold well in Europe?

21. What piece of furniture was invented by Benjamin Franklin and became popular in Europe?

22. Name one of the most famous American silversmiths.

23. Who was the Mennonite schoolteacher that greatly influenced American schools?

The Great Awakening

Revival

One of the most important things that happened in colonial America was the **Great Awakening,** a spiritual revival that swept through the colonies between 1730 and 1760. The leaders of the Great Awakening have been called the spiritual Founding Fathers of America, and their teaching did much to shape America's spiritual heritage.

It may surprise you that such faithful churchgoers as the colonists needed a revival. They went to church and were good citizens and lived good lives, but many had never accepted Christ as their personal Savior. Many were depending on their good lives to save them.

Most of the colonies had laws saying that only church members could vote. Nine colonies had official churches, and the people of the colonies had to pay taxes to support those official churches. Often, people joined churches to please the government officials rather than in obedience to the Bible. This kind of religion was good for the church leaders who wanted many members, but it was not good for the people, because it did not help them to personally accept Christ.

Jonathan Edwards: A Great Puritan Preacher

Jonathan Edwards was one of the first leaders in the Great Awakening. Jonathan Edwards was born in Connecticut in 1703. He was the only boy in a family of eleven children, and he began to read almost as soon as he could speak. When he was just seven years old he could read books in English and Latin, and he knew some Greek and Hebrew, too. He was also very good at arithmetic and science. When he was twelve he studied spiders by observing their ways. Then he wrote an amazing paper about them, describing their size, kinds, flight, and web-spinning activities. When he was thirteen he went to college, where he was a top student.

Jonathan thought much about God when he was a boy, and he tried very hard to be good. He made up a list of very good resolutions that he tried to follow, and for a while he prayed five times a day. But none of this gave him peace with God. Finally, when he was eighteen years old, he stopped trusting his good works and accepted Christ as his personal Savior. From that time on he was a changed person.

Jonathan Edwards

In 1734, Jonathan Edwards preached a sermon about salvation in his Congregational (Puritan) church in Northampton, Massachusetts. A wonderful thing happened. The Spirit of God moved over the congregation convicting people of their sins and of their need for Christ. "There was scarcely a single person in the town, old or young," Edwards wrote, "who was left unconcerned about the great things of the eternal world." Good people and bad people, parents and children, wealthy and poor, "from day to day, for many months together," came "by flocks to Jesus Christ."

What a change this brought to the town of Northampton! Jonathan Edwards wrote this about it:

> This work of God, as it was carried on, and the number of true saints multiplied, soon made a glorious alteration [change] in the town; so that in the spring and summer following . . . the town seemed to be full of the presence of God: it was never so full of love, nor of joy, and yet so full of distress, as it was then.

There was a change in the homes of the town, too:

> There were remarkable tokens [signs] of God's presence in almost every house. It was a time of joy in families on account of salvation being brought unto them; parents rejoicing over their children as new born, and husbands over their wives, and wives over their husbands.

This great move of the Spirit of God upon individuals, households, and whole communities spread throughout New England and eventually to most of the colonies. However, opposition arose.

Jonathan Edwards's church, which was supported by the Massachusetts government, would not let him preach any more in Northampton. The wonderful things that were happening were too exciting for the strict Puritan leaders who wanted to be religious without personal salvation.

Edwards moved to the little frontier town of Stockbridge, Massachusetts, where he served as church pastor and missionary to the nearby Indians. He was poorer now, and it was harder for him to provide for his wife and the eight children who were still at home, but he was faithful in the Lord's service. He had more time here, too, and he was able to write some important books about the Bible. His preaching and writing did much to turn the American people back to the Bible, and it is the Bible, above all else, that has made America a great nation.

Jonathan Edwards was probably the most intelligent man in colonial America as

New Words

1. **Great Awakening**—spiritual revival that swept through the colonies between 1730 and 1760

New Names

2. **Jonathan Edwards**—great Puritan minister who was one of the first leaders of the Great Awakening
3. **John Wesley**—famous English preacher who started the Methodist church
4. **George Whitefield**—Great Awakening preacher who came to America from England seven times to preach the gospel
5. **David Brainerd**—young missionary who gave his life to take the gospel to the Indians
6. **Tattamy**—Indian who helped David Brainerd preach the gospel
7. **Isaac Backus**—Baptist pastor who worked to give America religious freedom

well as one of the best educated. (He became president of Princeton University, a Presbyterian school, before he died.) But it was his faithful preaching of God's Word that made him great and blessed America.

John Wesley: Founder of the Methodist Church

John Wesley, the founder of Methodism

Although **John Wesley,** <u>founder of the Methodist church</u>, came to America only once, his influence on our country was very great.

John Wesley was born in 1703 in England. The nineteen Wesley children owed much of their training to their wonderful mother, Susanna, who made sure that her children learned to obey and respect authority at a very early age. She taught them how to read, too.

When little John Wesley was six years old, the family home burned down and John was just barely rescued from the flames. He and his mother always believed that God had spared him for a special purpose.

While John was studying at **Oxford University,** he and his brother Charles studied many books with some friends and tried very hard to live good lives. In 1736, John and Charles Wesley went to Georgia as missionaries. You have already read about John's missionary work with the Indians there. Something was wrong, though.

Back in England, John studied the Bible with all his heart. Then, with the help of a friend, he discovered what was wrong—he needed to know Christ personally. Once he had accepted Christ, John Wesley began to preach in earnest. The ministers in the Church of England did not want him to preach in their churches, so he started preaching in the open air. He would travel by horseback from town to town and preach in the fields, sometimes to thousands of people at once.

People were saved wherever Wesley preached, and he organized the new Christians into Methodist societies to pray, study the Bible, and tell others about Christ. These societies sent out ministers to spread the gospel, and England became a changed country as her people began to turn back to the Bible. The Methodists sent many ministers to America as well, and they played a great part in preaching the Word of God throughout our land.

New Places

8. Northampton, Massachusetts—city where Jonathan Edwards pastored a church

9. Oxford—college in England attended by the Wesleys and George Whitefield

New Dates

10. 1730–1760—Great Awakening

11. 1734—revival breaks out in Jonathan Edwards's church

12. 1744—David Brainerd begins his missionary work among the Indians

Comprehension Check 8A

1. Why did such good people as the colonists need a revival?

2. What American Puritan preacher helped the Great Awakening get started?

3. Who founded the Methodist church?

George Whitefield: The Great Evangelist to America

While John Wesley was traveling throughout England, **George Whitefield** was doing the same thing in America. Whitefield first came to America from England in 1738, and he preached in many different kinds of churches. Soon the crowds were too big for buildings, and he started preaching in the fields. He preached to the people, and he also preached to the ministers. After hearing George Whitefield, many preachers started telling their own people how to get right with God, a thing they had sadly neglected to do.

George Whitefield was born in England in 1714. When he was eighteen he went to Oxford University, where he studied hard. He was concerned about his salvation, though. Somehow he knew that just being a member of the Church of England was not enough. He started to do good deeds. He visited poor people in jail and read to them to cheer them up. He joined John and Charles Wesley's group at Oxford University. He ate poor food; dressed in old, patched clothes; and wore soiled shoes. But nothing could bring him peace.

Finally he started studying books about the Bible, and then he turned to the Bible itself. It was in the Bible that he found the answers to his questions. "I got more true knowledge from reading the Book of God in one month than I could ever have acquired from all the writings of men," he said. In 1735 he came to understand that a person is saved by faith in Christ, and he preached this truth for the rest of his life.

Thousands came to hear George Whitefield preach.

Whitefield preached in England for a while, and then he sailed for Georgia in 1738, where he started America's first orphanage and preached the gospel. He returned to England the next year, but the Anglicans would not let him preach in their churches. Instead, Whitefield started preaching in the fields. (In fact, John Wesley got the idea of preaching outdoors from George Whitefield.) Sometimes Whitefield preached to crowds of 20,000 people at once. He traveled thousands of miles to carry the gospel to the people in England, Scotland, and Wales.

In 1739, Whitefield sailed to Philadelphia to begin the second of his seven tours of America. During his seven tours he preached throughout all the colonies, spreading the gospel and collecting offerings for his orphanage. Many churches in America that were supported by the colonial governments were against Whitefield's preaching, and so again he preached outdoors.

One good friend of George Whitefield was the great American inventor and statesman, Benjamin Franklin. We do not know whether Ben Franklin ever accepted Christ, but he was moved by Mr. Whitefield's preaching. When Whitefield preached in Philadelphia, the change that took place in the people impressed Franklin. Here is what Franklin wrote:

> It was wonderful to see the change soon made in the manners of our inhabitants. From being thoughtless or indifferent about religion, it seemed as if all the world were growing religious, so that one could not walk through the town in an evening without hearing psalms sung in different families of every street.

George Whitefield believed that the gospel is for all people. That belief made him want to help everyone—children, adults, Indians, black slaves, poor people, rich people, orphans, people with no education, and people with much education.

Whitefield was very concerned about the slaves in America. He got Ben Franklin to print a letter from him urging the colonists to treat the slaves with more kindness. Newspapers all over the colonies soon printed this letter. Many times Whitefield preached directly to the slaves and told them that they needed to come to Jesus just like everyone else. Here is what he said to them toward the end of one sermon:

> I must not forget the poor Negroes. No, I must not. Jesus Christ has died for them, as well as for others. Nor do I mention you last, because I despise your souls, but because I would have what I shall say make the deeper impression upon your hearts.
>
> Oh that you would seek the Lord to be your righteousness! Who knows but that He may be found of you. For in Jesus Christ there is neither male nor female, bond nor free; even you may be the children of God, if you believe in Jesus. Did you never read of the eunuch belonging to Queen Candace? A Negro like yourselves. He believed. The Lord was his righteousness. He was baptized. Do you also believe, and you shall be saved. Christ Jesus is the same now as He was yesterday, and will wash you in His own blood. Go home then, turn the words of the text into a prayer, and intreat the Lord to be your righteousness. Even so, come Lord Jesus, come quickly into all our souls! Amen, Lord Jesus, Amen and Amen!

Whitefield was also interested in the Indians, and he wrote a gospel tract for a trader to read to them.

George Whitefield preached over 18,000 sermons in his lifetime to over ten million people. Whitefield's preaching of the gospel—that each person needs to be saved—affected all areas of American life. His care for the orphans was an example to others to help and educate young children. His interest in the slaves and his efforts to preach to them helped others to feel more kindly toward them. His interest in the Indians encouraged many people to become missionaries. Because he saw the importance of education, he influenced the founding of about fifty colleges in America.

Missionary Work in America

Because of the Great Awakening, many Americans became missionaries. The first American missionaries went to settlers in the frontiers of America and to the Indians. Later, America would become known as a great missionary nation, and Americans would go to all corners of the earth to preach the gospel. Even today, America has more Christian missionaries around the

Great crowds gathered to hear preaching outdoors.

world than any other country. The missionary spirit of Americans is probably one of the great things that has caused God to bless America.

One man who gave his life as a missionary to the Indians during the Colonial Period was **David Brainerd.** David Brainerd was born in Connecticut in 1718. When he was fourteen years old he became an orphan and went to live with his older sister and her family. His parents had taught him the importance of reading the Bible, and he came to know Christ in 1739.

The next fall he went to Yale to prepare to be a preacher. From the start he was an excellent student. In 1740, many students at Yale suffered from smallpox. Brainerd became very ill and was forced to go home for several months. He returned to school as soon as he could and studied even harder than before, but soon it was clear that he had a much more serious illness—tuberculosis. Tuberculosis was a disease that killed many people in colonial America. David

Brainerd would not go home, though, and he kept up with his studies.

While Brainerd had been home with smallpox, the Great Awakening had come to Yale. George Whitefield had preached there often, and many students were living changed lives. Brainerd, moved by what was happening, felt that God was calling him to be a missionary to Native Americans. The tuberculosis made him very sick, but he was determined to reach the Indians for Christ.

In 1744 the Presbyterian church sent David Brainerd out to minister in Indian villages. He traveled regularly on horseback, preaching in villages wherever he could. His travels took him to Indians of New York, New Jersey, and Pennsylvania. He preached in English, and a faithful Indian helper named **Tattamy** interpreted his words into the Indian language. Later he trained six Indians to preach to their people.

When Brainerd went to the Crosswelksung Indians in New Jersey, a wonderful thing happened. Up to seventy Indians at a time came to hear him preach of Christ's salvation. They listened carefully to several sermons in one day. The Indians were having a Great Awakening!

Brainerd wrote this in his diary about one Indian woman who heard the preaching:

> A young Indian woman, who, I believe, never knew before she had a soul, nor ever thought of any such thing, hearing that there was something strange among the Indians, came, it seems, to see what was the matter. In her way to the Indians, she called at my lodgings, and when I told her I designed presently to preach to the Indians, laughed, and seemed to mock; but went however to them. I had not proceeded far in my public discourse, before she felt effectually that she had a soul; and before I had concluded my discourse, was so convinced of her sin and misery, and so distressed with concern for her soul's salvation, that she seemed like one pierced through with a dart, and cried out incessantly.

David Brainerd traveled about one hundred miles on his horse each week, even though the pain from his illness grew worse and worse. Finally, he could work no longer, and he had to leave his Indians for the last time. He went to Jonathan Edwards's home to rest, and there he died in 1747.

David Brainerd was one of the first missionaries spurred by the Great Awakening to do great things for God. Other great missionaries followed his example after his death. John Wesley, Francis Asbury, William Carey, and Jim Elliot (who was killed by the Auca Indians of Ecuador in 1956) all said that David Brainerd had greatly influenced their lives. Through the lives of great men who have followed David Brainerd's example, the effects of the Great Awakening are still being felt around the world.

Comprehension Check 8B

1. What Great Awakening preacher came to America seven times to preach the gospel?

2. Who was a famous American missionary to the Indians?

3. What was the name of Brainerd's faithful Indian helper?

How the Great Awakening Shaped America

The preaching of George Whitefield, John Wesley, Jonathan Edwards, and the other leaders in the Great Awakening helped the colonists to see more than ever that all men are equal in worth to God. The preaching of the Great Awakening did more perhaps than anything else to draw the colonists together so that our country would truly become one nation under God.

The colonists saw that since all men are equal in the eyes of God, then no man is better than any other man. Therefore, all men should be equal in the sight of the law. All deserve equal justice, no matter who they are and no matter what their religious beliefs may be. This truth paved the way for the colonists to write, just a few years later:

> **We hold these truths to be self-evident, that all men are created equal; that they are endowed by their Creator with certain unalienable rights; that among these are life, liberty, and the pursuit of happiness.**

Many years later, Calvin Coolidge, who was President of the United States from 1923 to 1929, said this:

> America was born in a revival of religion. Back of that revival were John Wesley, George Whitefield, and Francis Asbury.

The Bible truths of the Great Awakening also paved the way to the most wonderful freedom in America—the freedom of religion.

Methodist churches grew up in our land, and Methodist circuit-riding preachers rode on horseback to preach from town to town. Many Presbyterian, Congregational, and Dutch Reformed churches were brought back to preaching the gospel, and Baptist churches sprang up throughout the colonies. The Baptists were especially eager to bring freedom of religion to America, for they had often been persecuted for preaching the gospel in Europe, in England, and even in America.

The great idea of separation of church and state that Roger Williams and his Baptist friends gave to Rhode Island would soon spread to the whole country, and America would be seen as a vast mission field, open for the free spread of the gospel.

★ People Worth Knowing More About ★

Isaac Backus

Isaac Backus—Defender of Liberty

One colonist who came to know Christ during the Great Awakening was **Isaac Backus.** He became a traveling evangelist. In 1756 he became pastor of the First Baptist Church in Middleborough, Massachusetts, and he was pastor there for fifty-eight years.

During those fifty-eight years, he especially spoke out against the religious taxes that all the people of a colony had to pay to support the Congregational churches. He said that people should be free to support their own churches, not a state church that they did not believe in. Finally, partly because of the work of Isaac Backus, America became a land that had freedom of religion through the separation of church and state.

Answer the questions on notebook paper.

1. What was the Great Awakening?
2. Although most colonists attended church, they still needed revival. Why?
3. Who was Jonathan Edwards?
4. What happened to make Jonathan Edwards a changed person?
5. What was another name for the Puritan churches?
6. Why did Jonathan Edwards move to the frontier?
7. Jonathan Edwards became president of what university just before his death?
8. What church did John Wesley start?
9. Who was the mother of John and Charles Wesley?
10. Where did John and Charles Wesley go to college?
11. Why was John Wesley's first trip to America unsuccessful?
12. Why did John Wesley start preaching in the open air?
13. How many times did George Whitefield come to America to preach the gospel?
14. Why did George Whitefield preach outdoors?
15. Who was Whitefield's famous American friend?
16. What young missionary gave his life to take the gospel to the Indians?
17. Who was Tattamy?
18. In whose home did David Brainerd die?
19. How did the Great Awakening affect America?
20. Who pastored a church in Middleborough, Massachusetts, for fifty-eight years and also worked to make America a free country?

French soldiers and Indian warriors fought British soldiers during the French and Indian War.

The French and Indian War

New France and Its Colonies

In the year 1608, when the English were building their first permanent settlement at Jamestown, the French were also building their first permanent settlement in the land they claimed in the New World, **New France.** New France covered most of what is now Canada as well as land far down the Mississippi River that is now part of the United States. The first settlement in New France was **Quebec.**

New France was huge, but there were few settlements there. Most Frenchmen who came were interested in becoming fur traders.

Since the French fur traders depended upon the Indians' friendship, the traders were eager to become friendly. They came to New France with glass beads, knives, cloth blankets, and anything else that the Indians desired. The French traded these items with the Indians for beaver skins and other furs that were valuable in Europe.

The Differences between New France and the American Colonies

Unlike the English, most French colonists could not become farmers, so they had no desire to take land from the Indians. The king of France did not allow the French colonists the rights the English colonists had. The people who went to New France were expected to work as the king told them. He was not interested in family life or farm life. He was interested in the valuable fur trade. So while the English brought their families, most French colonists were unmarried men. As they moved about trading and trapping furs, they often lived with the Indians instead of building their own homes.

New France was a valuable colony for its natural resources, especially its valuable furs.

France was a Catholic country, and no one was allowed to go to New France except Catholics. The French sent Catholic missionaries (priests) to the Native Americans.

The French and English Become Enemies

France's claim that she owned land along the Mississippi and Ohio Rivers caused problems. To strengthen this claim, she built forts along the Ohio River.

Meanwhile, the English colonists of the thirteen colonies were beginning to move west of the Appalachian Mountains onto land that both the French and English claimed as their own.

The English began chopping down trees to clear the land and build homes. The French fur traders became angry. The forests were the homes of fur-bearing animals. If the English disturbed the forests, animals would move and become scarce and the French fur trade would be affected. As a result, the French strengthened their forts. Then they began talking to the Indians.

"The Frenchmen are your friends. We do not come to take your land. We do not chop down trees and destroy your hunting ground," the French told the Indians. "We think of you as our brothers. The English think of you as enemies. The English come

Indians attack and burn English homes without warning.

as enemies of both of us. When they chop down trees, they destroy the Indians' hunting ground and the Frenchmen's trade. If we do not stop the English from coming, both the French and the Indians will be forced to move off this land. Will you allow this to happen? Will you help the French fight the English?"

Many Native Americans listened and nodded in agreement. They would fight with the French.

Bands of Indians encouraged by the French began raiding English frontier settlements in the early 1700s. Without warning,

New Names

1. **French and Indian War**—war that decided who would be the most powerful country in North America—England or France
2. **George Washington**—young soldier who became a well-known hero during the French and Indian War
3. **Edward Braddock**—famous English general who was killed in the French and Indian War

New Places

4. **New France**—France's land in the New World
5. **Quebec**—first settlement in New France
6. **Fort Le Boeuf**—French fort in the Ohio Valley
7. **St. Lawrence River**—river that flows by Quebec

New Dates

8. **1608**—the settlement of New France begins
9. **1754–1763**—French and Indian War

in the early morning hours, the Indians would attack an English settlement while the settlers were still in their beds. They would burn the cabins and kill most of the men. Often the Indians killed the women and children, but sometimes they took them captive. The Indians would then either sell them as servants to the French colonists or keep them as slaves. Many times white children taken as captives were adopted into the Indian tribes. They were then treated as real Native American children.

Comprehension Check 9A

1. What was the name given to France's territory in America?

2. The French were aided by whom in their war against the British?

3. Why did the French oppose England's westward movement in the New World?

The French and Indian War

Both France and England were powerful countries. Each wanted to control the New World. As a result, between the years 1689 and 1763, France and England fought four wars. The first three wars did not have a great effect on America. The last war, however, the **French and Indian War,** lasted from 1754 to 1763 and <u>decided who would be the most powerful country in North America—England or France</u>.

Events Leading to the French and Indian War

"The Ohio country belongs to England. The French have no right to build forts on our land," insisted the governor of Virginia. "I shall send a messenger to the French officer at **Fort Le Boeuf** [lə bŭf] and ask them to leave. Fort Le Boeuf is hundreds of

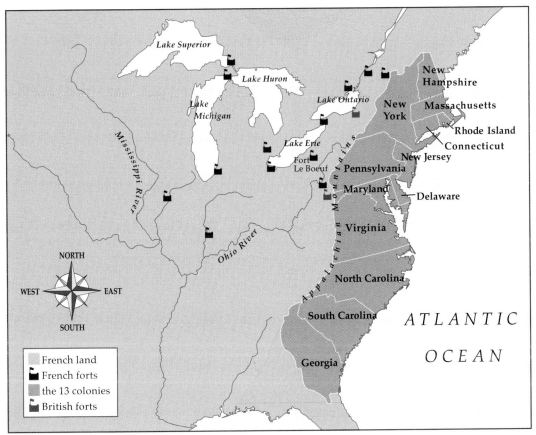

America at the Time of the French and Indian War

Lake Superior

Lake Huron

Lake Michigan

Lake Ontario

Lake Erie

Mississippi River

Ohio River

Appalachian Mountains

Fort Le Boeuf

New Hampshire

New York

Massachusetts

Rhode Island

Connecticut

New Jersey

Pennsylvania

Maryland

Delaware

Virginia

North Carolina

South Carolina

Georgia

ATLANTIC OCEAN

NORTH

WEST — EAST

SOUTH

- French land
- French forts
- the 13 colonies
- British forts

miles from Virginia. Whom can I trust to take a letter that far? He certainly should be a brave man, one that is not afraid to spend weeks in the wilderness."

George Washington, a young man from Virginia, already had a reputation for being both wise and brave. He was chosen to deliver the message.

Several men went with him. They left on a chilly October day. Together they crossed the mountains and watched for Indians. After weeks of traveling through the wilderness, they reached Fort Le Boeuf. The French officer took the message that young George Washington handed him from the governor of Virginia and read it. Then the French officer politely explained that the French had claimed this land for France. "We do not intend to give up what is ours," he told Washington.

Discouraged, the men from Virginia began their long trip home. It was now winter. The men had to battle heavy snowstorms. Once George Washington nearly drowned when he fell off a log raft into an icy river. After several weeks of hardships, Washington finally reported the bad news to the governor of Virginia.

The governor decided that there was only one thing left to do. He must raise a small army of colonists to drive the French out of the Ohio Valley. George Washington's brave trip through the wilderness to Fort Le Boeuf had made him a hero among the Virginians. The governor made Washington

George Washington led the first battle of the French and Indian War.

an officer of the Virginia army. Washington led his men bravely, but the colonists were not trained to fight as soldiers. The French army defeated them. The year was 1754. George Washington had led the first battle of the French and Indian War.

Help Arrives from England

Since the colonists could not defeat the French by themselves, the king of England sent an army of trained soldiers to America. Along with them came **General Edward Braddock,** who would command the English army.

Colonists from the thirteen colonies were asked to volunteer. Among the volunteers was George Washington.

The English army was very fine looking in their red uniforms. They could march together in perfect step. They knew all the rules for war in Europe. The English soldiers would not think of hiding behind a tree or rock to shoot. To them, that would be cowardly. The rules for war in Europe said that they must fight out in the open. There was only one thing wrong with their plans. This was not Europe. This was America. The Indians had their own rules for fighting a war.

The colonial soldiers had clothes made from homespun material and buckskin. They could not march in perfect step, nor did they know the rules for fighting in Europe. Yet they knew better than anyone else the rules for fighting in America.

Washington and other colonists tried to warn General Braddock. "If you are fighting Indians, you have to fight like an Indian. Indians hide behind trees and bushes while they shoot. Your red uniforms will make fine targets."

"My men will not fight like cowards," came the answer.

With drums beating, General Braddock led his army through the forest. The forest was thick with trees and bushes. The English had to make a narrow road as they moved forward so that their wagons of food and supplies could move through the forest. A long line of unprotected soldiers and wagons stretched out for miles.

Suddenly shots seemed to ring out from nowhere. The woods were full of French soldiers and Indians hiding behind trees, rocks, and bushes. The English army had not noticed them until it was too late.

The colonists jumped behind bushes and fought back Indian style. But the British soldiers fought where they stood. Because they could not see their enemy, they did not know where to aim their guns. The British soldiers were easy targets for the well-hidden Indians. Many were killed. Suddenly, a bullet hit General Braddock.

With their leader wounded, the British soldiers lost courage and ran. George

General Braddock and his men marched through the forest in a narrow line.

TIME LINE OF IMPORTANT DATES

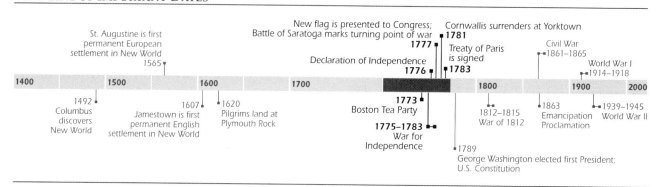

St. Augustine is first permanent European settlement in New World
1565

New flag is presented to Congress; Battle of Saratoga marks turning point of war
1777

Cornwallis surrenders at Yorktown
1781

Declaration of Independence
1776

Treaty of Paris is signed
1783

Civil War
1861–1865

World War I
1914–1918

| 1400 | 1500 | 1600 | 1700 | | 1800 | 1900 | 2000 |

1492 Columbus discovers New World

1607 Jamestown is first permanent English settlement in New World

1620 Pilgrims land at Plymouth Rock

1773 Boston Tea Party

1775–1783 War for Independence

1812–1815 War of 1812

1863 Emancipation Proclamation

1939–1945 World War II

1789 George Washington elected first President; U.S. Constitution

The American War for Independence

Thirteen English Colonies in America

With the close of the French and Indian War in 1763, England became the most powerful kingdom in the world. Many American colonists were proud to be a part of their mother country. England allowed her colonists in the New World much more freedom than France had allowed hers. The colonists of New France could not own homes or land. They could not have any part in making their laws. English colonists could own their homes and lands, and they had a part in making their own laws.

Though 3,000 miles of ocean separated England from her American colonies, the colonists were promised the same rights that the people in England had. This promise had made the colonists happy. Would the king of England ever dare to break it?

The American Colonies Demand Their Rights as Englishmen

Money Problems

England may have become the greatest power in the world, but she had also become very poor. She had fought four expensive wars with France. France and Spain still wished for a larger part of the New World. If they fought England, England wanted to be powerful enough to win. England must find a way to make money.

Stamp Act

At that time, **King George III** was king of England. He decided that the colonists themselves must pay for the protection that the English army had given them during the French and Indian War. This sounds fair, but remember, the colonists believed that they were to have a part in making their own laws. This was part of the rights which Englishmen were supposed to have. King George put aside this promise when he told the British government to pass laws for the Americans to obey. The colonists had no part in making these laws.

One law was known as the **Stamp Act.** Special stamps were to be sold by the British government to the American colonists. These stamps were really seals. The law said that all newspapers, marriage certificates, almanacs, and other documents bought by the colonists had to have a seal or stamp placed on them. The colonists were to buy the stamps when they bought the paper. Each stamp was really a tax that the colonists had to pay. A **tax** is money that people pay to help run their government.

In England, the people had **representatives,** <u>men chosen by the people to make decisions for them</u> about the tax. The colonists in America had no such representatives in England; they had no say in the taxes they had to pay. They believed that the laws of England said that the colonists were supposed to have a say in their taxes, for they believed they were supposed to have the rights of Englishmen. In their minds, King George was breaking the law of England as well as breaking his word.

The Stamp Act aroused the anger of the colonists. A group of colonists is burning a pile of the hated British stamps.

More Problems

Some laws had been passed years before, but the colonists had never really had to obey them. Now, the English government tried to force the colonists to follow them.

Most colonists were hard working. They grew crops such as tobacco, cotton, sugar, and indigo with hopes of selling their products to other countries. But England said, "No, you may not sell your products to any

New Words

1. **tax**—money that people pay to help run the government
2. **representative**—person chosen by the people to make decisions for them
3. **massacre**—the cruel killing of many people at one time
4. **patriots**—American colonists who wanted America to be free from England's rule
5. **Loyalists or Tories**—American colonists who remained loyal to England
6. **Hessians**—German soldiers who were hired by the British to fight against American colonists

New Names

7. **King George III**—king of England at the time of America's War for Independence
8. **Stamp Act**—unfair tax law that angered the colonists
9. **Boston Massacre**—a fight between angry colonists and British soldiers in which five colonists were killed
10. **Crispus Attucks**—black patriot killed during the Boston Massacre
11. **Boston Tea Party**—a protest by American colonists who dumped over 300 chests of British tea into Boston Harbor
12. **Continental Congress**—group of men who met before and during the War for Independence to decide what the colonies would do about England's unfair treatment
13. **Minutemen**—Massachusetts soldiers who said they could be ready to fight at a minute's notice
14. **Patrick Henry**—young patriot known for saying, ". . . as for me, give me liberty or give me death!"
15. **Paul Revere** and **William Dawes**—two men who warned the colonists of a British attack
16. **Ethan Allen**—daring American soldier who led the Green Mountain Boys to capture Fort Ticonderoga from the British
17. **Declaration of Independence**—document which stated the reasons why American colonists wanted freedom from English rule
18. **Thomas Jefferson**—author of the Declaration of Independence
19. **John Hancock**—president of the Continental Congress
20. **General George Washington**—commander in chief of the colonial army; called "the Father of His Country"
21. **Nathan Hale**—brave American spy who gave his life for his country; known for saying, "I only regret that I have but one life to lose for my country."

other country, except England." The colonists were forced to accept the low prices that England offered them, because they could not sell their products anywhere else.

Some colonists made cloth and began using it to make beautiful clothes. England told the colonists that they could make only enough clothes for their own families. Clothes made in one colony could not be sold in another colony. Where could a wealthy colonist buy fine clothes? He had to order them from England.

Iron was important to the colonists, for many utensils, pots, and pans of that time were made from iron. England said the colonists could make their own iron, but they were not allowed to make anything with the iron. The colonists must sell their iron to England where it would be made into the things that the colonists needed. Then, the English ships would take the iron products back to the colonies, where they would be sold for high prices.

Who would get wealthy under such laws? Who would become poor? Since the colonists had no voice as to the price of their products, they were the ones to become poor.

Such things would not happen to the people who lived in England. Where had the colonists' rights as Englishmen gone? The king had little concern for the colonists in America except for the money he made from them.

You can imagine how upset the colonists became when the Stamp Act was passed. The colonists decided not to buy the stamps.

22. **Betsy Ross**—lady said to have stitched together the first American flag with stars and stripes
23. **Flag Day**—celebrated on June 14; the anniversary of the day on which George Washington presented our country's new flag to Congress
24. **George Rogers Clark**—soldier who captured British forts in the Northwest Territory for America
25. **John Paul Jones**—brave sea captain who was one of the first officers of the American navy; he was determined our first navy would be successful
26. *Bonhomme Richard*—John Paul Jones's ship
27. *Serapis*—British ship captured by John Paul Jones in his most famous sea battle
28. **General Lord Cornwallis**—British general who surrendered to George Washington
29. **General Nathanael Greene**—American general who fought the British in the Southern Colonies
30. **Treaty of Paris**—agreement which ended the War for Independence, giving the colonies their independence from England

New Places
31. **Lexington** and **Concord**—towns in Massachusetts where the first battle of the War for Independence took place

32. **Bunker Hill**—place where Americans showed the British that they would not be easily defeated
33. **Fort Ticonderoga**—strategic fort captured by Ethan Allen
34. **Trenton**—town in New Jersey where the American army overtook the Hessians and captured many supplies
35. **Saratoga**—site of the turning point of the War for Independence
36. **Valley Forge**—area of Pennsylvania where Washington's army stayed during the harsh winter of 1777–1778
37. **Northwest Territory**—part of the land given to the Americans by the British in the Treaty of Paris
38. **Yorktown**—place where the British surrendered at the end of the war

New Dates
39. **1775**—War for Independence begins
40. **July 4, 1776**—Declaration of Independence is signed
41. **1781**—General Cornwallis surrenders at Yorktown
42. **1783**—Treaty of Paris is signed

"If we buy the stamps, the king will soon tax other things, too," they told each other.

The Colonists Speak Out

Although there were some colonists who agreed with England, many colonists felt that England was treating them wrongly. Men from nine colonies decided to hold a meeting in New York. In this meeting, it was decided that the colonists should complain to the king. At last the British government felt forced to drop the Stamp Act.

New Taxes

King George III was not happy at all after the Stamp Act was dropped. He was determined to make the colonists pay taxes without their consent. He now had the British government place a tax on glass, paint, paper, and tea sold in the American colonies. Again, the colonists refused to buy the goods that carried the new tax.

The Boston Massacre

The people of Boston, Massachusetts, grew very angry and restless at the new taxes. England sent soldiers to Boston to help keep the peace and force the colonists to obey. Because the British soldiers wore red coats, some colonists teased them and called them "redcoats" or "lobster-backs."

One cold, snowy evening, a small mob began throwing things at a British soldier. Other British soldiers came running to stop the fight. Suddenly, without orders, and perhaps by accident, a gun was shot. In the confusion, more soldiers fired their guns. <u>Five colonists were killed</u>, including **Crispus Attucks,** a black patriot.

Each side was partly to blame for this terrible mistake. The colonists were teasing, irritating, and threatening the British soldiers; the British soldiers fired without orders.

The people of Boston angrily called this incident the **"Boston Massacre."** A **massacre** is <u>the cruel killing of many people at one time</u>. Preachers preached against what the British were doing, and many of their sermons were printed in pamphlet form so that many people could read them. As always, the ministers had a great influence on the people.

England saw that the tax on the glass, paint, paper, and tea was not worth all the trouble it was causing. All the taxes were dropped except one. Because England wanted to show the colonists that the British government still had the right to tax the colonists, a small tax was still kept on tea. You can imagine what drink the colonists refused to buy from England—tea!

The Boston Tea Party

Three years had passed since the Boston Massacre. Most colonists still refused to buy tea from England. The British government decided to force the colonists to accept the

Hot tempers on both sides erupted in the Boston Massacre in 1770.

Americans disguised themselves as Indians and threw British tea into Boston Harbor at the Boston Tea Party.

tea. Three ships loaded with tea sailed into Boston's harbor.

On a chilly December night in 1773, about fifty colonists dressed up to look like Indians. Carrying tomahawks, they boarded the three ships where there were 342 chests of tea. <u>Each chest was smashed open with a tomahawk and then thrown over the sides of the ships into the water</u>. When they destroyed the last chest of tea, they quietly went back to their homes. This event became known as the **Boston Tea Party.**

News of the Boston Tea Party spread quickly to the other colonies. Many colonists cheered the people of Boston for their courage. Others wondered with fear, "What will England do now?"

The English government saw no excuse for the Boston Tea Party and passed harsh laws to punish the thousands of people in Boston, even though only fifty men did the damage.

England sent more soldiers to Boston and closed the harbor there. Since no ships could sail in or out, the people of Boston had no way of buying supplies or food.

"The port of Boston shall stay closed until its people pay for the tea they destroyed," the British government said. If the harbor remained closed, the people of Boston could starve to death.

The other colonies soon heard of the unfair laws forced upon the people of Boston. South Carolina sent gifts of food. Connecticut and New York sent herds of sheep and cattle. Other colonies also sent gifts. The English were able to keep ships from sailing into Boston, but they couldn't keep other colonists from traveling over the New England paths and hills to help the people of Boston.

"How can we protect ourselves from these regulations that the government of England has no right to impose upon us?" each colony asked itself.

One of the patriots suggested that representatives from each colony meet together in Philadelphia to decide what to do.

Comprehension Check 10A

1. Who was the king of England just before the War for Independence began?
2. What was the Boston Massacre?
3. What was the Boston Tea Party?

The War Begins

The First Continental Congress

About fifty men met in Philadelphia in September 1774. They all agreed that England was unfair to her colonies, but they did not agree about what to do. Most men only wanted England to be fair to the colonists. Only a few men had decided that it was time America became independent from England.

Finally they made a list of complaints against England. They were supposed to have the same rights that all Englishmen had; the king acted as though they had no rights at all. The colonists asked that their rights as Englishmen be respected. Then they agreed that the people of Massachusetts should not obey the laws that England had forced upon her. To show that they meant business, the colonists agreed not to buy goods made in England. <u>This meeting was called the</u> **First Continental Congress.**

"If England does not listen, then we will return in May to hold a second Continental Congress."

How did King George react? He sent warships and more soldiers to the colonies. He was determined to force the colonists to obey.

The Colonists Prepare to Fight

The British warships and soldiers upset the colonists. They began to drill and train as soldiers. Colonists began to hide gunpowder and ammunition.

Many Massachusetts men called themselves **"Minutemen"** because they said <u>they could be ready to fight at a minute's notice.</u> Colonists from all walks of life volunteered to join the Minutemen and fight for their rights as Englishmen. Many were farmers, and some little more than boys. One Minuteman, **Lemuel Haynes,** was a black Congregationalist minister. The colonists thought that once King George realized they meant business, he would give the colonists their rights again.

Meanwhile, in Virginia, a young man named **Patrick Henry** gave a stirring speech that began changing the minds of many colonists. In his argument for fighting for independence, Patrick Henry cried:

Patrick Henry

Gentlemen may cry, peace, peace—but there is no peace. . . . Why stand we here idle? What is it that gentlemen wish? What would they have? Is life so dear, or peace so sweet, as to be purchased at the price of chains and slavery? Forbid it, Almighty God! I know not what course others may take; but <u>as for me, give me liberty, or give me death</u>!

Those who, like Patrick Henry, now <u>wanted America to be free from England's rule</u> were called **patriots.** Those who <u>remained loyal to England</u> were called **Loyalists** or **Tories.**

How did the British react to the colonists in Massachusetts? The British general heard that the patriots had secretly stored guns and ammunition in the town of Concord. He also knew that two patriot leaders, John Hancock and Samuel Adams, were staying in the town of Lexington. Both Concord and Lexington were close to Boston. The British began making plans to march to Lexington and Concord where they hoped to capture the patriot leaders and capture the patriots' supply of guns and ammunition.

The Midnight Ride of Paul Revere

Fortunately, a patriot had heard of the British plan. If the Minutemen were warned, perhaps they could stop the British.

Paul Revere, a patriot from Boston, and another man named **William Dawes,** jumped on their horses and rode through the countryside. It was night. To wake and warn the colonists, they shouted, "The British are coming!"

The Minutemen jumped out of their beds and prepared to fight. John Hancock and Samuel Adams were warned just in time to escape being captured.

When the British soldiers reached Lexington that night in April, 1775, they met a group of brave Minutemen. Suddenly, the sound of a gunshot shattered the silence at Lexington. No one knows who fired the shot, but it started the War for Independence, and it signaled the birth of American freedom. From this shot would come a fight for liberty that the whole world watched with interest. And from this shot would come the creation of a new country that would play a great part in world history. Because that one shot changed history, it has come to be called the "shot heard 'round the world." Ralph Waldo Emerson, a famous American poet, wrote a poem about this famous shot.

> By the rude bridge that arched the flood,
> Their flag to April's breeze unfurled,
> Here once the embattled farmers stood,
> And fired the shot heard round the world.

After the fighting at **Lexington,** the British marched to **Concord,** but Minutemen were there to meet them. As the British troops marched back to Boston, they were fired upon by Minutemen all along the way. The war had begun, but the purpose of the war still was not clear. Were the colonists going to fight for their rights as Englishmen, or were they fighting for their independence?

Comprehension Check 10B

1. Who were the patriots? Who were Loyalists or Tories?

2. Who were the Minutemen?

3. Who rode across the countryside, warning of a British attack?

4. Where did the first battle of the War for Independence take place?

The first shots of America's War for Independence were fired at Lexington, Massachusetts.

Paul Revere rode through the countryside warning the colonists that the British were coming.

The American Colonies Fight for Independence

The Second Continental Congress

Because the king of England refused to listen to the colonists' list of complaints, representatives met in Philadelphia for another meeting—the **Second Continental Congress.** It was May 1775. Many important decisions were made at this meeting. Two of the most important were:

1. America must have an organized Continental Army; and
2. <u>George Washington would command the American army</u>.

The Battle of Bunker Hill

At the time, the British soldiers were staying in Boston. They did not feel that the American colonists had the strength or power to chase the powerful British army out of Boston.

In the darkness of night, while the British army was sleeping, more than a thousand colonists climbed Bunker Hill and Breed's Hill, which overlook Boston. All through the night, they dug trenches, holes or ditches to protect themselves. When the British woke, they were very surprised.

On June 17, 1775, the **Battle of Bunker Hill** was fought. Many people who lived in Boston climbed on their roofs to watch the battle. The British attacked, but the colonists beat them back. Again the British tried, and again they were beaten back. When the British tried the third time, the colonists ran out of gunpowder. This time, the Americans were beaten back.

Though the Americans were beaten back, they did show the British that the colonists could fight with determination even though they were not trained soldiers.

British soldiers marched straight into deadly American gunfire. Although the patriots fought bravely, the British eventually won the Battle of Bunker Hill.

Ethan Allen and the Green Mountain Boys

The British held **Fort Ticonderoga,** which was located on the main road between Canada and New York. This fort was important to the British because of its location, and it also contained supplies of guns, cannons, and ammunition that the colonists so badly needed.

In the land that is now Vermont lived **Ethan Allen** and a group of patriots who called themselves the **"Green Mountain Boys."** They decided that they would <u>take Fort Ticonderoga from the British</u>.

In the early morning hours while the unsuspecting British slept, the Green Mountain Boys surrounded Fort Ticonderoga. Then Ethan Allen knocked on the British commander's door. The sleepy commander opened the door, and Ethan Allen demanded that he surrender the fort "in the name of the Great Jehovah and the Continental Congress." The stunned commander looked outside. When he saw that the fort was already surrounded, he knew he had no choice. He surrendered the fort to the daring Ethan Allen.

Ethan Allen roused the British commander and demanded that he surrender Fort Ticonderoga to the Green Mountain Boys.

The supplies inside the fort were valuable to the Continental Army, for the colonists had few guns and little gunpowder to fight a war with the British. Cannons taken from Fort Ticonderoga finally drove the British army out of Boston.

More Decisions

Meanwhile the Second Continental Congress continued meeting in Philadelphia. It was now 1776. Many of the representatives still hoped that King George would change his mind. Then the Americans could become peaceful colonists of England once again. These hopes were soon crushed when the colonists received the cruel news that King George had <u>hired German soldiers</u> called **Hessians** to help fight against the Americans.

The king had a hard time finding Englishmen who were willing to fight against the American colonists. Many English believed that the colonists were right and just in their demands. Many people of England themselves did not agree with King George or some of the men in the English government. That is why the king was forced to hire soldiers from another country. This news destroyed most of the remaining loyalty the colonists had for England. From now on, the king was their cruel enemy. They realized they must fight for their independence from England.

Although the great evangelist John Wesley was a loyal Englishman, he felt that the English would have real problems if they kept fighting the Americans. He knew that the colonists were fierce lovers of liberty and that they would be united in their fight for it. He wrote to the English leader, Lord North, about the colonists:

> These men will not be frightened, and it seems they will not be conquered as easily as was at first imagined. They will probably dispute every inch of ground, and, if they die, die with sword in hand. . . . They are as strong men as you; they are as valiant as you if not abundantly more valiant, for they are one and all enthusiasts, enthusiasts for liberty.

Someone had told Lord North that the colonists were divided among themselves. Wesley wrote to tell him that this was not true. "My lord," he wrote, "they are terribly united." And united they were, because of their beliefs about human freedom.

The representatives of the Second Continental Congress now asked that a **Declaration of Independence** be written, <u>stating the reasons why the colonists wanted their independence</u>.

Comprehension Check 10C

1. Who was chosen to command the American army during the War for Independence?

2. Why was the Battle of Bunker Hill so important?

3. Who captured Fort Ticonderoga?

4. What were the Germans called who fought for England?

The Declaration of Independence Is Written

Five men in the Second Continental Congress were asked to work together to write the Declaration of Independence. They were Thomas Jefferson, John Adams, Benjamin Franklin, Roger Sherman, and Robert Livingston. **Thomas Jefferson** did the actual writing of the great document.

After the writing of the Declaration of Independence was finished, the members of Congress discussed it and changed a few words. On July 2, 1776, they agreed that the thirteen colonies should be free and independent states. On July 4 (the day that we know as Independence Day or the Fourth of July), the Declaration was signed by **John Hancock,** who was president of the Continental Congress then. He knew what great danger he had put himself in by signing the Declaration of Independence. The English would know who he was, and they might want to hunt him down for signing his name to this document.

Benjamin Franklin turned to the other members of the Continental Congress and said, "Gentlemen, we must all hang together, or assuredly we shall all hang separately."

The People Hear the News

An order was given to make copies of the Declaration. Immediately it was taken to the printing press. Copies were made to take to each colony.

On July 8, the **Liberty Bell** in Philadelphia was rung to call the people of the town together. On the bell are written these words from the Bible: "Proclaim liberty throughout all the land unto all the inhabitants thereof" (Leviticus 25:10).

The bell rang that day to proclaim liberty. When the people of Philadelphia gathered, the Declaration of Independence was read to them. They heard these wonderful words for the first time:

We hold these truths to be self-evident:— That all men are created equal; that they are endowed by their Creator with certain unalienable rights; that among these are life, liberty, and the pursuit of happiness.

The Declaration went on to state, clearly and simply, exactly why the war was being fought:

To secure these rights, governments are instituted among men, deriving their just powers from the consent of the governed . . . whenever any form of government becomes destructive of these ends, it is the right of the people to alter or to abolish it, and to institute a new government. . . .

The history of the present King of Great Britain is a history of repeated injuries and usurpations, all having, in direct object, the establishment of an absolute tyranny over these States.

We, therefore, the Representatives of the United States of America . . . do, in the name

Members of the Continental Congress signed the Declaration of Independence on July 4, 1776.

The Liberty Bell can still be seen in Philadelphia. Because of the crack, the bell has not been rung since 1835.

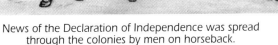

News of the Declaration of Independence was spread through the colonies by men on horseback.

and by the authority of the good people of these colonies, solemnly publish and declare, That these united Colonies are, and of right ought to be, Free and Independent States; that they are absolved from all allegiance to the British crown, and that all political connection between them and the state of Great Britain is, and ought to be, totally dissolved. . . .

And, for the support of this declaration, with a firm reliance on the protection of Divine Providence, we mutually pledge to each other our lives, our fortunes, and our sacred honor.

Of course, there were no telephones, televisions, or airplanes to speed the news to the other colonies. Riders packed copies of the Declaration in their saddle bags and jumped on their horses. Over dusty roads, through shallow streams, and over creaking bridges they quickly rode to carry the good news. Even so, it took as long as two months for the people in some settlements to hear the news. So our country's first Fourth of July was celebrated on many different days, as each town or settlement heard the news.

The people cheered! They rang church bells. They fired guns and cannons to salute the new United States.

The people were excited because they were hearing all that they believed about government, written in an almost perfect form. This Declaration was what they were fighting for!

Almost all the people in the churches throughout the land supported American independence. Most of the Anglican (Church of England) ministers did not, because of their ties with the Church of England, but many of the Anglican church members did. Pastors and people in the other churches— Congregational, Presbyterian, Baptist, Dutch Reformed, and many Catholics—supported the patriot cause, and many ministers served as chaplains in the army. Many Quakers, Mennonites, and Moravians did not believe in fighting, but they helped the patriot cause in other ways, such as caring for the wounded and providing food and clothing for those who needed help.

One Presbyterian preacher, James Caldwell, helped in an unusual way. His wife had been shot by the Hessians, and his house was burned to the ground. The people of the town rose up to defend themselves and were fighting the Hessians and British in a lot next to Caldwell's church. They were using long guns called muskets as weapons, and they ran out of the paper that they had to stuff into the muskets to keep the powder and ball from falling out. Caldwell ran into the church and gathered all the hymn books he could carry. The books were written by Isaac Watts. He tore pages out of the hymn books and shouted, "Put Watts into 'em, boys! Give 'em Watts!" The soldiers were able to keep on with their defense.

The Americans knew that they would have to set up a whole new government to protect their freedoms. No longer were they fighting for the rights of Englishmen. They were fighting to become free and independent from England. All the world was watching to see what would happen.

Comprehension Check 10D

1. What important document was signed on July 4, 1776?

2. Who was president of the Continental Congress when this important document was signed?

3. In Philadelphia, what was used to call the people together for the reading of the Declaration of Independence?

The War Continues

The Declaration of Independence did not end the war, neither did it give the colonists their freedom. Americans would have to prove to the world that they meant what they said. They must win the war.

Congress made George Washington commander in chief of the colonial army.

General George Washington

Congress made **George Washington,** who had been fighting so bravely for the colonists, <u>commander in chief of the colonial army</u>. Washington worked without pay to lead the Americans, and he even gave some of his own money to buy supplies for the army. George Washington did perhaps more than any other man to help the United States gain independence. That is one reason why he is called "the Father of His Country."

The Colonial Army at New York City

You will remember that the first fighting began around Boston. Now the British made plans to capture New York City. New York City had an excellent harbor. If the British controlled this harbor, British ships could easily bring fresh food and supplies to the British army.

General Washington moved his army to New York and prepared for a battle against the British. Just before the battle, Washington made an inspiring speech to his soldiers. He challenged them by saying that if they failed, America would lose its freedom. He made it clear to the men that if they did not conquer, they would die:

The time is now near at hand which must probably determine whether Americans are to be freemen or slaves; whether they are to have any property they can call their own; whether their houses and farms are to be pillaged [robbed] and destroyed, and themselves consigned [given over] to a state of wretchedness from which no human efforts will deliver them. The fate of unborn millions will now depend, under God, on the courage and conduct of this army. Our cruel and unrelenting enemy leaves us only the choice of a brave resistance, or the most abject [shameful] submission. We have, therefore, to resolve to conquer or to die.

Washington and his men fought bravely, but they could not win. Now the British army controlled New York City. General Washington moved his army to New Jersey.

Patriots Who Risked Their Lives

Despite the discouraging defeat at New York, the Americans kept on fighting for their freedom. **James Armistead,** a black slave, served the colonial army as a spy, risking his life to obtain important information from the British. Armistead, like many other slaves who fought for the colonies, was granted his freedom after the war for his courageous military service.

"I only regret that I have but one life to lose for my country." The American spy Nathan Hale met death bravely.

Another patriot, **Nathan Hale,** a young schoolteacher from Connecticut, volunteered to sneak behind enemy lines and find out what the British army was planning. He knew that if he were captured, he would be executed as a spy. But Nathan Hale did not worry about his own life; he wanted to serve his country no matter what the cost.

The British did capture Nathan Hale and condemned him to death. He was not a coward. He did not beg for mercy, and he did not betray his country. The last words he spoke before the British executed him still ring through history: "I only regret that I have but one life to lose for my country." Nathan Hale died, but his words lived on.

Even the British were impressed with the bravery and patriotism of these great heroes. American soldiers everywhere were stirred and reminded that they, too, should be willing to give their lives to make America a free land.

The Colonial Army at Trenton, New Jersey

It was almost Christmas. General Washington's army was very discouraged. Their food and supplies were almost gone. Their clothes were ragged. Few battles had been won. Some soldiers gave up and went back to their homes.

Washington was discouraged, too, but he would not give up hope. He knew that over a thousand Hessians were staying at **Trenton,** a town in New Jersey.

"If only my army could capture Trenton," he said to himself, "we could take and use the British guns, ammunition, and supplies." Then he made a plan.

In a brilliant move, Washington crossed the Delaware River on Christmas night and easily defeated the Hessians the next morning.

According to tradition, Betsy Ross stitched together the first American flag with stars and stripes.

Christmas night was very cold. Large chunks of ice floated down the Delaware River. From dark until dawn Washington's men worked. He had over 2,000 soldiers. By dawn, every one of his soldiers had safely crossed the dangerous, icy Delaware River in small boats. In the early morning hours, his soldiers surrounded Trenton and took the Germans by surprise.

What were the German soldiers doing while Washington's men were crossing the Delaware? They had been celebrating Christmas. Now they were fast asleep. Imagine their surprise when they woke up to find themselves surrounded by the American army. The Hessians had no choice but to give up. They became Washington's prisoners, and their supplies of guns and food were taken. Hope began to return to the American army.

A Flag for Our Country

The Second Continental Congress was still making important decisions. Americans had wanted their own flag for a long time. Many people had made their own flags with their own designs. Now Congress made this decision:

Resolved, that the Flag of the United States be thirteen stripes, alternate red and white, that the "Union" be thirteen stars, white in a blue field. . . .

The thirteen stripes and thirteen stars stood for the thirteen colonies. Later, a new star would be added for each new state that became a part of the United States of America. According to an old story, **Betsy Ross** stitched together the first American flag with stars and stripes. On June 14, 1777, George Washington gave our new flag to Congress. June 14 has become known as **Flag Day**.

Comprehension Check 10E

1. What brave American patriot said, "I only regret that I have but one life to lose for my country"?

2. In what city did the Americans win an important victory at Christmastime, 1776?

3. What happened on June 14, 1777, the day now known as Flag Day?

America Wins Its Freedom

The Colonial Army at Saratoga, New York

The British had already captured New York City. Now they made plans to capture all of New York state. Why? Because New York separated the New England Colonies from the other colonies. If the British controlled New York, the Northern Colonies would have no way of communicating with those in the South.

Fortunately, the American army was able to stop the British from capturing New York in the **Battle of Saratoga.** The Battle of Saratoga is often called <u>the turning point of the War for Independence</u>. This battle did not end the war, but it did prove to the world that America had a chance of winning the war. France had been watching. The Battle of Saratoga persuaded the king of France to help the Americans. However, news traveled slowly in those days. French help would not arrive for a while.

The Colonial Army at Valley Forge, Pennsylvania: Winter of 1777–1778

More trouble and hard times lay ahead for the colonists. The British had captured the city of Philadelphia. Winter was coming, and the British planned to spend the winter in the warm homes of the colonists in Philadelphia.

Washington's men were not so fortunate. Even the victory at Saratoga did little to cheer them. They had no warm place to spend the winter. Washington's army had tried to win back Philadelphia but failed. Afterward, Washington marched his men to **Valley Forge,** near Philadelphia.

Here, Washington's men would spend the worst winter of the war. <u>Hunger and cold</u>

The British general surrendering at Saratoga

<u>were the real enemies at Valley Forge</u>—not the British.

Log huts were built to give some protection against the cruel winter storms, but the huts certainly would not be warm. Little money was available to buy badly needed food, clothes, blankets, or supplies for the men.

Soldiers had only thin, ragged clothing. Many men did not even have shoes for their feet. As they walked, they left blood in the snow from their cold, sore feet. For the sick, there was very little medicine.

Cold, hungry, weak, sick, and discouraged—these are the words that described General Washington's army at Valley Forge.

George Washington and his troops
at Valley Forge, Pennsylvania.

What would you have done under such hardships? Some of Washington's men gave up and went home. Some complained about their leader, but enough men stayed on to wait for springtime when they would begin fighting again. If these men hadn't been brave enough to stay, there would never have been a United States of America. The thought of a free country—their own country—gave them the strength to continue.

The thought of their brave leader gave them courage, too. Someone has painted a picture of George Washington praying in the snow at Valley Forge. From what we know about Washington's character, this is probably exactly what he did, and he probably did it more than once.

George Washington praying at Valley Forge

The War on the Frontier

Some colonists had moved out of the colonies into the western frontier. The frontier had only a few small settlements, but the British decided to stir up trouble there, too.

Just as the French had gone to the Indians during the French and Indian War, so the British talked to the Indians during this war. "If the colonists win this war, they will keep moving west," the British told them. "They will build houses on your land.

They will take away your hunting grounds. You must help us stop them."

Although there were Indian tribes that decided to help the Americans, other tribes made war on the frontier settlements, killing and burning as they went.

A bold young man named **George Rogers Clark** decided to help. He led a group of men from Virginia down the Ohio River. Then they marched through swamps and forests. One by one, they captured three British forts on the frontier—two in the land that is now Illinois and one in what is now Indiana. The British had lost control of the northwest frontier.

Because of George Rogers Clark's courage, the Indians became less of a problem to the frontier settlements in the land north of the Ohio River. This land would soon be known as the Northwest Territory.

A New Navy

Before the War for Independence, the American colonists did not need a navy because the British navy had protected her colonies. Now the Americans needed a navy to protect themselves *against* the British navy. Of course, with little money, our new country could not build a large, powerful navy. Our navy would have to be a small navy run by determined men.

Before the war, **John Paul Jones,** a Scottish seaman, had come to America. He became <u>one of the first officers of our navy</u>. His courage and determination helped our first navy to be successful.

Of his sea battles, the most famous is the one between the American ship named the ***Bonhomme Richard*** (named after Benjamin Franklin's *Poor Richard's Almanack*) and the British ship named the ***Serapis.*** John Paul

Jones brought his ship so close to the *Serapis*, that the cannons of the two ships almost touched.

The British officer on board the *Serapis* shouted, "Are you going to surrender?"

With a clear, determined voice, John Paul Jones answered back, "<u>I have not yet begun to fight</u>!"

With that, guns of both ships boomed. Many on both sides were killed. Finally, the Americans were able to board the British ship and fight hand to hand. At last, the British officer surrendered his ship.

John Paul Jones's bravery and determination helped build the U.S. Navy.

When called upon to surrender, John Paul Jones said, "I have not yet begun to fight." Jones kept fighting and defeated the British ship *Serapis*.

The War in the South

In 1778, the British decided to move their fighting to the Southern Colonies. From this time until the end of the war, most of the fighting took place in the southern part of America.

First the British captured Georgia and then almost all of South Carolina. The <u>British leader at this time</u> was General Lord **Cornwallis.**

General Washington sent one of his trusted generals, **Nathanael Greene,** <u>to fight in the South</u>. With Greene's help, South Carolina and Georgia were won back from the British.

English General Cornwallis then moved up to Yorktown, Virginia. At last General Washington saw the chance he had been waiting for.

Victory at Yorktown: October 1781

The French had sent their navy to help the Americans. When English General Cornwallis moved into **Yorktown,** he expected help from the British navy. However, before the British navy could help, the French navy sailed into the Chesapeake Bay and blocked the bay. Now, no help could get to the British without attacking the powerful French

Famous Quotations
George Washington: "We have to resolve to conquer or to die."
Paul Revere and William Dawes: "The British are coming!"
John Paul Jones: "I have not yet begun to fight!"
Nathan Hale: "I only regret that I have but one life to lose for my country."
Patrick Henry: "Give me liberty, or give me death!"

navy. Cornwallis was in a trap. He could not sail out to escape, and no British ship could sail in to help him.

Meanwhile, General Washington began marching his army to Yorktown. Thousands of French soldiers joined him, until General Cornwallis's army was surrounded by both sea and land. Although it was hopeless, Cornwallis fought bravely.

At last, <u>the entire British army surrendered</u>. The date was October 19, 1781. The Americans had fought for six long, hard years. At last they had won their independence.

Americans realized that God had been with them in their struggle for freedom. Now, as General Washington himself recommended, prayers of thanksgiving could be heard in the American army, in the churches across this new nation, and in the homes and hearts of thankful Americans.

The Treaty of Paris

A **treaty** is <u>an agreement or understanding between two or more countries</u>. The fighting had stopped in 1781, but almost two more years passed before England signed the agreement known as the **Treaty of Paris** in **1783**. In this treaty, <u>England gave up her thirteen American colonies. These colonies were now free and independent states</u>.

How big was our country then? The Treaty of Paris gave the Americans the land from Florida to Canada, and from the Atlantic Ocean to the Mississippi River. The northern part of this new land that was not a part of the thirteen colonies became known as the **Northwest Territory.** You will remember that George Rogers Clark had battled his way through this wilderness to win three forts from the British. His triumph in winning these forts was of great importance to our country.

★ ★ ★ ★ Chapter 10 Checkup ★ ★ ★ ★

(*Lesson 55 (1-15)*)

Answer the questions on notebook paper.

1. What king of England angered the colonists by taking away their rights as Englishmen?

2. What law that added to the cost of newspapers, documents, etc., was thought unfair by the colonists?

3. What is a tax?

4. What is a representative?

5. What is a massacre?

6. How many colonists were killed in the Boston Massacre?

7. Who was Crispus Attucks?

8. How did the colonists respond when King George III tried to force them to accept British tea?

   What was this event called?

9. Name the group of representatives who met to decide what to do about England's unfair treatment of the colonies.

10. Who said, "Give me liberty or give me death"?

11. What were the colonists who wanted to be free from England's rule called?

12. What were the colonists who remained loyal to England called?

13. Name the soldiers who said they could be ready to fight at a minute's notice.

14. What did Paul Revere and William Dawes do?

15. What happened at Lexington and Concord?

16. What is a trench?

17. Name the commander of the American army during the War for Independence.

18. During which battle did the colonists show the British that the Americans would not be easy to defeat?

19. What important fort did Ethan Allen and the "Green Mountain Boys" capture?

20. Who were the Hessians?

21. When was the Declaration of Independence signed?

22. Near what city did Washington and his men cross an icy river to surprise the Hessians at Christmastime?

23. On what day did George Washington present the new American flag to Congress?

24. What is often called the turning point of the War for Independence?

25. Where did General Washington's army spend the harsh winter of 1777–1778?

26. Whose bold adventures captured British forts in the Northwest Territory for America?

27. What Scotsman was determined to help the American Navy be successful?

    What was the name of his ship?

    In his most famous victory, what ship did Jones capture?

28. Which general led the British army near the end of the war and eventually surrendered to Washington?

29. When the war shifted to the Southern Colonies, who was sent to lead the American forces?

30. What treaty ended the War for Independence?

Building a New Nation

After the War for Independence

The thirteen colonies had gone through a hard struggle to become thirteen free and independent states. They had faced the problems of fighting the British. Now that they had won, they would face problems of a different kind—those of building a new nation.

The thirteen states did not feel united as one country. The people from Georgia thought of themselves as Georgians. Those from Virginia thought of themselves as Virginians, those from Pennsylvania as Pennsylvanians. Hardly anyone thought of himself first as an American. Instead of one big country, the thirteen states were acting as if they were thirteen small countries, each ruling itself.

Many people were afraid of one strong government. They feared that it would be like the powerful British government from which they had just won their freedom!

The Articles of Confederation

The first plan of government that the states agreed upon was called the **Articles of Confederation.** Under this plan, the government could not be strong.

The government had no power to tax the people of the United States. Requests went out to the states for money, but very little came in, because the states knew that the government could not force them to give. The government had little money to do anything.

This government had no power to settle quarrels that might arise between two states. The states could refuse to do anything that the government asked them to do. In order for this government to work, each state would have to agree with all the others all the time. Do you think this was possible?

Already you can see problems that would arise. This government was too weak to work.

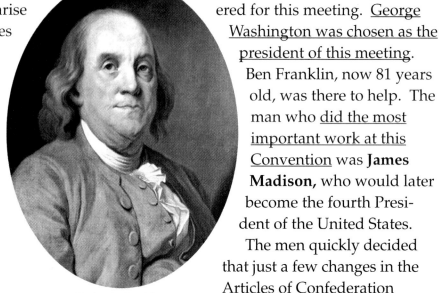
Benjamin Franklin

The Constitution of the United States

A meeting was held in **Philadelphia** to discuss what could be done to make our government stronger. This meeting was called the **Constitutional Convention.** The meeting lasted all through the summer of 1787. It was held in Independence Hall, where the Declaration of Independence had been signed eleven years earlier. Many wise and important men gathered for this meeting. George Washington was chosen as the president of this meeting. Ben Franklin, now 81 years old, was there to help. The man who did the most important work at this Convention was **James Madison,** who would later become the fourth President of the United States.

The men quickly decided that just a few changes in the Articles of Confederation would not do. Our country needed a brand new government. The plan for that new government, which our government still follows, is the **Constitution of the United States.**

Many discussions were held. Many committees met. Many ideas were talked about. In debate after debate the men challenged one another to find what was best for America. In the history of the world there

New Words

1. **President**—head of government; has the power to see that the nation's laws are obeyed
2. **Congress**—part of government that has the power to make our country's most important laws
3. **houses**—the two groups that make up the Congress: the Senate and the House of Representatives
4. **Senate**—house of Congress with one hundred members: two Senators from each state
5. **House of Representatives**—other house of Congress; the number of representatives from each state is determined by the size of the state
6. **Supreme Court**—highest court in the United States; its job is to judge whether the Constitution has been obeyed
7. **republic**—government run by representatives of the people
8. **Inauguration Day**—day when a President of the United States takes the oath of office

New Names

9. **Articles of Confederation**—the first plan of government the states agreed upon after the War for Independence
10. **Constitutional Convention**—meeting of representatives which created a new government for the United States of America

has probably never been such an assembly of wise men. The wisdom about politics that our Founding Fathers showed at the Convention has never been equaled. The writing of the **Constitution of the United States** and the writing of the **Declaration of Independence** are two of the most important events that have contributed to the happiness and progress of all mankind. These documents were written for America, but the whole world has learned a lesson from them—what it means to be free men. Everyone was convinced that the hand of God was in the work that was being done at this Convention and that no country can be strong without God's continuing help. At one point during the Convention, Benjamin Franklin stood and said:

> I have lived a long time, and the longer I live the more convincing proofs I see of this truth: that God governs in the affairs of men. And if a sparrow cannot fall to the ground without His notice, is it probable that an empire [great country] can rise without His aid?

Everyone agreed on the purpose of the new government. The government would protect the freedoms that the Declaration of Independence talks about and that the War for Independence was fought over. Everyone wanted this. They disagreed, though, over just what kind of government could best protect our freedoms. The government would have to be strong enough to protect people from criminals and yet not so strong that it could take away the freedoms of people who obey the laws.

Here are some of the questions that the delegates discussed:
- What powers should the government for the whole country have? How much power should be left with the states?
- How should the government for the whole country be set up so that it could protect the country from foreign enemies but not become the enemy of the country it was supposed to protect?
- Should there be limits on what the state governments could do?
- What could be done to keep bad men from using government for selfish purposes?

---

11. **James Madison**—man who did the most important work at the Constitutional Convention; later became the fourth President of the United States
12. **Constitution of the United States**—the new plan of government for our country after the Articles of Confederation failed; the plan of government still used in our country today
13. **Bill of Rights**—a list of rights or freedoms added to the Constitution to protect the freedom of individuals and groups
14. **George Washington**—first President of the United States
15. **John Adams**—first Vice President; later became the second President of the United States

16. **Benjamin Banneker**—first black American to write a scientific book; helped to plan the city of Washington, D.C.

New Places
17. **Philadelphia**—city where the Constitutional Convention was held
18. **New York**—first capital of the United States
19. **Mount Vernon**—George Washington's home
20. **Washington, D.C.**—capital of the United States

New Dates
21. **1787**—Constitutional Convention is held

The men working on the Constitution realized that no one person or state could have its own way completely. Each side had to give a little. In this way, the men began to work together through the long, hot summer months to answer these questions:

Who would carry out the laws of our new nation?

The delegates of the Convention decided that the head of our new government would be a **President.** The President <u>would have the power to see that the laws were obeyed</u>.

Who would make our country's laws?

Congress <u>would have the power to make our country's most important laws</u>. Congress was to be made up of <u>two groups called **houses.**</u>

One house was to be the **Senate.** <u>Every state</u>, no matter how large or small, <u>was to send two senators</u> to represent their state in the Senate.

The other house was the **House of Representatives.** Each state would send representatives to the House of Representatives. How many representatives? This depended upon how many people lived in a state. A large state like Virginia could send more representatives than the small state of New Jersey.

The idea of a Senate pleased the small states, for there every state, no matter what size, had the same power. The House of Representatives pleased the larger states, for there they had more power. Yet neither house was more important than the other. The Senate and the House of Representatives both have to agree on a law before it becomes a law. Who would settle our country's arguments? Who would decide between right and wrong?

The new government would make and enforce many new laws. A new set of courts and judges was needed. <u>The highest court in the land</u> is known as the **Supreme**

This painting includes a picture of every man who signed the Constitution. It hangs in the United States Capitol in Washington, D.C.

Court. Its job is to judge whether the Constitution has been obeyed.

A Brand New Government

The Constitution was now complete. Each state thought carefully before taking a big step and signing the Constitution. Each state gave up its power to completely govern itself when it signed. The American people were putting their trust in a brand new government, a government of the people, by the people, and for the people.

The Constitution began with these words:

We the people of the United States, in order to form a more perfect Union, establish justice, insure domestic tranquillity, provide for the common defense, promote the general welfare, and secure the blessings of liberty to ourselves and our posterity, do ordain and establish this Constitution for the United States of America.

Comprehension Check 11A

1. What was the first plan of government that the states agreed upon after the War for Independence?
2. Where was the Constitutional Convention held?
3. Why did this first plan of government fail?
4. What plan of government did the Convention draw up?
5. By signing the Constitution, what did each state agree to give up?

The Bill of Rights

The people of the United States knew from the very beginning that it was important to make sure that no government—even our own government—could take away freedoms that God has given us. To protect the freedom of individuals and groups, they added a **Bill of Rights** to the Constitution. The Bill of Rights is a list of people's rights or freedoms. The Bill of Rights forbids the federal government from taking these freedoms from us.

The Bill of Rights includes the right to print and read what we want, within certain limits. It also includes the right for someone accused of a crime to be tried by a jury in a court of law.

The new government could not interfere in these areas. The Bill of Rights also protected the states and their powers from being taken over by the new government. Americans believed it was wise not to give too much power to any one person or group, or even to the government.

The Bill of Rights is written in the form of ten amendments, or changes, to the Constitution. The First Amendment is especially important. It guarantees us freedom of religion, freedom of speech, freedom of the press, and freedom of assembly. It says:

Congress shall make no law respecting an establishment of religion, or prohibiting the free exercise thereof; or abridging the freedom of speech, or of the press; or the right of the people peaceably to assemble, and to petition the government for a redress of grievances.

The Bill of Rights protects the rights and freedoms of all Americans.

The New Republic

It has been said that as Benjamin Franklin left the Constitutional Convention, a woman walked over to him and asked, "What kind of government has been

Washington became the first President on April 30, 1789. He took the oath of office with his hand placed on the Bible.

formed?" His thoughtful answer was, "A republic, if you can keep it!"

"A republic, if you can keep it!" What did Benjamin Franklin mean by this statement?

A **republic** is <u>a government run by representatives of the people</u>. Franklin knew that it was dangerous for only one man to rule a country. Yet never before in history had any country as large as ours tried to have self-government. The Constitutional Convention had worked hard to plan a government in which our President could not rule like a king.

A republic is also a government in which <u>no particular group has all the power</u>. Franklin also knew that it is dangerous for the people to have too much power. He knew that in self-government the people can sometimes act like a harsh king. We are fortunate that the Constitution guards against this.

America has so far kept the republican government set up by the Constitution. May we as Americans never let our government take away the freedoms that were guaranteed to us by our Constitution and the Bill of Rights.

An Election

Now there was another decision to make. Who would be the first President of the United States? This was not a hard decision. The man who had led our country through the War for Independence was already loved and trusted. **George Washington** was elected <u>our first President</u>; **John Adams** was <u>our first Vice President</u>.

After being elected, Washington traveled in a horse-drawn coach to <u>our nation's first capital</u>—**New York.** Washington, D.C., did not exist yet.

People crowded the roads that George Washington's coach traveled. All along the way, he was met by cheering crowds. Little girls threw flowers in his path. Guns were fired to salute the first President of the United States. On the first **Inauguration Day,** Washington asked that a Bible be brought to him. With his hand resting on the Word of God, Washington took the oath of office. Washington set a good example that day; all the Presidents since then have been sworn in on a Bible.

George Washington was a good President. He was well aware that, as the first President, he would be setting an example for all the Presidents who would come after him. Therefore, all his official actions were done carefully, cautiously, and thoughtfully. Because he set such a good example, Washington is regarded by historians as one of the greatest of all Presidents. He served his first term of four years so well that the people elected him for a second term. When it came time for the third election, the people wanted to elect him again—but this time he refused. He and his wife, Martha, returned to their beautiful plantation farm, **Mount Vernon,** in Virginia.

Before he left office, Washington wrote a long farewell address. In the address he thanked the people of America for voting for him and for allowing him to serve his country as President for eight years. Then he warned the people that unless they acted like responsible citizens, the freedom for which they had fought so hard might disappear. He told them that respect for and obedience to the nation's laws are vitally important. He warned people that loyalty to their country should never be replaced by loyalty to a political party. He urged people from the North, South, East, and West not to think about what would be good for their part of the country, but what would be good for the country as a whole. Above all, he stressed that this new government could work only in an atmosphere of strong morality (doing right according to God's laws). He said that morality would result only when religion held its proper place in the lives of its citizens.

A short time after writing this address, Washington retired to Mount Vernon. Honest, hard-working John Adams took his place and became the second President of the United States.

Comprehension Check 11B

1. Who was elected the first President of this country?

2. What do we call the day on which a new President is sworn into office?

3. What was the first capital of this country?

4. Who became the second President of our country?

John Adams became the second President of the United States.

A New Capital

You will remember that our nation's first capital was New York. Soon plans were made to build a new capital. **Benjamin Banneker,** the first black American to write a scientific book, helped to plan the new city. Both Virginia and Maryland gave land to build the city on the banks of the Potomac River. Although George Washington never lived there, the city was named Washington, in his honor. The land that the city was built on was called the District of Columbia. Thus, we get the name **Washington, D.C.**

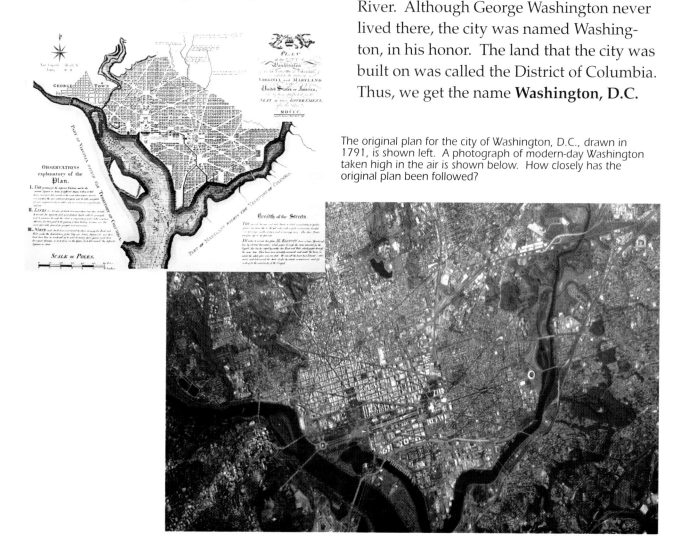

The original plan for the city of Washington, D.C., drawn in 1791, is shown left. A photograph of modern-day Washington taken high in the air is shown below. How closely has the original plan been followed?

★ ★ ★ ★ Chapter 11 Checkup ★ ★ ★ ★

Answer the questions on notebook paper.

1. How did most Americans feel about having one strong government over them?
2. What plan of government did the states first form after the War for Independence?
3. Was the government under the Articles of Confederation weak or strong?
4. What important power did the government lack?

5. At what meeting was the decision made to create a brand new government?

6. In what building was the Constitutional Convention held?

7. Who was the president of the Convention?

8. Who did the most important work at the Convention?

9. What new plan of government was formed during the Constitutional Convention?

10. Who has the power to see that our nation's laws are obeyed?

11. Who has the power to make our country's most important laws?

12. Name the two houses that make up Congress.

13. Which house gives equal representation to all states, no matter what size?

14. In which house do the larger states have more power?

15. What is the highest court in the land?

16. What did each state give up when it signed the Constitution?

17. What was added to the Constitution to insure that certain rights and freedoms could never be taken away from the people?

18. What is a republic?

19. Who was our first President?
    Who was our first Vice President?

20. Where was our country's capital when George Washington was President?

21. What do we call the day the new President takes the oath of office?

22. How many terms did Washington serve?

23. Who was our second President?

24. Near what river was the country's new capital built?
    Which states gave land for the city?

25. What was the name of the new capital?
    What was the land that the city was built on called?

Oregon Country
1846

Mexican Cession
1848

Louisiana Purchase
1803

1818 ‡

Lake Superior

Lake Huron

Lake Ontario

Lake Michigan

Lake Erie

Northwest Territory

UNITED STATES
1783

Original
13 Colonies

Missouri River

Mississippi River

Ohio River

Gadsden
Purchase *1853*

Texas Annexation
1845

Pacific
Ocean

Mississippi River

1810 ‡   *1813* ‡

New Orleans

Florida
1819

Atlantic
Ocean

Gulf of Mexico

1842

Alaska
Purchase
1867

Hawaii
Annexation
1898

* This section of land, like the Northwest Territory, was given to
the United States by the Treaty of Paris following America's War
for Independence. However, it was never widely called one
name as the Northwest Territory was.

‡The yellow areas of land were in dispute for part of America's history—
more than one country claimed them at a time.

TIME LINE OF IMPORTANT DATES

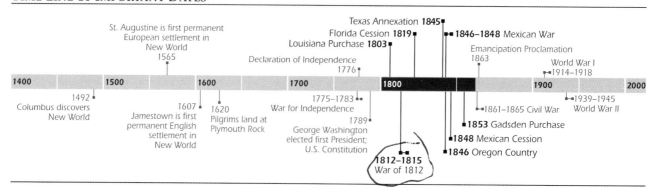

St. Augustine is first permanent
European settlement in
New World
1565

Texas Annexation **1845**

Florida Cession **1819**

Louisiana Purchase **1803**

1846–1848 Mexican War

Declaration of Independence
1776

Emancipation Proclamation
1863

World War I
1914–1918

| 1400 | 1500 | 1600 | 1700 | 1800 | 1900 | 2000 |

1492
Columbus discovers
New World

1607
Jamestown is first
permanent English
settlement in
New World

1620
Pilgrims land at
Plymouth Rock

1775–1783
War for Independence

1789
George Washington
elected first President;
U.S. Constitution

1861–1865 Civil War

1853 Gadsden Purchase

1848 Mexican Cession

1846 Oregon Country

1939–1945
World War II

1812–1815
War of 1812

Our Nation Grows

America Pushes Farther West

What area of the country would you think of if you heard someone say that he was moving to the West? Perhaps you would say "California" or "Oregon." In today's America, you would be correct. But if you had lived back in the early 1800s, your idea of the "West" would have been completely different. In those days, the "West" meant any land that was still frontier land. The "West" kept moving farther west as America continued to grow.

Daniel Boone and the Wilderness Road

Even before the American War for Independence, there were pioneers who were eager to see the West. Most of these early pioneers were unmarried men who wanted to hunt and trap animals for furs. Few had horses. Most walked through the wilderness without even a path to guide them. It was impossible to take wagons because of the many trees and rocks. For these reasons, few women and children were among the early pioneers.

Daniel Boone yearned to see the wilderness of Kentucky. When some friends offered to go along with him, Daniel decided to leave his family for a while and see Kentucky. The trip was filled with new experiences. Daniel and his friends were even captured by Indians.

When he returned home, Daniel certainly had many stories to tell his wife and children. He hoped for the day when he could move his family to Kentucky.

Daniel Boone is shown here leading a group of settlers to the Kentucky territory.

The next year, Daniel Boone was asked to return to Kentucky to clear a trail so that other pioneers could follow. Daniel chose thirty strong men to work with him. The trail that they made was barely more than a path through the thick forests and over the mountains. At first, the path was so narrow that it was still impossible for a wagon to travel over it. Yet this path was called the **Wilderness Road.** The first pioneers who traveled this road would have to walk or ride a horse.

Almost the same time that the War for Independence started, a settlement was built in Kentucky and named **Boonesborough** in honor of Daniel Boone. Then Daniel returned to his home and brought his family back to live in Kentucky.

Although the Wilderness Road was at first only a rough path, it led many of the first pioneers to the West. For this reason, Daniel Boone has been called "the pioneer of pioneers." With the passing years, the Wilderness Road was made wider. Thousands of wagons and families traveled over it.

As the population grew in each new section of the country, new states were added to the original thirteen states. Vermont, which had been considered frontier at the time of the War for Independence, became the fourteenth state. Later, Kentucky, Tennessee, Mississippi, and Alabama—which were part of the land given to us by England following the War for Independence—joined the Union.

Settling the Northwest Territory

The **Northwest Territory** became part of the United States after we won the War for Independence. One day this large piece

New Words

1. **frontier**—land with few people west of settled areas
2. **flatboat**—long boat with a flat bottom
3. **dictator**—one who rules by force and allows his people little or no freedom
4. **ghost towns**—former mining towns full of empty buildings where no one lives

New Names

5. **Daniel Boone**—pioneer who began the settlement of Kentucky; called "the pioneer of pioneers"
6. **Wilderness Road**—trail cleared by Daniel Boone in Kentucky
7. **Land Ordinance of 1785**—law that divided the Northwest Territory into townships and demanded that one section of land in each township be set aside for a public school
8. **Northwest Ordinance of 1787**—law that guaranteed that the freedom and democracy the original states enjoyed would also be present in the territories
9. **Louisiana Purchase**—section of land purchased from France by President Jefferson that doubled the size of the United States
10. **Captain Meriwether Lewis** and **Captain William Clark**—young men who led an expedition to explore the Louisiana Purchase
11. **Sacagawea**—Indian woman who went with the Lewis and Clark expedition to translate the Indian language
12. **Napoleon Bonaparte**—French ruler who sold the Louisiana Territory to the United States
13. **War of 1812**—war fought between the United States and England; neither country won the war
14. **Francis Scott Key**—man who wrote "The Star-Spangled Banner" during the battle of Fort McHenry
15. **President James Monroe**—President who purchased Florida from Spain
16. **Francis Asbury**—famous circuit-riding preacher
17. **Peter Cartwright**—one of the best-known circuit-riding preachers of the Second Great Awakening
18. **General Santa Anna**—Mexican dictator who tried to crush the Texas rebellion
19. **Davy Crockett**—famous frontiersman who died fighting at the Alamo

of land would make up the states of <u>Ohio, Indiana, Illinois, Michigan, Wisconsin, and part of Minnesota</u>.

Because our government knew that many settlers would flock to the Northwest Territory, Congress passed <u>laws that would bring order and government to the territory</u>. These laws were called the Land Ordinance of 1785 and the Northwest Ordinance of 1787.

The **Land Ordinance of 1785** divided land into large townships measuring 6 miles on each side. Within each township were 36 smaller sections measuring one mile on each side. These one-square-mile sections would be sold to settlers for not less than $1.00 an acre. The Land Ordinance also demanded that one of these sections of land in each township be set aside for a public school. Thus, settlers who wanted to move to the Northwest Territory were sure that schools would be there for their children to attend.

Within two years, large numbers of settlers began moving into the new territory, and a plan of government became necessary. Congress met this need with the **Northwest Ordinance of 1787.** The Ordinance of 1787 made sure that the freedom and democracy that the original states enjoyed would also be present in the territories. It guaranteed freedom of religion, outlawed slavery, and set up territorial assemblies.

Perhaps the most important part of the Northwest Ordinance of 1787 was the promise that "education shall forever be encouraged." Finally, the Northwest Ordinance said that when the population of an area reached 60,000, that area could become a state and enter the Union.

20. **General Sam Houston**—leader of the Texans in their fight for independence
21. **President James K. Polk**—President during the Mexican War
22. **Gadsden Purchase**—section of land in the Southwest purchased from Mexico in order to build a railroad
23. **John Sutter**—man on whose land gold was discovered in California in 1848
24. **"forty-niners"**—nickname for the people who flocked to California to find gold in 1849
25. **Gold Rush**—name given to the great movement of gold seekers to California
26. **Marcus and Narcissa Whitman**—husband and wife who were missionaries to the Indians in Oregon
27. **Noah Webster**—writer of the first American dictionary and history and reading textbooks, including the *Blue-backed Speller*
28. **William H. McGuffey**—author of a series of readers that were used in American schools

New Places
29. **Boonesborough**—pioneer settlement in Kentucky named after Daniel Boone

30. **Fort McHenry**—during a siege on this fort, "The Star-Spangled Banner" was written
31. **Northwest Territory**—large piece of land that eventually became the states of Ohio, Indiana, Illinois, Michigan, Wisconsin, and part of Minnesota
32. **Alamo**—Spanish mission where 187 men fighting for Texas were killed by Mexicans
33. **San Jacinto**—place where the Texans defeated the Mexican army
34. **Rio Grande**—river that forms the border between Texas and Mexico
35. **Oregon Territory**—land that eventually became the states of Oregon, Washington, and Idaho, as well as part of Montana and Wyoming

New Dates
36. **1803**—Louisiana Purchase
37. **1812–1815**—War of 1812
38. **1819**—Florida is purchased from Spain
39. **1846–1848**—Mexican War
40. **1848**—gold is discovered in California
41. **1853**—Gadsden Purchase

There were men who desired to move their families into the Northwest Territory. Some felt too crowded where they were and wanted to move on. Others just wanted adventure and a new way of living. Together, they formed one courageous group of pioneers, helping our country to grow.

There were no highways to lead these pioneers. Since Ohio was first to become settled in the Northwest Territory, let's see how a pioneer family traveled to Ohio from Pennsylvania.

First the settlers bought a covered wagon and loaded it with the supplies they knew they could not get in Ohio—seeds for gardens, a plow, tools, nails, guns, an iron kettle, cooking utensils, a spinning wheel, and blankets. They had to pack enough flour, salt, bacon, and other food to last them until they reached Pittsburgh.

To one side of the wagon, they tied a crate of chickens. To the other side they might tie a crate of piglets. Behind the wagon walked a cow. As you can see, there was not much room left to take furniture or fancy dishes. They would have to make their own homemade furniture when they reached Ohio. With chickens cackling and piglets squealing, the wagon began creaking down the rough road.

In a few days, the covered wagon reached the city of Pittsburgh in Pennsylvania. Here, the father sold the wagon and bought a **flatboat,** which was a long boat with a flat bottom. Then the family unloaded their supplies from the wagon and placed them on the boat. Even the chickens, piglets,

These settlers on their way west have stopped to make camp for the night.

horses, and cow were placed on the boat. More food and supplies were bought.

Men gave advice to the family before they began their trip down the Ohio River to their new home:

"Beware of Indian traps! To avoid them, keep your distance from the shore."

"Keep your eyes open for fallen trees and sharp rocks in the river. They can tear the bottom of your boat open!"

The trip by flatboat could be even more dangerous than traveling in the bumpy covered wagon. Once the pioneers traveled west of Pittsburgh, they left the protection of forts and soldiers.

When the family finally reached their new home in Ohio, their flatboat was carefully taken apart to save the lumber and nails. Then their home was built and a garden was planted. There was plenty of work to do.

As more and more pioneers moved into Ohio, it was no longer considered the frontier. Schools were built as well as stores and churches. Then new pioneers who wished to settle in the frontier of the Northwest Territory no longer stopped in Ohio.

They kept moving westward into Indiana, Illinois, Michigan, and Wisconsin.

Ohio's population grew so quickly that in 1803, it became our seventeenth state. As the years passed, more frontier became settled and more states were formed.

Comprehension Check 12A

1. What famous pioneer opened up Kentucky to settlers?
2. What trail into Kentucky did Daniel Boone clear?
3. What states were formed from the Northwest Territory?

The United States Doubles Its Size

Thomas Jefferson, author of the Declaration of Independence, became our third President. He made many good decisions for our country. One decision had to do with the city of New Orleans at the mouth of the Mississippi River. Jefferson knew how important this city could be to the United States. American ships could load and trade here freely if the city belonged to America.

The land surrounding New Orleans was called the Louisiana Territory. It had belonged to Spain, but Spain gave the land to France. Jefferson quickly asked the French ruler if he could buy New Orleans for two million dollars. The French decided to sell not only New Orleans, but also all of the Louisiana Territory. The price for all this land would be fifteen million dollars. This may seem like a large amount of money, but it was a small price to pay for so much land. Thomas Jefferson gladly accepted France's offer and bought the Louisiana Territory in 1803.

The **Louisiana Purchase** more than doubled the size of the United States. In the years to come, the Louisiana Purchase was to provide all or part of the land for fifteen new states.

Exploring the Louisiana Territory

Hardly anything was known about the land that made up the Louisiana Territory. President Jefferson chose **Captain Meriwether Lewis** to lead a group on an expedition to explore this new land. Lewis chose **Captain William Clark** to join him.

Along the way, Lewis and Clark's group met Indians, but the explorers had a hard time understanding the Indians' language. Fortunately, they met a French trapper whose wife was an Indian. Her name was **Sacagawea** [săk′ə·jə·wē′ə]. Sacagawea and her husband agreed to go with Lewis and Clark's expedition to translate the Indian language for them.

Together they climbed over mountains. When they came to rivers, they built boats. At last they saw the Pacific Ocean. When the expedition finally returned to Washington, D.C., Lewis and Clark had important reports to make to President Jefferson.

Americans heard about Lewis and Clark's exciting trip to see the West. Many people from the original thirteen states in the East became eager to move west. As a result, pioneers began pushing their way west to make new homes.

The War of 1812
The French Purpose in Selling Louisiana

At the time we purchased the Louisiana Territory, the French were being governed by a very powerful soldier, **Napoleon**

During the War of 1812, British soldiers set fire to Washington, D.C. Here, the President's House is seen going up in flames.

During the battle at Ft. McHenry, Francis Scott Key wrote "The Star-Spangled Banner." His poem became our national anthem.

Bonaparte. Napoleon sold the Louisiana Territory to the United States, but he was not selling it to be generous to us. At the time, he was trying to become the ruler of all Europe. He needed money to carry on his wars in Europe. Selling Louisiana was a good way to get the money he needed. Although America was certainly far away from Europe, she became a part of the war between France and England.

Problems Arise for American Ships

The powerful French and English navies were fighting each other. If an American ship tried to sail with goods to England, France tried to prevent the American ship from reaching England. On the other hand, if an American ship tried to take goods to France, England did her best to prevent the ship from reaching France.

Then English warships began stopping American ships. The British would go on board the American ships and capture some American sailors. These Americans were then forced to fight in the British navy. Soon hundreds of American sailors had been kidnapped and were being forced to serve in the British navy.

American ships had no respect on the seas. Since England was causing most of the problems, the United States declared war on England in 1812, and the **War of 1812** began.

The British and the Americans fought for over two years. The American army and navy were still new and weak. In 1814, the British marched into Washington, D.C., where they burned the Capitol building and the President's house.

Our National Anthem

The British next planned to capture Baltimore, Maryland. During the battle of **Fort McHenry** in Baltimore, an American lawyer named **Francis Scott Key** was seeking the release of an American prisoner on board an English warship. The battle continued during the night.

As the bombs burst and the rockets gave off a red glare of light, Key had enough light to see that our flag was still flying over the fort. When dawn finally came, Key saw plainly that our flag was still there. The British had failed to capture Baltimore. The sight of our battle-torn flag inspired Francis Scott Key to <u>write our national anthem,</u> <u>"The Star-Spangled Banner."</u>

The Results of the War of 1812

The last battle of the War of 1812 was fought in 1815. The Americans soundly defeated the British at this battle, but <u>neither side won the war</u>. After three years of war, each side gladly made peace. England finally respected our ships on the seas. We also gained the respect of other countries who were watching to see what the outcome would be. <u>The United States</u> <u>proved to herself and others that she was</u> <u>strong enough to protect herself</u>. The people of the United States became prouder than ever of being Americans.

Comprehension Check 12B

1. Which President purchased the Louisiana Territory?
2. What two young men led an expedition to explore the Louisiana Territory?
3. What city was burned during the War of 1812?
4. Who wrote "The Star-Spangled Banner"? During what battle?

The Purchase of Florida

You will remember that Florida belonged to Spain. However, Spain did not rule Florida well. Men who had broken the law often ran to Florida to hide, and Spain did little to stop them. Many Indians of Florida were warlike. Spain did nothing to control these Indians from crossing over Florida's

border into Georgia, where they terrorized the settlers. After burning and killing, these Indians would run back to Florida. Florida was not a safe place to live in the early 1800s.

The United States finally had enough of Spain's poor control. President **James Monroe** offered to buy Florida from Spain for five million dollars. However, this money would not be paid to Spain. Instead, the United States planned to use it to pay back the people of Georgia and other United States citizens who had property damaged by Florida's Indians.

<u>Spain accepted our offer and sold Florida</u> <u>in 1819</u>. The United States as we know it today was beginning to come together like pieces of a puzzle.

The Second Great Awakening

As more and more people poured into the western regions and settled there, the need for churches and preachers was great. But the people of the territories were spread out over a large area, and many were too poor to build churches and hire full-time pastors.

One Methodist who came to America from England was **Francis Asbury.** He had learned from John Wesley the method of riding from town to town on a horse to preach in as many towns each week as possible. When Asbury became a Methodist leader in the American colonies in 1771, he, too, spread the gospel in this way and taught many other Methodist preachers to do it.

These men were called **circuit-riding preachers,** because regularly <u>they would</u> <u>make the same circuit (circle) of towns,</u>

preaching wherever they went. They preached every day of the week, and sometimes as many as six sermons a day. You can imagine what a great number of colonists heard the gospel when this method was used!

Through the years, the preaching of many circuit riders started what some people call the Second Great Awakening. This great revival began in Kentucky (the territory that Daniel Boone had opened up to settlers), spread to neighboring areas, and then moved up into the Northwest Territory. Soon many people were being converted under the preaching of Baptist, Methodist, and Presbyterian evangelists in Indiana, Ohio, Kentucky, and Tennessee.

One of the best-known circuit riders was **Peter Cartwright,** who preached the gospel for over fifty years. Cartwright was a strong and rugged man who seemed to enjoy the life of a circuit rider. Here is his description of what it was like to be a traveling preacher on the frontier:

> A Methodist preacher in those days, when he felt that God had called him to preach, . . . hunted up a hardy pony of a horse. . . . He started, and with a text that never wore out or grew stale, he cried, "Behold the Lamb of God, that taketh away the sins of the world." In this way he went through storms of wind, hail, snow, and rain; climbed hills and mountains, traversed [crossed] valleys, plunged through swamps, swam swollen streams, lay out all night, wet, weary, and hungry, held his horse by the bridle all night, or tied him to a limb, slept with his saddle blanket for a bed, his saddle or saddlebags for his pillow, and his old big coat or blanket, if he had any, for a covering.

Circuit-riding preacher

Clearly, a circuit rider had to be a strong man to face up to the many difficulties of his job. The West was not a place for weaklings, and it was not a place for a preacher who wanted to make a lot of money, either. Peter Cartwright says that in his day the average salary paid to preachers in the West was thirty to forty dollars per year. So why did these men spend their lives doing such hard work? They preached because they loved God, and they wanted to see the frontier people come to Christ.

Eventually the Second Great Awakening made its way east. New England, where the first Great Awakening had taken place, experienced another great revival.

For many years the spirit of revival was kept alive in America by **camp meetings.** Each year a camp meeting was held in many places throughout every state. People from all around gathered together for a solid week to hear gospel preaching. Because people lived so far apart, many traveled several miles to the campsite. There they would set up a tent and live and cook camp-style throughout the week.

Comprehension Check 12C

1. Which territory did President Monroe buy from Spain?
2. What were circuit-riding preachers?
3. Who was one of the most famous circuit-riding preachers during the Second Great Awakening?

The United States Gains the Southwest

In 1821, the country of Mexico fought for and won her independence from Spain. At that time Texas, New Mexico, Arizona, and California were all part of Mexico.

Mexico Invites Americans to Texas

The Mexican government was eager to have more settlers come to Texas. Mexico offered to sell land cheaply to Americans if they agreed to become Mexican citizens and obey Mexico's laws.

Thousands of Americans accepted Mexico's offer. By 1834 there were more Americans in Texas than there were Mexicans. The Mexican government began to worry, "What if the Americans try to take over Texas?"

As a result Mexico decided to stop any more Americans from coming to Texas. Mexican soldiers were sent to guard the Texas border. Then the Mexican government tried to take away the freedoms of the Americans already in Texas. You can imagine how freedom-loving Americans felt about that!

Texas Decides to Fight for Independence: The Alamo

In 1833, a Mexican general named **Santa Anna** took complete control of Mexico. He allowed the people no freedom. Such a leader is called a **dictator.**

Finally, the Americans in Texas could take no more. In 1836, they declared Texas an independent country, free from Mexico's rule. Santa Anna replied by sending an army to beat the Americans.

Inside an old Spanish mission called the **Alamo,** 187 men gathered and prepared to fight. Not all the men in the Alamo were Texans; some had come down from the United States to help the Texans fight. One group from Tennessee was led by the famous frontiersman **Davy Crockett.** Why did Crockett go to Texas to fight even though Texas was not yet part of the United States? Because the people of Texas wanted to be free, and Davy Crockett was willing to fight anywhere for any people that wanted to be free.

When Davy Crockett had left his home state of Tennessee to head for Texas, he had an idea that he might not ever return. So he wrote a beautiful farewell poem to his home and his family:

> The home I forsake where my offspring arose;
> The graves I forsake where my children repose;
> The home I redeemed from the savage and wild;
> The home I have loved as a father his child;
> The corn that I planted, the fields that I cleared,
> The flocks that I raised, and the cabin I reared;
> The wife of my bosom—Farewell to ye all!
> In the land of the stranger I rise or I fall.

The Alamo can still be seen in San Antonio, Texas.

But Davy was not afraid. He always said that his life's motto was, "Be always sure you're right—then go ahead!" That was his motto when he fought bravely in the War of 1812. And now he felt it was right to fight for Texas's freedom—so he went ahead!

Crockett and the other men in the Alamo fought bravely, but they were no match for the 3,000 Mexican soldiers. However, the Texans did make the Mexicans pay dearly for a victory. For eleven days the Mexicans could not get near the Alamo. Finally the Texans ran low on ammunition, and the Mexicans poured into the old mission. The men fought on until all 187 were killed. Not a man would give up. Even Davy Crockett died in the battle. The night before his death, Crockett made this last entry in his diary:

March 5. Pop, pop, pop! Bom, bom, bom!—throughout the day. No time for memorandums now. Go ahead! Liberty and independence forever!

Davy Crockett and the other men in the Alamo gave their lives for liberty and independence.

The cry "Remember the Alamo!" swept through Texas as men prepared to fight Santa Anna. Texans led by **General Sam Houston** took the Mexican army by surprise in the battle of **San Jacinto** [săn′ jə•sĭn′tō]. <u>Santa Anna himself was captured along with the Mexican army.</u> Texas now considered herself a free nation. Sam Houston was elected to be her president.

Texas remained independent until 1845, when she became the twenty-eighth state to join the Union (the United States).

Davy Crockett and many other brave Americans met their death at the Alamo.

The Rio Grande forms the border between Texas and Mexico.

War with Mexico

Mexico never recognized Texas as being independent. When Texas became a state, Mexico became bitter toward the United States.

Then there was an angry quarrel over the boundary line that separated Texas from Mexico. Texas claimed that the **Rio Grande** was her western boundary, while Mexico claimed another boundary that gave Texas less land.

President James K. Polk <u>sent an army to guard the Rio Grande boundary line</u> that Texas claimed was hers. Of course, the

Mexicans claimed this land was theirs and attacked the American army for being on their land. In the fight, some Americans were killed. The United States then declared war on Mexico.

The Mexican War began in 1846 and lasted for two years. The United States easily won. By the treaty of peace, the Rio Grande was accepted as the border between Texas and Mexico. Mexico gave the United States a large area of land that makes up the present states of California, Nevada, Utah, and parts of Arizona, New Mexico, Wyoming, and Colorado. The United States agreed to pay Mexico fifteen million dollars for this piece of land. It became known as the **Mexican Cession.**

The Gadsden Purchase

Only five years later, in 1853, the United States bought a strip of land from Mexico. This land, known as the **Gadsden Purchase,** made up the southern parts of what are now New Mexico and Arizona. One reason for making this purchase was to build a railroad through the Southwest.

The Great Rush to California

In 1848, gold was discovered in California on **John Sutter's** ranch. One day a hired worker saw what he thought might be flakes of gold. Gathering some, he took them to John Sutter.

John Sutter studied the flakes for a long time as his worker, James Marshall, watched. Finally, Sutter whispered, "You have found pure gold! But don't tell anyone, for if you do, my land will be destroyed as people search for gold."

The news did spread. "Gold has been found in California! Go to California and become rich."

Before long the whole United States had heard the exciting news. Many people from the North, South, and East left their jobs and homes to go to California. In those days, such a trip was long and dangerous, for there were mountains and deserts to cross and warlike Indians to deal with.

Gold! Gold! Gold was the only thing these people thought about! So great was their desire for gold that it became known as "gold fever"!

Although gold was discovered in 1848, it was 1849 before the great crowd of gold seekers began arriving in California. For this reason, the gold miners were often called **"forty-niners."** This movement was called the **Gold Rush.**

Most miners did not find enough gold to pay for all their troubles in reaching California. True to John Sutter's words, thousands of greedy, uninvited gold miners swarmed over his land. These men cared nothing about the crops that John Sutter had planted or the animals he was raising. Although gold was discovered on his land, John Sutter's farm was ruined.

A "forty-niner" searches for gold.

Life in a California Gold-mining Town

Towns grew rapidly as thousands of gold miners made their way into California. They found that life was not easy in a gold-mining town.

Storekeepers demanded that their goods be paid for in gold dust rather than money. Perhaps you have heard your parents talk about the high cost of food today, but can you imagine paying these prices? One egg cost as much as fifty cents to a dollar, and one pound of flour often cost more than a dollar's worth of gold! With prices like these, the storekeepers often became richer than those who found the gold.

Along with the honest gold miners came the dishonest who would steal or kill to gain more gold. Why didn't the law stop them? At the time, California was not a state. There was little or no law; the people had to protect themselves.

Lumber was so expensive that many men chose to live in tents rather than to build buildings. Some cities had many wooden buildings; others were made up almost entirely of tents. As long as gold was found, towns remained prosperous.

What happened to those towns whose miners could no longer find gold? Some became **ghost towns**—towns with empty buildings where no one lived. In other towns, some miners finally decided to settle down and build farms or businesses.

California Becomes a State

By 1850, only two years after gold was discovered, California's population had grown so much that the people who lived there asked if it could become a state. In that same year, California became the

Pioneers traveled west to settle the wilderness. This painting shows a group of pioneers traveling to the Oregon Territory.

thirty-first state to join the Union. Then our country stretched from "sea to shining sea."

Comprehension Check 12D

1. At what Spanish mission did the Americans in Texas fight against Santa Anna?

2. Whom did the Texans choose to be their leader?

3. What was the Mexican War fought over?

4. What river forms the boundary line between Mexico and Texas?

5. What purchase was made so that a railroad could be built in the Southwest?

The Oregon Territory

Meanwhile, Americans had become greatly interested in the land called the **Oregon Territory.** This land would include the present states of Oregon, Washington, and Idaho as well as part of Montana and Wyoming. At the time, the Oregon Territory was owned by both England and the United States. They both agreed to be joint owners of the land, which at the time even included part of Canada.

If you have ever traveled in these states, you know what beautiful country there is to see. You might then ask, why did it take so long for the Oregon Territory to be added to the United States? Perhaps it was because it involved a long, dangerous trip to get there. The Oregon Trail was almost 2,000 miles long, stretching over wild country and hazardous mountains. Before Oregon could be settled, someone had to see it to know how rich and beautiful it was. Then someone had to travel all the way back to the East to tell people how wonderful the Oregon Territory was so that pioneers would be persuaded to come.

Missionaries were among the first to travel to Oregon. They were interested in teaching the Indians. The most famous missionaries to Oregon were **Dr. Marcus Whitman** and his wife **Narcissa.** They worked hard to teach the Indians, and they worked hard to bring pioneers to Oregon. During one winter, Marcus Whitman traveled back east to tell people about Oregon. When he returned, he brought several pioneers with him.

Slowly, people back in the East heard about Oregon. To make this journey, Oregon-bound pioneers traveled to Independence, Missouri, where the Oregon Trail began. Here they waited until enough pioneer families came to form a wagon train.

All of the families had to work together to make the 2,000-mile journey a success. Each man would be needed to keep the wagons repaired and rolling on their way. Each man would be expected to defend the wagon train in an Indian attack. Many pioneers would die of sickness or be killed before they reached Oregon.

By 1845, thousands of pioneers had been successful in reaching Oregon. It became clear to both England and the United States that there would have to be a boundary line dividing Oregon into British-owned land and American-owned land. In 1846, an agreement was reached giving us the border between Canada and the United States that we have today.

In 1859, the state of Oregon joined the United States. The state of Oregon did not include all of the Oregon Territory. Later on, Washington and Idaho also became states.

New Schools and Schoolbooks

As America grew, schools began springing up everywhere. There were several reasons for the growth of our schools. First, Americans believed that each person should get a good education so he could think and work on his own. Those who had been converted during America's great revivals especially wanted to see schools built so that their children could learn to read the Bible. Second, you will remember that the Land Ordinance of 1785 provided land for public schools. Finally, many states began to pass laws requiring that schools be built in each city. Before long, children throughout the country were going to school.

Noah Webster was concerned because textbooks used in American schools still contained many British words and spellings. In the late 1700s, Webster decided to write textbooks himself that would be truly American. These books taught children to read, but they also taught children to do right, to be loyal Americans, and to love God and His Word. Webster's most famous book was *The American Spelling Book,* nicknamed the "Blue-backed Speller." Some sixty million copies of this book were sold during the fifty years that it was printed. Later he also wrote the first American dictionary.

Between 1836 and 1857, **William H. McGuffey** also <u>wrote a series of textbooks</u>. These McGuffey readers sold over 122 million copies. Some of the stories in these readers contained useful information about geography and science, some taught valuable lessons, and some were simply filled with good fun. But they all helped children learn.

Webster, McGuffey, and other textbook writers helped America become a great country because their books taught children to love freedom, to be good citizens, to fear God, and to serve Him by obeying His Word.

What Schools Were Like

Millions of American children in the 19th century went to one-room schoolhouses. Classes did not meet separately: all the boys sat together on one side of the classroom, all the girls on the other side. The teacher would call the students by groups to the front of the classroom to recite their lessons. First she might help the fourth graders with their history; then she might quiz

Although one-room schoolhouses were small and simple, children could receive a good education.

a sixth grader on his spelling words; then she might help the first graders with their phonics. The teacher always stayed busy teaching the students and making sure they behaved themselves.

The schoolhouse was small and simple, but the children took pride in it and kept it clean. Few maps or globes were available, and of course there were no computers, CD players, etc. But still the children learned! They learned because they had the right tools for learning—good textbooks and a teacher who loved them and wanted to help them learn.

★ ★ ★ ★ Chapter 12 Checkup ★ ★ ★ ★

Answer the questions on notebook paper.

1. What state did Daniel Boone open up to settlers?
2. Why did Daniel Boone clear the Wilderness Road?
3. What early settlement in Kentucky was named in honor of Daniel Boone?
4. What laws established the rules for settling the Northwest Territory?
5. How did pioneer families travel down the Ohio River?
6. Which purchase doubled the size of the United States?
7. Who was our third President?

8. What piece of land did he purchase for our country in 1803?

9. Who led the expedition to explore the Louisiana Territory?

10. What Indian woman translated the Indian language for the Lewis and Clark Expedition?

11. Why did America declare war on England in 1812?

12. During what war did the British burn Washington, D.C.?

13. What is our national anthem?

14. Who wrote our national anthem?

15. During what battle did he write "The Star-Spangled Banner"?

16. Which side won the War of 1812?

17. Which President purchased Florida from Spain?

18. Who was one of the most famous circuit-riding preachers during the Second Great Awakening?

19. What dictator tried to take away the liberties of Texans?

20. How many men were killed defending the Alamo?

21. Who led the Texans in the battle of San Jacinto?

22. At what battle was Santa Anna captured and defeated?

23. What did Texas claim to be her boundary with Mexico?

24. Who was President during the Mexican War?

25. How long did the Mexican War last?

26. Why was the Gadsden Purchase made?

27. On whose ranch was gold found in California in 1848?

28. Why were the men who went to California looking for gold called "forty-niners"?

29. Why did many people in gold-mining towns decide to live in tents?

30. What were deserted, empty towns in the West called?

31. From what territory were the states of Oregon, Washington, and Idaho formed?

32. What missionary couple helped Indians and pioneers in Oregon?

33. Who wrote the first schoolbooks especially for American schoolchildren? What was the name of his first schoolbook?

34. What man wrote a series of famous readers in the middle of the 19th century?

TIME LINE OF IMPORTANT DATES

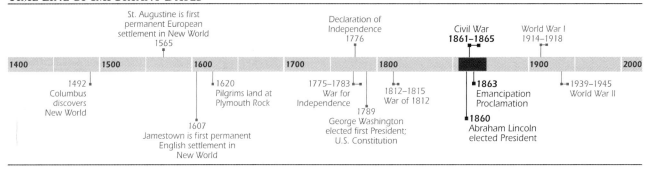

St. Augustine is first
permanent European
settlement in New World
1565

Declaration of
Independence
1776

Civil War
1861–1865

World War I
1914–1918

| 1400 | 1500 | 1600 | 1700 | 1800 | | 1900 | 2000 |

1492
Columbus
discovers
New World

1620
Pilgrims land at
Plymouth Rock

1775–1783
War for
Independence

1812–1815
War of 1812

1863
Emancipation
Proclamation

1939–1945
World War II

1607
Jamestown is first permanent
English settlement in
New World

1789
George Washington
elected first President;
U.S. Constitution

1860
Abraham Lincoln
elected President

The Civil War

Before the War

While our country was growing in size, its problems were also growing. For many years, the North and the South had misunderstood each other. This misunderstanding slowly turned into anger in the minds of some people. The states from the South began talking about withdrawing from the **Union,** the United States, and forming their own country. Those states from the North said that no state could leave the Union.

States quarreled with each other. Neighbors argued. Even many families were split with quarrels. These quarrels led to the **Civil War.** To better understand the problems that arose we will first study the differences in the way the people of the North and the South lived.

The North and Slavery

You will remember from our study of colonial life, that life in the North was very different from life in the South. Until the late 1700s, some slavery existed in all American colonies. Then slavery began to disappear from the North. Most Northern farms were small. The Northern farmer could not afford to buy many slaves.

Because Northerners could not depend on slaves to do their work, they knew they would have to work hard themselves. They knew they would have to think of other ways to get a great deal of work done. Factories began growing in importance in the North.

The South and Slavery

Many Southern farms were very large. These large plantations usually grew only one or two crops—cotton and tobacco.

When **Eli Whitney,** a young schoolteacher from Massachusetts, moved to Georgia, cotton was not a very important crop. Separating the seeds from the cotton fibers (lint) by hand took so long that the cost of preparing cotton was very high. In 1793, Whitney invented the **cotton gin,** a machine

Eli Whitney's cotton gin removed the seeds from the cotton plant much faster than workers could do it by hand.

that quickly removed the seeds from the cotton and greatly increased the speed of turning cotton into cloth. The cotton gin made cotton cloth cheaper to make, and cotton became a valuable crop in the South. Not only the Northern states but also England and France bought cotton from the South.

Tobacco had been an important crop since early in the colonial days of America, but smoking tobacco was becoming a more and more popular habit. The climate of the North is too cold to grow either cotton or tobacco. Because the world wanted these two crops, the Southern planters happily grew them.

As they sold more crops, Southern planters bought more land in order to plant more cotton and tobacco. Who could take care of such large fields? The Southern planter could never *hire* enough people to get his work done. Some people in the South believed that *buying* slaves was the answer. However, only one out of every ten Southerners owned slaves.

Southern weather was warm and the slaves stayed healthy. The South had no need for factories, because growing cotton and tobacco helped her to prosper. The North, which depended largely on its factories for a living, began to dislike slavery. If slaves ran away from their owners in the South, there were some Northerners who were willing to help them get to freedom.

"How can we call this a free country when we allow one man to own another?" the North asked the South. By this time, the South depended on its slaves. If Southerners freed their slaves, how would they be able to make a living? There was no easy answer to this question.

Troubled Times

As new states were added from the territories, a new argument arose. Should the states be admitted as **free states,** states not allowing people to own slaves, or should they be added as **slave states,** states that allowed people to own slaves?

New Words

1. **cotton gin**—machine that quickly removed seeds from cotton
2. **free states**—states that did not allow people to own slaves
3. **slave states**—states that allowed people to own slaves
4. **compromise**—a decision that tries to satisfy both sides of an argument
5. **blockade**—the Union's move to block all major seaports of the South in order to keep them from receiving valuable supplies
6. **ironclad**—ship covered with thick iron plates so that cannon balls or gun shells would bounce off
7. **emancipate**—to set free
8. **proclamation**—an important statement

New Names

9. **Union**—name used to refer to the United States during the Civil War
10. **Civil War**—war fought between the North and the South from 1861 to 1865; also called the War between the States
11. **Eli Whitney**—man who invented the cotton gin
12. **Missouri Compromise**—decision to allow Missouri to enter the Union as a slave state and Maine as a free state to preserve the balance of slave and free states represented in Congress
13. **Abraham Lincoln**—President during the Civil War
14. **Confederate States of America**—name that the Southern states gave themselves after they withdrew from the Union to form their own nation

$150 REWARD

RANAWAY from the subscriber, on the night of the 2d instant, a negro man, who calls himself *Henry May*, about 22 years old, 5 feet 6 or 8 inches high, ordinary color, rather chunky built, bushy head, and has it divided mostly on one side, and keeps it very nicely combed; has been raised in the house, and is a first rate dining-room servant, and was in a tavern in Louisville for 18 months. I expect he is now in Louisville trying to make his escape to a free state, (in all probability to Cincinnati, Ohio.) Perhaps he may try to get employment on a steamboat. He is a good cook, and is handy in any capacity as a house servant. Had on when he left, a dark cassinett coatee, and dark striped cassinett pantaloons, new—he had other clothing. I will give $50 reward if taken in Louisville; 100 dollars if taken one hundred miles from Louisville in this State, and 150 dollars if taken out of this State, and delivered to me, or secured in any jail so that I can get him again. WILLIAM BURKE.

Bardstown, Ky., September 3d, 1838.

Many slaves tried to reach freedom in the North by means of the Underground Railroad.

Why did this turn into an argument? Remember that each state has two representatives in the Senate. If there were more slave states, the Senate would be more careful to look out for the slave states. However, if the free states controlled the Senate, it would be more interested in the free states. To keep both the free and slave states happy, there had to be an equal number of free and slave states.

In 1819, both Maine and Missouri were asking to become states. Maine would enter as a free state. To keep the Senate equal, Missouri would have to be admitted as a slave state. The people who lived in Missouri, however, did not agree. Some wanted to own slaves while some were against it.

Finally, in 1821, Congress admitted Missouri as a slave state, but only after a compromise was made. A **compromise** is a decision that tries to satisfy both sides of an argument. Since Missouri was to become a slave state, no other states north of an established boundary line could enter the Union as slave states. This decision was called the **Missouri Compromise.**

Many Southern states felt that the right of each state to do as it wanted was more important than the country as a whole, and they began to talk about separation from the United States. They wanted to form their own nation.

15. **Jefferson Davis**—President of the Confederate States of America
16. *Merrimac*—first Confederate ironclad
17. *Monitor*—first Union ironclad
18. **Emancipation Proclamation**—announcement made by President Lincoln that freed the slaves
19. **General Ulysses S. Grant**—general in command of the Union army
20. **General Robert E. Lee**—general of the Confederate army
21. **General William T. Sherman**—Union general who captured Atlanta, Georgia, then marched through Georgia to the sea, burning and destroying everything on the way
22. **John Wilkes Booth**—man who shot and killed Abraham Lincoln
23. **Andrew Johnson**—man who became President after Lincoln's death

New Places

24. **Fort Sumter**—fort in Charleston, South Carolina, where the first battle of the Civil War was fought
25. **Gettysburg**—battle which was the turning point of the Civil War
26. **Vicksburg**—city captured by the Union army so the North could control the Mississippi River
27. **Richmond**—capital of the Confederate States
28. **Appomattox Court House, Virginia**—place where General Lee surrendered to General Grant at the end of the Civil War

New Dates

29. **1821**—Missouri Compromise
30. **1861–1865**—Civil War
31. **1863**—Emancipation Proclamation is issued
32. **1865**—President Lincoln is shot

"After the War for Independence, we agreed to join the United States. Now, we can see no reason why we cannot agree to leave the Union," said the South.

"No state can leave the Union!" replied the North.

Indeed, our nation was in the midst of troubled times. A very sad and horrible war was about to begin within our own country.

the same decision: Mississippi, Florida, Alabama, Georgia, Louisiana, and Texas. These states formed their own nation called the **Confederate States of America.** They elected **Jefferson Davis** as their president.

The people of the United States listened as Abraham Lincoln begged the North and the South not to become enemies—but they had already become enemies.

Abraham Lincoln

Abraham Lincoln Becomes President

A new President of the United States was to be elected in 1860. Throughout the North and West, a tall man from Illinois, **Abraham Lincoln,** had become popular. Above all, Lincoln wanted our country to remain one strong Union. He did not want to see our country divided.

Abraham Lincoln cared about the South's problems, but the people of the South said they would not trust him as their President because they knew he disliked slavery. "If Abraham Lincoln becomes President, the South will leave the Union."

Abraham Lincoln was elected our President. True to their words the South began to carry out their threat of leaving the Union.

The South Leaves the Union

South Carolina was the first state to leave the Union. Within a short time, six other Southern states made

Comprehension Check 13A

1. What was the United States often called during the Civil War period?
2. What was the first state to leave the Union?
3. What did the states that left the Union call themselves?
4. Who was elected president of the Confederacy?

Being a soldier was not pleasant: food, uniforms, and supplies were scarce; sickness and disease were common.

The Civil War

A Divided Country: Its Soldiers

The Union Troops. When Abraham Lincoln asked for soldiers, thousands volunteered. The Northern soldiers wore blue uniforms. Besides being called the Union troops, they were sometimes called the "Yankees," "the Yanks," or "the Billy Yanks."

The Confederate Troops. The South called for soldiers, and thousands of men volunteered to join the Confederate army. They wore a gray uniform. Their own Confederate flag waved in the breeze. The Southern Confederate soldiers were sometimes called "Rebels" or "Johnny Rebs."

The First Battle

The United States Army owned several forts located in the Confederate states. The Confederate government demanded that these forts and their guns be given to the Confederate states. Of course, the United States would not give up her forts.

Fort Sumter in Charleston, South Carolina, stands on a man-made island of rock in Charleston's harbor. The Confederates wanted to remove the Union soldiers from Fort Sumter. "Fort Sumter belongs to us," the Confederates claimed.

Early on an April morning, in 1861, Confederate troops aimed their guns at Fort Sumter. Although it was still dark, the people of Charleston came out of their houses to watch. At 4:30 in the morning, the Confederates fired the first shot. This shot began the Civil War.

The Union troops inside Fort Sumter had few supplies. They fought for two days, but at last they had to surrender the fort. The United States flag was taken down from the fort and the Confederate flag was raised in its place.

The Confederates cheered, for they had won the first battle of the war. Little did they realize what a long, horrible war lay before them. They thought the North would not want to keep fighting. They also thought that England and France would come to help them. But the Confederates were wrong.

The Union Must Be Saved

The battle at Fort Sumter saddened President Lincoln. He knew that the Union must be saved, even if it meant war. He

The first shot of the Civil War was fired at Fort Sumter, in South Carolina.

The battle between the North's *Monitor* (right) and the South's *Merrimac* (left) was probably the strangest-looking navy battle that ever took place.

asked for 75,000 Union men to volunteer as soldiers. Within days, thousands of men volunteered to join the Union army.

The Confederacy Grows

The Southern states of Virginia, North Carolina, Tennessee, and Arkansas had not joined the Confederacy. When President Lincoln's call for soldiers came, these states could not bear the thought of fighting against their own Southern neighbors. Instead, they left the Union and joined the Confederate states.

The Confederate government now represented eleven states; the Union government represented twenty-two.

A Blockade against the South

The North had many factories and many small farms that grew large supplies of food. The North could depend on these farms and factories for supplies during the war.

The South did not have many factories, and it had depended mainly on cotton and tobacco for making a living. Southerners could not eat tobacco, and they could not wear cotton unless it was turned into cloth by the factories of the North or of Europe. President Lincoln knew that the South now depended on trade with Europe for guns, ammunition, war supplies, and even some food. Without these things, the South did not have a chance of winning the war.

In order to stop the South's trade with Europe, President Lincoln sent Union ships to block all major seaports of the South. Such a plan is called a **blockade**. The blockade did hurt the South. A few ships managed to fool the North and slip through, but most Southern ships were stopped.

The **Merrimac** and the **Monitor**

The Southern navy had very few ships compared to the Northern navy. The South badly needed to break the blockade that was preventing her from getting important supplies. Since she did not have as many ships as the Union, she must come up with a wise plan and at least one powerful ship!

The Confederates raised the **Merrimac,** an old ship that the Union had sunk. As you can imagine, there was much work to be done before the *Merrimac* could sail.

How could an old, sunken ship be fixed to be better and stronger than the Union's ships?

The Confederates covered the *Merrimac* with thick iron plates. Now cannon balls and gun shells would simply bounce off. Then they fitted guns on each side. They also fitted a sharp piece of iron to the boat's bow so that the *Merrimac* could ram into the sides of the Union's ships.

At this time, all Union and Confederate ships were made of wood. An **ironclad** ship could easily destroy wooden ones without receiving any harm itself. The *Merrimac*'s first battle was a tremendous success. Within a short time, she destroyed two of the best ships in the Union navy.

However, the South did not know that the Union was also building its own ironclad ship, the ***Monitor.***

Soon afterward, the South's *Merrimac* met the North's *Monitor* in battle. What a strange-looking battle that must have been! People have described the *Merrimac* as looking like an upside-down bathtub, and the *Monitor* as looking like a cheese box on a raft. These two ships shot at each other and tried to ram each other, but neither could do any better than dent the sides of the other. <u>The battle was a draw—neither side won</u>.

Even so, the battle did have an important result. It proved the value of ironclad ships to the navy. Gradually, wooden ships became outdated. From then on, ships were built with iron and steel.

The Emancipation Proclamation

The question of what he should do with the slaves bothered President Lincoln. If he set them free, what would happen to them after the war was over? They had no homes to live in nor jobs to make a living from. Very few had any education. How could they get jobs in order to buy homes, food, and clothing? How could a nation, already weak from war, help them?

As the war dragged on, President Lincoln felt that he could weaken the South and shorten the war by setting the slaves free. <u>He made an announcement that on January 1, 1863, all slaves would be considered free in any states that were fighting against the North</u>. This announcement is known as the **Emancipation Proclamation.** To **emancipate** means <u>to set free</u>. A **proclamation** is <u>an important statement</u>.

Lincoln reads a copy of the Emancipation Proclamation to members of his Cabinet. Lincoln said about the Proclamation, "If my name ever goes into history, it will be for this act, and my whole soul is in it."

The Emancipation Proclamation did *not* do several things. It could not really free the slaves until the North won the war. Also, it did not free any slaves who were owned in states that were not fighting against the Union. After the war, an **amendment** or <u>change</u> would be added <u>to our Constitution</u> giving all slaves in the United States and her territories their freedom.

However, the Emancipation Proclamation did have one immediate result. For many people, it changed the reason for fighting the Civil War. Before the proclamation was read, the Union army was fighting to keep our country from dividing. Now the Union army was also fighting to free the slaves.

Before the Emancipation Proclamation, England had considered helping the South become a separate country. However, England was against slavery and had no wish to help the South continue slavery. So, the Emancipation Proclamation ended the South's chance of receiving English help.

A Divided Country: Its Military Leaders

Ulysses S. Grant, Union General. All through his life, **Ulysses S. Grant** was a very determined person. Once he made up his mind to do something, he tried his best to succeed. In 1864, President Lincoln made Grant the <u>commander of all Union armies</u>. His determination always to win did lead the Union to victory.

In victory, he proved to be a gentleman, being generous and forgiving to those he had defeated.

Robert E. Lee, Confederate General. The thought of war greatly troubled Rob-

Ulysses S. Grant   Robert E. Lee

ert E. Lee. He loved the United States and could not bear the thought of its dividing. He hated slavery and had even set his own slaves free.

Why then did he become the <u>general of the Confederate Army</u>? He loved his home state of Virginia. When Virginia left the Union, he felt it was his duty to follow his state, for he could not stand the thought of fighting against his own state. Lee was one of the greatest generals in the Civil War.

The Battles

During the Civil War, many different battles were fought. At first, the war did not go well for the North. During the first two years, the North lost more battles than it won. The fighting so far had only been in the South. The Confederates fought hard to keep the North from sweeping over the South.

Then the Confederates decided to fight in the North. General Robert E. Lee marched 70,000 men from Virginia to Pennsylvania. There, the South lost the three-day **Battle of Gettysburg.** <u>The Battle of Gettysburg was the turning point of the war.</u> General Lee sadly marched his men back to Virginia.

Abraham Lincoln delivering the Gettysburg Address.

The Gettysburg Address

The Battle of Gettysburg took a terrible toll on both the Northern and Southern armies. Thousands of men died in this one battle. After the battle, Gettysburg became a great cemetery. A special ceremony was held to honor the men who had been killed there. Many famous men were scheduled to speak, including President Lincoln.

The main speaker at Gettysburg on November 19, 1863, was a famous orator (speaker) named Edward Everett. He gave an address that lasted two hours. Then came the President's turn to speak. Instead of a long speech, Lincoln spoke for less than three minutes. He spoke ten simple, direct sentences, and then sat down. But those ten sentences—now known as the Gettysburg Address—make up one of the most famous and familiar speeches in American history. Edward Everett's long speech has been forgotten, but everyone is familiar with the Gettysburg Address.

In the speech, Lincoln quoted a historical document. He borrowed Thomas Jefferson's words in the Declaration of Independence when he said that "all men are created equal." To Abraham Lincoln, that was the most important part of the Declaration. He believed that the secret to America's greatness was the idea that all men are created equal in worth to God. He reminded everyone that America still believed that all men are created equal. Lincoln wanted to honor those men who had given their lives so that all men—blacks and whites, Northerners and Southerners—could be free. Lincoln's words challenged the people then, and still challenge us today, to be willing to die for our country. Our Constitution, which promises freedom and equality under the law to all Americans, must be preserved, no matter the cost.

General Lee would have been even sadder if he had known that on that same day, the fourth of July, 1863, General Grant had defeated Confederate troops and taken over Vicksburg, Mississippi.

Why was the **Battle of Vicksburg** so important? Vicksburg was an important city on the Mississippi River. The Mississippi River divided the Confederate states. By gaining control of Vicksburg, the Union army was also winning control of the Mississippi River. No longer could the Confederates on one side of the river send supplies to Confederates on the other side. The South was cut in two, yet she would not give up.

Comprehension Check 13B

1. Who was President of the United States during the Civil War?
2. At what fort did the Civil War begin?
3. What was Lincoln's announcement that freed the slaves called?
4. Who was the leader of the Confederate army? Of the Union army?
5. What battle was the turning point of the war?

Sherman's March to the Sea

Everyone was tired of fighting. General Grant made plans that he hoped would hasten the end of the war. He chose **General William T. Sherman** to carry out this plan. This time, Grant's plan included capturing Atlanta, Georgia, which was a very important city to the Confederates. From there, he wanted Sherman to march to Savannah, Georgia, on the Atlantic coast.

Sherman carried out his orders. Knowing that the only way to make the South surrender was to discourage the Confederates even further, he gave orders for his Union troops to burn or destroy everything they found, including homes, barns, animals, food, and crops. The South could not possibly keep fighting much longer after such destruction.

The Surrender at Appomattox Court House

Meanwhile, General Grant had been fighting General Lee to capture **Richmond, Virginia.** Richmond was the capital of the Confederate States just as Washington, D.C., is the capital of the United States.

After many months of hard fighting, the Union troops surrounded the Confederate army. The Confederates had been beaten in too many places. General Lee knew there was nothing else his troops could do. He told General Grant that he would surrender.

On April 9, 1865, Lee met Grant in a farmhouse in the town of **Appomattox Court House, Virginia.** Grant wrote very generous terms of surrender. Like President Lincoln, Grant was glad the fighting was coming to an end. He had no wish to hurt the South more.

In his terms of surrender, Grant wrote that there would be no prisoners of war. General Grant did not take away all the horses from the Confederate soldiers, for he realized that the Southern farmers would need these animals to help plant crops for a now starving South.

The officers of the Confederate army were allowed to keep their guns. General Lee was allowed to keep his sword.

When Lee read the terms of surrender that Grant had written, he said gratefully, "You have been very generous to the South."

After four years of courageous fighting, General Lee surrendered to General Grant at Appomattox Court House, Virginia.

Now that the Confederate army had surrendered, Grant ordered that food be taken to the starving Confederate soldiers.

Results of the War

Soldiers began returning to their homes. Peace had come after four years of bitter fighting. The fighting had not been in vain—the war settled two important problems:

1. no state could leave the Union, and
2. there would be no more slavery in the United States.

Comprehension Check 13C

1. What Union general led a destructive march to the sea?
2. What city served as the capital of the Confederacy?
3. What was the site of Lee's surrender to Grant?

Plans for Peace

Some people in the North felt bitter against the South. They said that the South should be punished because it had begun the war.

Great Plans for Peace

Just before the war had ended, President Lincoln was elected for the second time as President of the United States. He made it clear that he looked forward to the time when our nation would be whole again. He did not intend to hate or punish the South.

He spoke these words to our nation: "With malice [hate] toward none, with charity [love] for all." He then asked the people "to bind up the nation's wounds; to care for him who shall have borne the battle, and for his widow, and orphan—to do all which may achieve . . . a just and lasting peace."

Did you notice that in Lincoln's speech, he did not say, "only the North" or "only the South." Instead, he referred to "all." Yes, President Lincoln was making great plans to bring peace again to our whole country. Unfortunately, he never lived to carry out his plans.

Our Nation Mourns

The Civil War had been over for only five days. A very tired but happy President Lincoln took his wife to see a play at Ford's Theatre in Washington, D.C. While they were watching the play, a half-crazed actor named **John Wilkes Booth** slipped through the theater to where the President sat watching the play and shot Lincoln, probably because he blamed Lincoln for the Civil War.

Men carried the President to a house across the street from the theater, where he died the next morning. Our whole nation mourned the death of this great man. Even the South was beginning to realize the friend they had had in President Lincoln.

A Bitter Peace

Andrew Johnson became President in Lincoln's place. Although he wanted to carry out Abraham Lincoln's wishes, there were many men in Congress who felt nothing but bitterness toward the South. These men were able to make Congress strong enough to stop President Johnson's plans. As a result, for several years Congress passed laws that punished the South. In return, the South grew bitter.

Slowly, with the passing of time, the bitterness and hatred caused by the Civil War was forgotten. Once again, the men from the North and the South were willing to stand side by side to help their country.

Abraham Lincoln was killed by John Wilkes Booth at Ford's Theater.

Abraham Lincoln: the Man Who Saved the Union

Many people consider Abraham Lincoln to be the greatest President this country has ever had. He is truly one of the great men of all time. He is also a good example to show that America is a land of freedom and opportunity.

Abraham Lincoln was born in Kentucky in 1809, but his family soon moved to Indiana. There Abe grew to be a strong boy who helped his father farm. Because he was so busy farming, he had little chance to go to school. Abe did not want to be ignorant, so he read what few books he could get his hands on. He especially enjoyed reading the Bible, *Pilgrim's Progress,* and a biography of George Washington.

Abe grew very wise. Men would come from all around to swap stories with young Abe at the general store. When a war with the Indians started, the men chose Abraham Lincoln as their leader. He won their respect for his leadership in the war.

Once as a young man Lincoln traveled down the Mississippi River to New Orleans. He enjoyed himself there, but he saw something that deeply disturbed him. He saw men, women, and children being sold like animals at an auction. This was the first time he had seen what slavery was, and from that time on he wanted to do something for those poor people.

Mr. Lincoln decided to move to Illinois to seek a better life. That is one of the great things about America: if you are not satisfied with the job you are doing, you are free to move anywhere you want and try your hand at any job you choose. That is what Lincoln did in Illinois; after several years of study, he became a lawyer. Soon he had built up a successful practice. People liked Abe because he was honest and kind-hearted. He was called "Honest Abe."

Lincoln was bothered by the trouble in the country. He saw hatred and conflict over the slavery issue. He knew that sooner or later America would have to reach a decision: either America would accept slavery or America would reject it. He quoted a Bible verse to prove his point: "'A house divided against itself cannot stand.' I believe this government cannot endure permanently half slave and half free. I do not expect the Union to be dissolved—I do not expect the house to fall—but I do expect it will cease to be divided. It will become all one thing, or all the other."

Lincoln hoped that by becoming President he could keep the Union from falling apart. When the Southern states withdrew from the Union, it hurt him deeply. He saw that war was the only way to bring the country back together again. Before he died he did see his beloved country reunited.

Because America is a free country, Lincoln was able to overcome his poverty and become President. Being the son of a poor farmer did not stop him. Not being able to go to college did not stop him. This was America; he was free to work toward his goals. Because he was from the common people, he understood and loved the common people. The American people were saddened when he died; they have loved and honored him ever since because he fought to save the Union. He has also helped many young people reach for high goals in their lives. Because of the example of Abraham Lincoln, many young people would like to some day become President of the United States of America.

★ ★ ★ ★ Chapter 13 Checkup ★ ★ ★ ★

Answer the questions on notebook paper.

1. What was America often called during the Civil War period?
2. Why did slavery disappear in the North?
3. What were the South's two main crops?
4. Who invented the cotton gin?
5. Why was the cotton gin such a help to Southern farmers?
6. What two states were brought into the Union under the terms of the Missouri Compromise?
   Which was slave and which was free?
7. Who was elected President in 1860?
8. Why did the South dislike Lincoln?
9. Which state left the Union first?
   Name the other six states that left the Union.
   What name did the Southern states choose for their new nation?
10. Who was Jefferson Davis?

11. What were the Northern soldiers called?

12. What were the Southern soldiers called?

13. Where was the first battle of the Civil War fought?

14. How many states made up the Confederacy?

    How many states stayed with the Union?

15. What did the North set up against the South to weaken it?

16. What was the name of the first Southern ironclad ship?
    What was the name of the first Northern ironclad ship?
    Which ship won the battle when they fought each other?

17. What document issued by Lincoln freed the slaves?

18. What important effect did the Emancipation Proclamation have on the Civil War?

19. Who was General Ulysses S. Grant?

20. Who was General Robert E. Lee?

21. What was the turning point of the Civil War?

22. What battle put the Mississippi River under Northern control?

23. Which Union general marched his troops to the sea, destroying everything on the way?

24. What was the capital city of the Confederacy?

25. What was the site of Lee's surrender to Grant?

26. What two things did the Civil War make certain?

27. Who shot and killed President Lincoln?

28. Who became President after Lincoln's death?

New Frontiers

Rebuilding the South

After the Civil War, much of the South was desolate. Many farms had been ruined. Worst of all, millions of slaves had been freed but left with no jobs, no property, no homes, and no education.

Two black Americans spent their lives trying to improve conditions for the blacks in the South. The first was **Booker T. Washington.** Booker grew up with a deep love of learning. As a boy, he taught himself to read by using an old, battered copy of Webster's *Blue-backed Speller*. Booker was tremendously excited when he heard that a teacher was coming to his town. That first day at school was one of the greatest days of Booker's life.

Booker continued to learn. When he was fifteen, he left home to go to a school named Hampton Institute. It was there that Booker learned to love the Bible. He also learned many skills.

Booker T. Washington, the great educator who founded Tuskegee Institute

In 1881, a town named Tuskegee in Alabama asked Booker T. Washington to teach school there. Washington was thrilled—his own school building, his own books, his own students! But when Washington reached Tuskegee, he received a shock. There was no building. There were no books. And there were just a handful of students. So Washington went to work to build a school. He worked harder than he ever had before in his life, but he didn't mind, because he knew that his hard work was worthwhile. "Nothing ever comes to one, that is worth having, except as a result of hard work," he said.

The Tuskegee school started out in a leaky, ramshackle old building, but it grew rapidly. More and more black students came to be taught by Booker T. Washington. Washington wanted to teach his students that they should work hard to support themselves. He and his students worked to plant a garden at the school. They used the crops for food and sold whatever was left over to get money for books. When more buildings were needed, Booker taught the students to make bricks and build their own buildings. Extra bricks were sold to get money. The school, which came to be known as Tuskegee Institute, prospered and grew. It still provides excellent training for men and women.

Booker T. Washington's school, now called Tuskegee University.

In 1896 Booker T. Washington was looking for a good chemistry teacher for his school. He wrote a letter to a man who had just earned a degree from Iowa State College and invited him to come down to Tuskegee for a lifetime of "hard, hard work." The man's name was **George Washington Carver,** and he was not at all afraid of hard work. He had been born a slave, but after the war ended, his former master treated him as a son and let him read and study all he wanted. He was fascinated by nature, and he taught himself all about the plants of the forest. His knowledge of trees and plants amazed his teachers in college. He decided that he could put his knowledge to good use at Tuskegee, so he accepted Washington's invitation to teach there.

George Washington Carver amazed the world with his accomplishments. It seemed that he was <u>a genius who could do anything with plants</u>. He studied the chemistry of plants very thoroughly and knew what could be done with them. For example, <u>he found 118 uses for the sweet potato</u>. He made flour, starch, paste, vinegar, ink, rubber, chocolate, dyes—all from sweet potatoes! <u>From the peanut he made over 285 products</u>, including milk, butter, cheese, candy, coffee, shaving lotion, lard, soap, shampoo, and ink! One time Carver served a delicious meal to a group of visitors. After the meal, the guests complimented Carver on his cooking. Only then did Carver reveal that all the food in the meal had been made from peanuts!

We do not remember Carver simply because he stayed in his laboratory and discovered many uses for peanuts and sweet potatoes. He did far more valuable work when he helped poor farmers in the South become prosperous. For years, cotton was practically the only crop planted by Southern farmers. But cotton wears out the soil and makes the soil unable to grow crops. Carver found crops which helped the soil,

New Words

1. **soybeans**—one of the most profitable crops a farmer can grow
2. **reservations**—pieces of land set aside by the United States for the Indians
3. **transcontinental**—crossing the continent; from one coast to the other
4. **stampede**—a sudden rush of animals or people

New Names

5. **Booker T. Washington**—great educator who built Tuskegee Institute
6. **George Washington Carver**—scientist whose work with plants helped Southern farmers; taught at Tuskegee Institute for many years
7. **American cowboys**—men whom ranchers hired to take care of their cattle
8. **Cyrus McCormick**—inventor of the first successful mechanical reaper

George Washington Carver's knowledge of plants helped rebuild farms in the South.

and he traveled around the South convincing farmers to plant them. He encouraged farmers to plant peanuts, which nourished and enriched the soil instead of wearing it out. He urged farmers to grow **soybeans.** Today, <u>a crop of soybeans is one of the most profitable crops a farmer can grow</u>. Years and years of growing cotton had exhausted the soil and had made Southern farmers poor. George Washington Carver encouraged farmers to plant many different crops. He helped the South get on the road back to prosperity.

Comprehension Check 14A

1. Who founded and built Tuskegee Institute in Alabama?

2. What famous scientist found many uses for the peanut and the sweet potato?

3. Why did this famous scientist urge Southern farmers to plant crops other than cotton?

The Last Frontier

After the end of the Civil War, Americans once again began to feel the urge to move West. Many Northerners could not find jobs when they got back from the war. Many Southerners came home to find that their farms and cities had been destroyed in the fighting. These returning soldiers had heard stories of the West. Eager to forget the hardships of the war and make a new way of living for themselves, Northerners and Southerners alike began to look to the West, where there was still plenty of free land waiting for them. Thousands of pioneer families joined them. Before long, wagons were once again rumbling over the western trails, headed for the last frontier.

This was to be the last great westward movement. It was a period of cowboys and Indians and farmers, each trying to gain control of the West. It was a period of great danger and great excitement.

9. **Union Pacific Company** and **Central Pacific Company**—the two railroad companies that built the transcontinental railroad

10. **Homestead Act**—law that promised 160 acres of free land to settlers in the West who would cultivate or homestead the land for five years

11. **Oklahoma Land Rush**—time in 1889 when the government opened Oklahoma for settlement; settlers raced to find land they could call their own

New Places

12. **Promontory Point, Utah**—place where the Union Pacific Company and the Central Pacific Company met and completed the transcontinental railroad

New Dates

13. 1862—Homestead Act is passed

14. 1869—transcontinental railroad is completed

15. 1889—Oklahoma Land Rush

We have seen that the "West" kept moving over as settlers moved into a region. Many years had passed since Daniel Boone led many of the first pioneers into Kentucky. Since then, there had been a continual movement of pioneers traveling westward. Bit by bit, the frontier was shrinking. By the middle of the 1800s, California and Oregon had already begun settlement. The West had reached the Pacific Ocean! The Great Plains and the area around the Rocky Mountains remained the last frontier to settle.

When the West reached the Pacific Ocean, what was once called the West became known as the Midwest. From ocean to ocean, all regions were becoming settled, and modern America was taking shape.

The Indians of the West

At the time of the Civil War, many Native Americans lived in the Great Plains region. Huge buffalo herds roamed through this country. The buffalo was an important animal in an Indian's life. It provided the Indians with meat to eat. The buffalo hides (skins) were used to make clothing and tepees. Even the bones were used to make tools. No other animal could provide these Indians with food, shelter, and clothing.

After the Civil War, pioneers began to build settlements on the Great Plains. Little by little, the Native Americans watched land that they considered theirs being taken away. Many could not understand that their way of life would have to change as the United States grew. Soon the white men began to kill off the buffalo herds. Some men came from the East to hunt the buffalo for its hides that could be sold back East. Some men came just to shoot the buffalo for sport. Soon there were fewer and fewer buffalo.

The white men had broken many promises. Many Indians decided they must not be forced to move again. They determined to fight for what they believed was theirs.

Indian wars followed. There was cruelty on both sides in this sad part of our country's history. The Indians had many false religions that influenced their way of life and which made it hard for the Indians and the white men to get along. Yet few white men tried earnestly to teach the Native Americans about Christianity. Many on each side made little effort to understand the other. Each side fought for what they believed was theirs.

Finally, the United States government sent great numbers of soldiers to the West to fight the Indians. One by one, the Indian tribes were defeated and forced to move onto **reservations,** pieces of land that the United States has set aside for the Indians. Here they were promised protection.

In 1924, our government passed a law which made Native Americans citizens of the United States. Gradually, since that

The buffalo provided Indians with food, shelter, and clothing.

time, a greater understanding and friend-ship has developed between the white man and the Indian. Today, Indians are an important part of the American population.

A Gold Spike for a Railroad

In the early part of the 1800s, some people felt that California and Oregon were too far from the East to become states. However, the coming of the railroad changed people's minds. Little by little, railroads were im-proved. Men began to dream of a railroad that could connect the East with the West. Soon, plans were made to build <u>a railroad that would cross the continent from coast to coast</u>—our country's first **transcontinental** railroad.

Building a transcontinental railroad would be a long, difficult job. The track would not only have to be laid across prai-ries and plains, but also around and up and down mountains. Two railroad companies would work on this tremendous job: the **Union Pacific Company** and the **Central Pacific Company.** Work was begun in 1862, during the Civil War.

The Union Pacific began work in Omaha, Nebraska. A railroad had already been built this far from the East. The Union Pacific workers built their tracks westward from Omaha.

The Central Pacific began work in Sac-ramento, California, and built their tracks toward the East. Somewhere in the middle, these two railroad companies would meet and join to form our first transcontinental railroad.

Many years of hard work went into this job. There were no stores along the way to buy supplies and food for the twenty thousand workers. Trains would carry the needed supplies to the workers as far as the new tracks were finished. Buffalo were shot for fresh meat.

The workers did not have an easy job. Summer days were hot and the winter days cold. Indians often attacked the working men.

Day by day, the two sets of tracks came closer and closer to joining each other. The two railroad companies raced each other to see which company would finish the most miles of tracks. Finally on May 10, **1869,** a Union Pacific locomotive traveling west met a Central Pacific locomotive traveling east. The <u>place where the two railroads met</u> was **Promontory Point, Utah.**

Building the transcontinental railroad was not an easy job.

The transcontinental railroad was built across rugged mountains, through deep valleys, and over miles of endless plains.

Work on the transcontinental railroad continued during the cold winter months.

But the great railroad was not finished yet. The last long nail, or spike, needed to be driven into the rails at their meeting place. An ordinary spike could not be used for such a great event. Amidst the sound of cheers and the blows of sledge hammers, a gold spike was driven into the last rail.

This transcontinental railroad brought tremendous changes to our country:

1. It helped to settle the West.
2. The East was brought closer to the West.

Settlers began traveling West in trains rather than in the slow wagons. People from the East could visit people who had moved West. Farmers and businessmen from the West could send their products back East by train to sell them. In return they could buy supplies from the East.

Comprehension Check 14B

1. What animal provided the Indians with food, shelter, and clothing?

2. What is a reservation?

3. What is a transcontinental railroad?

4. When and where was the transcontinental railroad finished?

The American Cowboy

Even before the transcontinental railroad was built, the Great Plains was an ideal place to raise beef cattle. By the time of the Civil War, many ranchers from Texas were raising large herds of half-wild cattle called longhorns. Over the next few years, ranches spread to other parts of the Great Plains including Wyoming, Montana, Colorado, Nebraska, and Kansas.

In those days, there were no fences to control the cattle. They roamed where they pleased. Often, a herd was made up of a thousand or more cows.

American cowboys were hired by ranchers to look after their vast herds.

The rancher needed help in looking after a herd this size. The <u>men whom the rancher hired to take care of his cattle</u> were the **American cowboys.**

The cowboy practically lived with the cattle, making sure they had food, water, and protection. Since there were no fences to keep one rancher's cattle from mixing with the cattle from another ranch, the cattle were branded with a hot iron. <u>The brand burned a special mark onto the cow's or calf's hide</u>. Every ranch had its own special brand, different from any other ranch. During the spring, the cowboys would round up all the new calves for branding.

The Long Drive

After the Civil War, <u>beef was scarce in the East but plentiful in the West</u>. How could a rancher get his cattle over the great distance to the East? The coming of the transcontinental railroad provided the answer. But you must remember that there was not a railroad in every city or even every state. <u>Most ranchers had to move their herds over several hundred miles to the nearest railroad that would handle cattle</u>. Such a town with a railroad was called a cow town.

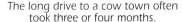

The long drive to a cow town often took three or four months.

Most ranchers had to move their herds hundreds of miles to the railroad.

The three or four months' journey to a cow town was called the long drive. Since the rancher had his ranch to look after, he usually hired many cowboys for the long, hard job. During the long drive, there were always dangers to look out for—Indian attacks, a wild animal, or a storm. Any one of these, or even a sudden noise, could cause a **stampede** <u>in which the cattle would wildly run</u>.

At night cowboys would take turns keeping watch over the herd. <u>To soothe the tired animals and prevent stampedes, cowboys often sang soft songs</u>, such as:

> Whoopee ti yi yo, git along, little dogies;
> It's your misfortune and none of my own.
> Whoopee ti yi yo, git along, little dogies;
> You know that Wyoming will be your new home.

Even though the cowboy was devoted to his work, you can be sure he was glad to reach the cow town. Here, the cattle were sold and placed on the train. Then the cowboy was paid for the work he had just accomplished.

The Cowboy and the Farmer Disagree

By this time, many families were moving West to buy land and build farms. The <u>cowboy was used to letting his herd roam the open range for grass to eat. As farms were built, the farmers planted fields of wheat and corn. You can imagine the trouble that arose when the cowboy's herd of cattle spied a young green cornfield or wheatfield. Of course, the cattle preferred young tender wheat and corn to the grass they could eat every day on the plains.

The angry farmer would not stand to see his crops trampled and ruined. When there were few farms, this was easy to correct. All the cowboys had to do was drive their herd where there were no farms. But as the West became more settled, this became impossible.

You must realize that the cowboy did not own the land over which he drove his cattle. Neither did he pay for using it. The United States government owned this land and had begun selling it to farmers. Since the farmers were now the owners of this land, they had a right to keep the roaming cattle from destroying their crops. The farmers began putting barbed-wire fences around their farms.

For a time, the farmer and the cowboy fought. Slowly, the cowboy realized that if he was going to succeed in raising cattle, he must buy his own farm and fence in large pastures for his cattle to graze or feed on the grass.

The Homestead Act

In 1862, our government passed the **Homestead Act.** This was a law that said that any family that settled in certain areas of the West could receive 160 acres of land. To keep this land for his own, the head of the family had to live on that land and farm it for five years.

This sounds like a good offer, but there were several problems with it. At the time the law was passed, the Civil War was going on. Families were concerned with the problems of the war. There were also still problems with the Indians in the West. Many men did not want to risk the lives of their families for a free farm. There was also another problem. Many people wondered how they could farm in the West because of the hot, dry summers of the Great Plains. What crops could survive this weather?

A homesteader's house was often built of bricks cut from the tough, sunbaked prairie sod.

Thousands of people joined the Oklahoma Land Rush the instant the borders of Oklahoma were opened.

But when the Civil War was over, many people were willing to try. By this time, the Indians were being placed on reservations. New methods of farming with less water made it possible to grow some crops. And many soldiers returned home from the war, restless and eager for a change.

As the years passed, there was less and less land for the government to give away in the West, for more and more people were settling there as a result of the Homestead Act. As the government made land available for settlement, there would be a great land rush. People would line up in wagons and on horses, waiting to claim their 160 acres that the government would give them.

The Oklahoma Land Rush

Originally, the government had given the territory known as Oklahoma to the Indians. But once again the Indians were moved and a date was set aside for the settlers to claim land in Oklahoma. The year was 1889.

The day came for the great **Oklahoma Land Rush.** Many thousands of people were lined up along the borders of Oklahoma. Some were in carriages, some in wagons, and some in trains. Some were on horseback, and some were on foot.

Soldiers guarded the borders. No one could move over the border until a signal was given. At last at noon, the signal was given. The eager settlers began the scramble to find some land that they could call their own. You can see why this was called a "land rush." Before the day was over, most of the land in the Oklahoma Territory was claimed.

In 1890, it was announced that there was no more frontier land left in the United States. There were still large, unsettled areas, and there were still some homesteads to be given away, but there was no longer a clear line drawn between an unsettled area and a settled area.

Cyrus McCormick

Thousands of people moved to the West to homestead. Most farmers planted wheat. The plains filled up with wheat so fast that it was hard to find workers to harvest it all.

Once again an ingenious American came up with the solution to a knotty problem. **Cyrus McCormick** was a Virginian who liked to tinker around with mechanical devices. One of his projects was a mechanical reaper that his father had tried unsuccessfully to build. Cyrus studied his father's designs and made improvements on them. In 1831, Cyrus invited his neighbors to watch the first demonstration of his mechanical reaper. He hitched horses to the reaper, climbed aboard, and headed into a wheatfield. The reaper cut down the wheat neatly and evenly. It would have taken several men hours and hours to cut down the

wheat in that field; Cyrus McCormick did it by himself in a brief time.

McCormick set up a factory for producing reapers in Chicago, near the plains. Farmers everywhere ordered McCormick reapers. Cyrus McCormick became a wealthy man, and his ingenuity helped make farming easier and more efficient.

★ ★ ★ ★ Chapter 14 Checkup ★ ★ ★ ★

Answer the questions on notebook paper.

1. What school did Booker T. Washington establish in Alabama?
2. What is George Washington Carver known for?
3. Which of the crops that Carver urged farmers to plant has become very profitable?
4. By the middle of the 1800s, what was the last frontier that remained to be settled?
5. What did the buffalo provide for the Indians?

6. Why were the buffalo disappearing?

7. Where were the Indians put when white men began to settle the Great Plains?

8. Which two railroad companies built the transcontinental railroad?

9. When and where was the transcontinental railroad finished?

10. What two changes were brought about by the transcontinental railroad?

11. What was the cowboy's main job?

12. Why were cattle branded?

13. What was the purpose of the long drive?

14. Why did the cowboys sing to their cattle?

15. What was the disagreement between cowboys and farmers?

16. What law promised 160 acres of land to anyone who would farm the land for five years?

17. What territory was opened to settlers in 1889?

18. Who invented the first successful mechanical reaper?

While his brother watches, Orville Wright makes
the first successful flight in an airplane.

Wilbur Wright sitting
at the controls

An Age of Progress

A Growing Nation

During the 19th century, our country saw great progress in many areas, including the rapid growth of our population.

In 1800 there were over four million Americans; in 1870, there were thirty-eight million; by 1916, there were almost one-hundred million Americans. Our country's population had multiplied at an amazing rate! Where did all these new Americans come from? Some of them were born here, but many of them were immigrants.

An **immigrant** is <u>a person who leaves his own country to make his home in another country</u>. The United States is truly a country made up of immigrants. From the days of early colonization, people had come to America from Europe for freedom of religion, freedom to work and own land, and freedom from oppressive governments.

As the years passed, the reasons for immigrants coming to America grew. Immigrants came <u>for the freedoms that America had to offer</u>—the freedom of speech, press, and religion—and <u>because America was a land of opportunity</u>. Some came from poor families where they faced starvation. Many came because they could not own their own homes, businesses, or farms in their

The oil industry played an important part in the Age of Progress.

Millions of immigrants came to America to find freedom and a better life.

One of the reasons God has blessed America is that the people of our land have done much to reach other people around the world through missionary activity. Changes took place in other lands as missionaries began to go out from America in large numbers during this period.

Adoniram Judson (1788–1850), the <u>Father of American Missions</u>, was one of the very first people to leave America and go to another country as a missionary. He spent many years preaching to the people of Burma. Other men and women followed in his footsteps and sought to take the gospel "to the uttermost part of the earth."

The 19th century was a time when people took Christianity seriously. They responded in large numbers to the preaching of evangelists. Many of those who responded desired to obey the Bible and to let the Bible change their lives and their society. So great were the advances made by Christianity during this time that one history writer called the 19th century "the greatest century that Christianity had thus far known."

★ People Worth Knowing More About ★

George Liele: Missionary Pioneer

<u>America's first missionary to a foreign land</u> was George Liele (17?–1828), a freed slave. In 1779, George Liele left America to preach the gospel to the black people of Jamaica.

George was born in Virginia and taken to Savannah, Georgia, by his master, Henry Sharp. When the people in the Baptist church where Sharp served as a deacon realized how much Liele loved the Lord and witnessed his wonderful ability to explain the Scriptures, they ordained him to preach. He was probably <u>the first ordained black preacher in America</u>. Liele's master freed him from slavery so he could spend all of his time preaching the gospel. The former slave preached in Georgia throughout the War for Independence. In 1779 he and his follower Andrew Bryan founded what may have been <u>America's first black Baptist church</u>, in Savannah. That same year, Liele went to Jamaica, hiring himself as an indentured servant to pay his way. He preached in the streets of Kingston, Jamaica, and eventually started Jamaica's first Baptist church, which grew from four members to 500 members in eight years. Liele organized a missionary society in Jamaica that sent fifty Jamaican missionaries to Africa and about twenty Jamaicans to the United States to minister to African Americans.

George Liele went to Jamaica fourteen years before William Carey, the Father of Modern Missions, went from England to India, and thirty-three years before Adoniram Judson, the Father of American Missions, went from the United States to Burma.

Comprehension Check 15A

1. Which brilliant lawyer became one of America's greatest revival preachers?

2. Who was the most famous evangelist at the end of the 1800s in America?

3. What famous evangelist of the early 1900s was once a baseball star?

4. Who was the Father of American Missions?

Steel and Oil: Ingredients for Success

The 19th century was a time of great prosperity and growth in industry. **Industry** is the manufacturing business, the kind of work that uses factories to make things. Two main products allowed American industry to grow rapidly: steel and oil. The leaders of these two industries became giants in American history. Their names were Andrew Carnegie and John D. Rockefeller.

Andrew Carnegie
Sees the Future of Steel

For many years iron had been the chief metal used by industry. However, there were problems with iron: it was heavy, it was expensive, and it was brittle (or easily breakable). Around 1856, an Englishman named **Sir Henry Bessemer** developed a method of turning iron ore into steel, a metal that is just as strong as iron but is much lighter and more flexible. The man who brought the steel industry to America was **Andrew Carnegie.**

Andrew Carnegie was an immigrant. In 1848, when he was a boy of thirteen, his family came to America from Scotland to find a better life. Andrew's father got a job in a mill factory and soon secured a position for his son as well. At first, Andrew was paid $1.20 a week. Since Andrew was

Andrew Carnegie made millions of dollars in the steel industry.

an able and willing worker, he soon moved on to better jobs. He became a messenger boy, then a telegraph operator, then a railroad clerk, and finally a railroad supervisor. As he earned more money, he used it wisely. He got involved in iron factories and prospered. However, when he saw Bessemer make steel from iron, Carnegie became a steel man at heart. He converted all his factories to steel production. People thought he was being foolish, but he disagreed. "The age of iron is over; the age of steel is here," he said. "All the railroads will want steel rails because their old iron rails break too easily. Bridges will be built of steel, and ships and tall buildings and many other things that we don't even know about yet. The future is in steel."

Carnegie was right. The steel industry became a huge success, and Carnegie's steel company was the most successful of all. After many years, Carnegie was very wealthy. He felt that the best thing to do with money is to give it away for worthy causes. "The man who dies rich dies disgraced," said Carnegie, who spent the last years of his life giving away his fortune. He loved good church music, and he donated over 7,000 pipe organs to churches. He paid for schools and colleges. As a boy, he had loved to read, and he wanted all boys and girls to have books to read. So he began building libraries in towns throughout America. Eventually Carnegie paid for the construction of over 3,000 public libraries. By the time of his death in 1919, Carnegie—who had once earned $1.20 a week—had given away over $350,000,000.

John D. Rockefeller Organizes the Oil Industry

Early farmers and settlers in Pennsylvania were often bothered by a sticky black liquid that muddied their streams. Then they heard from the Indians that the gooey substance had magical powers, so they bottled up the black liquid and sold it as medicine. The substance was oil. Soon people discovered that oil made a good fuel, and people flocked to Pennsylvania to pump oil out of the ground. Dozens and dozens of small petroleum companies were established.

John D. Rockefeller (1839–1937) decided that the oil industry could become successful only if someone organized it. He began to unite small companies into one big company. The results were lower prices for oil and better service to the consumer. Rockefeller called his company Standard Oil. He became the first billionaire in history, and was for many years the richest man in the whole world.

John D. Rockefeller, leader of the oil industry, was for many years the richest man in the world.

Rockefeller lived to be ninety-eight years old, and he gave away over $530,000,000 during his lifetime. He created the Rockefeller Foundation, an organization that handled the huge task of giving away all that money.

Both Andrew Carnegie and John D. Rockefeller were born poor. But because America is a land of freedom, both were free to work hard and to be rewarded for their work. As a result of their labor, both became wealthy. Through their efforts, American industry grew and prospered. And through their generosity the lives of millions have been improved in many different ways.

Comprehension Check 15B

1. Who developed a method for making steel from iron?
2. Who built the steel industry in America?
3. Who organized the oil industry and made it prosper?
4. Which man was the first billionaire in history and was for many years the richest man in the whole world?

Inventions: New Ways to Do Things

God has given each of us minds through which we are able to think of better or faster ways of getting jobs done. Since the creation of man, there have been inventions.

However, a good invention is never really finished. Someone else is bound to improve upon a good idea. For example, look at pictures of the first cars and planes. Can you imagine

Robert Fulton's *Clermont* was the first successful steamboat.

yourself still riding around in those early models instead of the modern ones? Aren't you glad that other inventors have continued to make improvements upon them? People will continue to invent new ways to improve the car and plane as well as every other important invention. This is called progress—moving forward to improve our way of life.

The First Successful Steamboat

For many years, the steam engine had been used to run machines in factories. The steam engine, run by burning wood and coal, interested several Americans who wondered if steam could also be used to make boats move.

Several men attempted to build a steamboat but were unsuccessful. Although most people laughed at the idea, **Robert Fulton** felt sure he could succeed. He was not successful at first, but he was willing to be patient and try again.

In 1807, just thirty-one years after America became a nation, Fulton's steamboat was completed in a New York shipyard. He named his boat the *Clermont.* Would the *Clermont* work? The only way to find out was to give it a trial run.

When the day arrived, crowds of people gathered on the river banks to watch. Many laughed and made fun of the *Clermont* before they even had a chance to see if it worked. Some people became frightened as smoke and sparks began to pour from the *Clermont*'s smokestack. Nearly everyone was surprised when the *Clermont*'s paddle wheels began turning and the *Clermont* began splashing its way up the river.

Before the steamboat, man had only sailboats and boats rowed by men to carry them up and down the river. Sailboats had depended upon the wind. It could take a sailboat several days to make the same trip that a steamboat could make in a day. Few people laughed at the steamboat now.

Men began working to improve the steamboat. Within a few years, steamboats replaced sailboats in carrying manufactured goods and passengers up and down large rivers. Soon, steamboats were even traveling across the oceans.

The Telegraph: Messages Sent by Electricity

People were now living all over the United States. How they wished they had

Being a pony express rider was a dangerous job. The mail for the pony express was carried in the leather pouches on the sides of the saddle.

Steamboats and railroads speeded up communication somewhat, but there were some men who felt there had to be a faster way. One of these was a Christian man named **Samuel Morse.** He believed that messages could be sent over long distances through a wire by electricity.

In the 1840s, electricity was still new and exciting. Samuel Morse set about drawing plans for his invention. Then he began building what was called the **telegraph.** The biggest problem that he ran into was lack of money. An invention may make a person wealthy, but the invention has to be built and proved before someone will become interested in buying it.

Samuel Morse needed money to finish his experiments. Most of all, he needed money to spread telegraph lines over long distances to prove that his experiment

a faster way of communicating with their loved ones who had moved or whom they had left behind! People tried many different ways of making communication faster. One of these was called the **pony express.** The pony express was <u>a mail route from St. Joseph, Missouri, to Sacramento, California</u>, that opened in 1860 and lasted only nineteen months. Boys or young men who were small and light and who were not afraid of riding through Indian country alone carried the mail. The mail carrier would ride a pony as fast as he could for a ten or fifteen-mile stretch. Then he would stop at a relay station to switch to a fresh pony and be on his way again in less than two minutes. The rider would cover from 75 to 100 miles in a day. A letter sent by pony express could travel from coast to coast in ten days. But the pony express was expensive (at first it cost $5.00 to send a letter) and very dangerous. Men continued to look for a faster means of communication.

Samuel F. B. Morse, inventor of the telegraph

worked. Morse was a poor man with a family to support. He often went without food himself so that he could work a little longer on his experiments.

Morse knew that his invention would greatly benefit our country. If he had the money to prove it would work, important messages could be sent from city to city in a matter of seconds instead of days. Knowing this, he decided to ask the United States Congress for money to prove his experiment.

At first, Congress voted no. Several years passed. Morse became discouraged, but he would not give up. Again, he asked Congress for the money, and this time, Congress voted yes. Thirty thousand dollars was given to build a telegraph line from Washington, D.C., to Baltimore, Maryland. The distance between the two cities is about forty miles.

Morse knew he could not send words over his telegraph wire. Instead, he figured out <u>a code of short and long dots and dashes to be clicked over the telegraph wire</u>. By this system of dots and dashes, known as the **Morse code,** the letters of the alphabet and numbers can be tapped over the telegraph wires.

In May of 1844, the telegraph was ready to test. Morse was at a telegraph set in Washington, D.C., while another man was at a telegraph set in Baltimore. A message was written down to send over the telegraph. This was the message: "What hath God wrought!" Morse tapped out this message on his telegraph set. Within seconds, the man waiting in Baltimore heard the message on his telegraph set. He then sent back to Morse the message he had just heard.

Samuel Morse's telegraph was a great success. Telegraph wires were run from city to city and state to state until finally, in 1861, a telegraph wire stretched from the East Coast to the West Coast of the United States.

When the transcontinental railroad was completed, it was the telegraph that sent the message of the railroad's success to cities across the United States. Now, thanks to the telegraph, newspapers in cities that were hundreds and even thousands of miles apart could print the nation's news the same day that it happened. People who were moving to the West no longer felt out of touch with those in the East. The telegraph had brought the East and the West together.

Talking over a Wire: the Telephone

Alexander Graham Bell sailed to America from Scotland when he was a young man. He loved America and the opportunities he had as an American. Bell was <u>a teacher of students who were deaf and mute</u>. This means that they could neither hear nor speak. Usually, these students could not talk because they had never heard words or sounds.

Bell was a very good and patient teacher who did his best to teach the deaf how to talk. He once made the comment, "If I can make a deaf-mute talk, I can make iron talk." The idea and plans for a telephone were already developing in his mind.

As we have found out from other inventors, inventing something worthwhile can be costly. Bell was not a wealthy man, but fortunately, he was offered help. The fathers of two of his students offered him money to help in his work.

Now Bell was able to hire a helper, **Thomas A. Watson,** to assist him with his work on the telephone. Watson became Bell's close friend as well as a hard worker.

In March 1876, Bell was in his attic workshop. Watson was in a distant room that was connected to Bell's only by a wire. Suddenly Bell said, "Mr. Watson, come here; I want you!" Excitedly, Mr. Watson came running. The telephone worked! He had heard Bell's voice over the telephone!

Americans were slow to realize the importance of Alexander Graham Bell's invention. They thought of the telephone more as a toy than as an important invention that could change their way of living.

In 1876, a world's fair was held in Philadelphia, Pennsylvania, to celebrate our country's one hundredth birthday. Our country had changed greatly since the Declaration of Independence had been written. Because new inventions had an important place in that change, many new inventions were shown at the world's fair. One of those inventions was the telephone.

Important men came from many different countries to judge the inventions. The American judges wanted to pass by Bell's invention, but the emperor of Brazil was too interested to pass by. He picked up the receiver and Bell talked to him from the other end.

"It talks!" said the excited emperor.

"This is the most wonderful thing in America!" said an interested English scientist.

Americans finally began to see the telephone's usefulness. One year later, the Bell Telephone Company came into being.

In 1915, another important telephone conversation took place between Bell and his friend, Watson. Again Bell said, "Mr. Watson, come here; I want you!" But Bell was joking this time. You see, Alexander Graham Bell was speaking in New York. Mr. Watson was in San Francisco, California! It was the first coast-to-coast telephone conversation.

What do you think Alexander Graham Bell wanted to be remembered for the most? If you said "the telephone," you are wrong. He wanted to be remembered first of all as a teacher of the deaf, for he greatly loved his students and did all that was within his power to help them.

Alexander Graham Bell is shown here speaking into his most famous invention, the telephone.

Comprehension Check 15C

1. Who developed the first successful steamboat?
2. What mail service was introduced in 1860 to speed up the mail?
3. What man invented the telegraph?
4. What is the system of dots and dashes called that is used to send messages over the telegraph?
5. Before he invented the telephone, what did Alexander Graham Bell do?

A Man of Many Inventions: Thomas Edison

An American whose daily life is not affected by the work of **Thomas Alva Edison** is a rare person indeed. How many times have you used electric lights today? Has your teacher ever used a science movie to help your class learn science? If your dad or mom works in an office, they may use machines that have been developed from Edison's ideas.

Edison was so interested in inventing that he built a large invention factory at **Menlo Park, New Jersey.** Here, Edison worked both day and night, stopping only for naps.

The electric light, motion pictures, the phonograph, and office machinery are a few of Thomas Edison's inventions. He designed over a thousand in all. There is only space here to tell you about two. To learn more, you might read a biography of Thomas Edison's life.

The most fascinating invention to Edison was the phonograph.

The first phonograph recorded a person's voice. The person spoke into a mouthpiece and at the same time, turned a handle. The person's voice was recorded. Adjustments were then made, and the handle was turned again. This time, as the handle was turned, the recorded sound could be heard. The machine talked!

At first, even Edison's workers did not believe that such a strange-looking machine could talk. As his workers watched, Edison thought of what he would say. Then he put his mouth down to the mouthpiece and began turning the handle. "Mary had a little lamb; its fleece was white as snow . . . ," he said and finished the nursery rhyme. His workers waited as he adjusted the machine. Then he began turning the handle again.

In Edison's voice, the machine repeated, "Mary had a little lamb. . . ." The workers were amazed! Then laughter and cheers filled the room. Edison himself was very

Thomas Edison invented the phonograph in 1877.

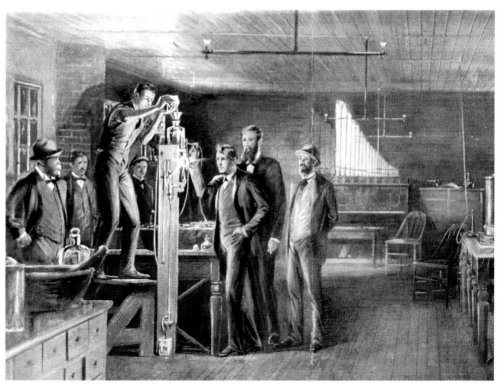

Thomas Edison was a tireless worker. He would perform hundreds of experiments until he had found the solution to his problem.

pleased. This invention would make him famous.

As in all of Edison's inventions, he was never through with his phonograph. He worked day and night to make an even better one. Imagine Edison's delight when the President of the United States asked him to come to the White House to demonstrate the phonograph.

After Edison finished his work on the phonograph, he worked on the electric light bulb. The idea of an electric light bulb was not a new one. Several different men besides Edison had been trying to invent one. Edison himself had the same problem they had. Many men had invented unsuccessful bulbs that would burn out in only a minute or two.

After two years of experimenting, Edison invented a successful bulb. When he turned the light on, he watched excitedly as it kept burning hour after hour. That first successful light bulb burned for forty hours. Then Edison and his workers kept working to make light bulbs that would burn even longer.

Edison's success with the light bulb gradually changed America's way of life. People had parades as electric lights lit up their streets. Soon stores and other buildings in big cities wanted electric lights too. Gradually, electric lights spread to homes throughout America.

To the end of his life, Edison worked on improving both his and other people's inventions. For example, he worked to improve the telephone. His ideas inspired other men to invent. As a result, today we can enjoy a better life because someone would not give up.

Edison was never content to put one of his successful inventions aside. He always worked to improve his inventions. Many people called him a "genius." To that remark, Edison replied, "Genius is one percent inspiration and ninety-nine percent perspiration." He meant that having a good idea was only a small part of being successful. Hard work is the largest part.

Perhaps you have a hobby at home or a subject in school in which you do very well.

Do not be content with your work because it is already good. Work hard to make it even better.

Did Thomas Edison's experiments ever fail to work the way he had planned? Yes! But no matter how many times "failures" slowed his experiments down, Edison never gave up. Once he was working on a special battery. Each one of the 8,000 tests he made on this battery failed.

"Aren't you discouraged?" asked his friends, as they wondered why he wouldn't give up.

"Discouraged?" he asked. "Why I've made progress! I have found out 8,000 things that won't work!" With that, he went back to work.

Each one of us has tried something that didn't work out just the way we planned. That doesn't mean that we should give up! We should work to make our "failures" into stepping stones on the road to success.

The First Cars

Today nearly every American family owns a car, but this was not always true. When the first "horseless carriage," or car, was invented, it was so expensive that only the very wealthy could afford to buy one. At that time, each car was made completely by hand. You can imagine how long it took to build one car.

Fortunately, a man named **Henry Ford** was interested in building cars. Henry Ford did not invent the car. While he was only a boy, a few people already owned cars.

Henry Ford with his first automobile (right) and his son Edsel with a Model T

Ford's dream was to make an inexpensive car that nearly every American family would be able to afford.

The first cars were costly and not very dependable. They were run by steam engines or electricity. Sometimes they would go and sometimes they would not go. A little later, the gasoline engine was invented. "Why could the gasoline engine not run a car?" Henry Ford asked himself. To answer this, he first had to learn how to build a gasoline engine.

After he built the gasoline engine, he had to build the body of a car in which to put his engine. The body of the car had four bicycle wheels for tires and was shaped like a box. Instead of a steering wheel, there was a stick. Finally the car was finished except for trying it out. Ford's first car with a gasoline engine ran successfully. Like the rest, however, it was completely made by hand and would still be expensive to buy. The year was 1896.

Henry Ford knew that his work was not finished. He built other cars, making improvements on each one. In 1903, the Ford Motor Company began, yet it was still only the wealthy that could afford to buy cars. Ford was determined to find a way of building a car for a low price. Finally, he found a way.

Ford built the Model T by developing a method that we call the **assembly line.** On an assembly line, each worker has his own special job to do. The worker becomes very skilled in this job and can work quickly. To make his work even faster, the car comes to the worker on a moving belt. The belt moves at just the right speed to allow the worker to finish his job. Then the belt moves the unfinished car on to the next worker who has another job to do. This keeps on until the car is completed at the end of the assembly line.

By hand, it had taken many days to assemble one car. With the assembly line, one car could be completely assembled in an hour! Because it took less time to build cars, cars could be made at a much cheaper price—a price most American families could afford.

The Model T was a very good car and sold for a reasonable price. By 1914, there were more than a million Model T Fords on the roads, and the number kept growing and growing.

Ford's dream did come true. He may not have been the inventor of the car itself, but he was the first to use the idea of the assembly line to build cars. By using the

This is part of Ford's Model T assembly line. Here, the Model T's are nearing completion. Using this efficient method, Ford produced 15 million Model T's.

assembly line, Henry Ford made his own reasonably priced car that most Americans could afford to buy.

Soon other factories were using Ford's idea to create other kinds of goods faster and cheaper. Because this good idea was put to work, Americans began enjoying a better and more modern way of life.

Comprehension Check 15D

1. What are among Edison's most famous inventions?

2. Where was Edison's laboratory?

3. Why is Henry Ford so important in automotive history?

4. What was the name of Ford's most popular car?

The Wright Brothers

Pop! Whirr—. Off flew the toy "helicopter" as its two young owners watched in delight. The year was 1878.

"What?" you ask. "Helicopters were not invented until the 1900s. How could children be playing with toy helicopters in 1878?"

These toys did not look much like the helicopters we see today. They were made from a piece of bamboo, cork, and paper. They were propelled by rubber bands. After the rubber band was twisted tightly and let go, the "helicopter" flew straight up.

The two boys were brothers, named **Wilbur and Orville Wright.** At the time, Wilbur was eleven years old and Orville was seven.

"Let's do it again," cried Orville.

Repeatedly they sent their prized "helicopter" into the air until it broke, but they were only saddened for a moment.

"Let's make another one!" Wilbur suggested.

"A bigger and better one!" nodded Orville.

They experimented by making several of their own helicopters, but they found out that the bigger they made their helicopters, the less they would fly. The two disappointed brothers wondered why.

Some men who were interested in flying were also asking themselves a question. Would it ever be possible for a man to fly? Men had flown in balloons, but a balloon is not the same as a flying machine. Some men had tried to fly by strapping wings to their arms. Some had built strange-looking machines. But all had failed.

After the Wright brothers grew up, they became the owners of a bicycle shop, but they were still interested in flying. Their bicycle shop soon became a place for experimenting and finding the answers to their questions.

Several men had experimented with gliders, airplanes with no engine. The Wright brothers decided to build their own. This took several years of work. When they

The Wright brothers—Orville (left) and Wilbur (right)—built and flew the first successful airplane.

were finished, with the advice of the United States Weather Bureau, they decided to test their glider at **Kitty Hawk, North Carolina.** Here there were sandy beaches to give their glider a soft landing and good ocean winds to help it fly.

Orville Wright lived to see many improvements made to the airplane.

Their glider was successful, but the brothers were not satisfied. They must build a better one. They built a second and then a third glider. The third flew more than 600 feet. They tried their third glider repeatedly until they had made almost one thousand flights. This was the best glider any man had ever made.

Now they were ready to build something even better! This time it would not be a glider. It would be a plane run with an engine. Men had been successful in building gliders before the Wright brothers, but no one had ever been successful in building a plane run by an engine. This kind of plane is called an airplane.

By that time, gasoline engines were already being built for cars, but they were not light enough to be carried by a plane. The brothers had to build their own light gasoline engine. They also had to build special propellers for their plane.

Their first airplane took almost a year to build. On December 17, 1903, the brothers were ready to test it. Orville warmed up the engine. The airplane started forward, slowly lifting itself into the air. That first airplane ride lasted twelve seconds. Orville had flown 120 feet.

The brothers made two more flights during that same day. Wilbur made the third flight. It lasted 59 seconds. He flew 852 feet!

These three flights were the first to be controlled by a man using an engine. It was a tremendous step forward for the progress of America. Wouldn't you think that all the newspaper reporters of America would have been eager to write the story of the Wright brothers' flight? The next day, only a very few newspapers in our whole nation carried the story. Why? They just could not believe that man could really fly! They thought the story was a joke.

The Wright brothers would not give up. They continued their work on the airplane and made improvements. By 1908, people finally became interested in the airplane.

Although Wilbur died in 1912, Orville lived until 1948. During his life, he had seen great improvements that other men had made on the airplane. By the time of Orville's death, large airline companies had been formed. Some men were even begin-

Robert Goddard with one of his rockets

ning to talk about flying to the moon. Most Americans at that time said flying to the moon was a silly joke. What do you think Orville Wright thought about such a flight?

Robert H. Goddard and the Rocket

Even when **Robert Goddard** was a boy, he dreamed of one day sending an object high into space. At that time, men were having enough trouble experimenting with an airplane. To most people then, the idea of an airplane was foolish enough. The thought of sending a rocket into outer space seemed ridiculous.

When Robert was a boy, people laughed at his dream, but when he graduated from college, Robert began work on making his dream come true. People continually made cruel jokes about his efforts. Although he was hurt by these jokes, he would not give up his experiments.

He began work on a rocket that would burn liquid fuel. He used a combination of gasoline and liquid oxygen. This was a new idea. Liquid oxygen is highly explosive and very dangerous. Goddard and his workers were very careful.

In 1926, <u>Goddard launched the first successful liquid-fuel rocket ever built</u>. In the following years, he built bigger and better rockets. For many years to come, people would not realize the importance of his work. Goddard himself realized he probably would never live long enough to build a rocket big and fine enough to fly to the moon. It often took years of work to make one improvement on the rocket. Goddard realized there were many improvements to be made.

Goddard must have realized that other scientists would follow in his steps, as indeed they did. As a result, we have seen not only rockets but also astronauts sent to the moon.

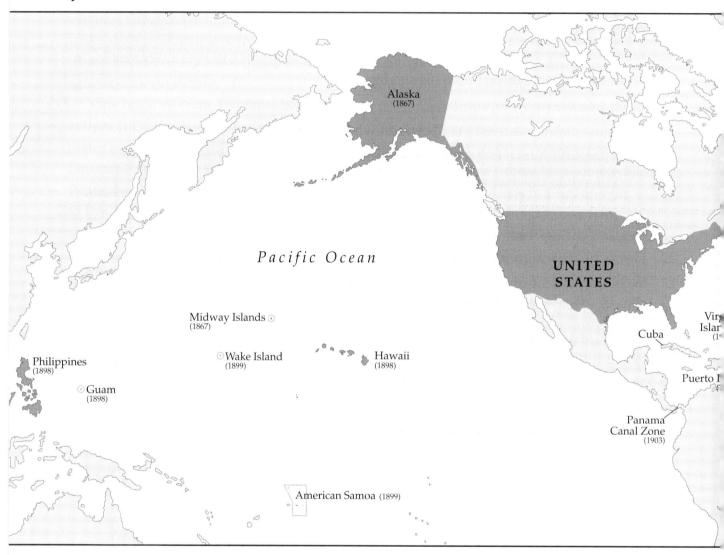

Beyond Our Borders

Alaska
(1867)

Pacific Ocean

UNITED
STATES

Midway Islands ⊙
(1867)

⊙ Wake Island
(1899)

Hawaii
(1898)

Philippines
(1898)

⊙ Guam
(1898)

American Samoa (1899)

Cuba

Vir
Islar
(1

Puerto I

Panama
Canal Zone
(1903)

TIME LINE OF IMPORTANT DATES

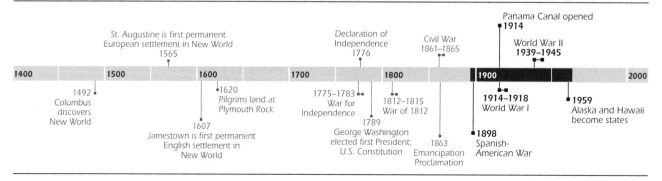

Panama Canal opened
■ 1914

St. Augustine is first permanent
European settlement in New World
1565

Declaration of
Independence
1776

Civil War
1861–1865

World War II
1939–1945

| 1400 | 1500 | 1600 | 1700 | 1800 | 1900 | 2000 |

1492
Columbus
discovers
New World

■1620
Pilgrims land at
Plymouth Rock

1775–1783
War for
Independence

1812–1815
War of 1812

1914–1918
World War I

■ 1959
Alaska and Hawaii
become states

1607
Jamestown is first permanent
English settlement in
New World

1789
George Washington
elected first President;
U.S. Constitution

1863
Emancipation
Proclamation

■1898
Spanish-
American War

Beyond Our Boundaries

Alaska

Until the end of the Civil War, the United States was interested mostly in its growth from coast to coast. But in the years just after the war, the last frontier would come to an end. What would happen then?

England, France, and Spain were not the only countries to have a part in the history of America. At the time the thirteen colonies won their independence from England, <u>Alaska belonged to Russia</u>. People called it **Russian America.** The Russians were interested in the furs and the fish they could find in Alaska.

In 1867 our country's Secretary of State, **William H. Seward,** received a visitor from the Russian government. During that visit, it became evident that <u>Russia was willing to sell Russian America for $7,200,000</u>.

Most Americans thought of Russian America as a worthless land of ice and snow. "What good would such a land be to

us?" many Americans asked one another. These people had never been to Alaska to see the beauty in its rivers and mountains. In southeast Alaska, there is rich farmland. At that time, no one knew of the great riches in gold and natural resources such as coal and petroleum (oil) that would one day be found there. These riches would make seven million dollars seem a very small price.

Seward urged our government to buy Russian America. He knew the wealth of valuable furs that could be trapped there. The purchase would also open the way for a large and profitable fishing industry. At

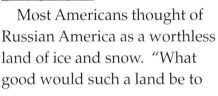
Mount McKinley in Alaska is the highest peak in North America.

last our government accepted the offer. Many Americans made fun of the purchase, calling Russian America "Seward's folly" and **"Seward's icebox."**

The United States changed the name of "Russian America" to Alaska. Fishing and furs soon proved to be very valuable. In 1896, gold was discovered and the Alaskan gold rush began. Alaska soon paid for itself many times. No longer could Americans make fun of the purchase of Alaska.

Alaska did not become a state when it was purchased. It became a **territory** of the United States. Because they lived in a territory, the people of Alaska could not vote in our elections or choose their own governor.

New Words

1. **territory**—an area of land owned by the United States that has not yet become a state; people living there cannot vote in elections or choose their own governor
2. **canal**—man-made waterway

New Names

3. **Russian America**—name for Alaska when Russia owned it
4. **William H. Seward**—Secretary of State who purchased Alaska from Russia for $7,200,000
5. **Seward's icebox**—name given to Alaska by those who thought that Alaska was a worthless frozen land
6. **Captain James Cook**—English explorer who discovered Hawaii
7. *Maine*—United States battleship that was sunk while stationed in Cuba; the event which led to the Spanish-American War
8. **Admiral George Dewey**—American admiral sent to the Philippine Islands to destroy the fleet of Spanish ships stationed there during the Spanish-American War
9. **Theodore Roosevelt**—leader of the Rough Riders during the Spanish-American War; later became President of the United States

Americans who think of Alaska only as a land of ice and snow have never seen Alaska.

oil, and natural gas supply a need for energy. Alaska is also important to the defense of our country. Both navy and air bases were built there to watch constantly and alert our country if an enemy tries to attack.

Hawaii: Our Fiftieth State

The state of Hawaii consists of eight large islands and over 110 smaller islands. The islands get their group name from the largest island, Hawaii. This beautiful group of islands in the Pacific Ocean is more than 2,000 miles away from the coast of California. How then did Hawaii become our fiftieth state? To answer that question, we must go back in time about 200 years.

Instead, the President of the United States appointed a governor for Alaska. The governor could then tell our government what Alaska needed.

Alaska was admitted as our forty-ninth state in 1959. Why did it take so long for Alaska to become a state? You must remember that a great distance separated the United States from Alaska. From the time it was purchased until 1942, there were no roads connecting Alaska to the United States, and the huge land of Canada lay in between.

Today, Alaska is very important to our country. Its natural resources such as coal,

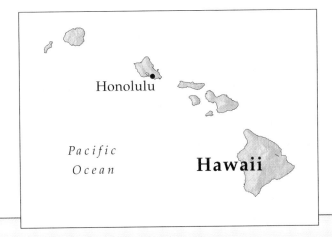

10. **Rough Riders**—group of soldiers led by Theodore Roosevelt which became famous for their part in winning the Battle of San Juan Hill

11. **Colonel William Gorgas**—army doctor who successfully destroyed the disease-carrying mosquitoes in Cuba and in the Panama Canal Zone

New Places

12. **San Juan Hill**—place where the most important land battle of the Spanish-American War was fought

13. **Philippines, Guam, Puerto Rico**—territories the United States received from Spain at the close of the Spanish-American War

14. **Isthmus of Panama**—narrow strip of land which connected North and South America until the Panama Canal was built

New Dates

15. **1867**—United States purchases Alaska from Russia

16. **1898**—Spanish-American War is fought

17. **1914**—Panama Canal is opened

18. **1959**—Alaska and Hawaii enter the Union as the forty-ninth and fiftieth states

Captain James Cook discovered Hawaii in 1778.

The English explorer, **Captain James Cook,** discovered Hawaii in 1778. For the next forty years, English and American explorers, adventurers, trappers, and whalers stopped at the Hawaiian Islands for food and supplies on their way to and from China. These visitors had a deep influence on the Hawaiian people, who had for years been worshiping false gods. Contact with people who believed in the one true God made the Hawaiian people want to find out more about God.

In 1820 Christian missionaries began arriving in the Hawaiian Islands from America. The Hawaiian people were ready for the message of salvation, and many accepted Christ. Many Christian churches and schools were started.

Other Americans came to Hawaii to raise pineapple and sugar cane. They hired islanders to work their fields. Most of the crops were sold to the United States. Soon the islanders began to depend on their trade with the United States.

As the years passed, Americans who were living in Hawaii wanted the islands to

Many people visit the warm, sunny beaches of Hawaii.

become a part of the United States. In 1898, the United States Congress voted to make Hawaii a United States territory like Alaska. Still, like the people of Alaska, the people of Hawaii wanted their land to become a state. However, the United States Congress did not vote to accept Hawaii as our fiftieth state until 1959.

Comprehension Check 16A

1. Who owned Alaska before the United States bought it?

2. What was Alaska called in those days?

3. Who discovered Hawaii?

4. When did the territories of Alaska and Hawaii enter the Union?

The Spanish-American War

You will remember that in the years following Columbus's discovery of America, the Spanish gained control of a large part of the New World. Then other European countries began to build colonies in the New World. As these colonies grew more powerful, they took Spain's colonies away from her.

The island of Cuba is located ninety miles south of Florida. It was one of Spain's last possessions in the New World. Though Spain struggled to keep Cuba, the people of Cuba constantly fought for their independence. In an effort to stop the fighting, the Spanish sometimes treated the Cubans cruelly. In time, the people of the United States grew sympathetic toward the Cubans. It was their wish that the people of all countries could be free and independent as Americans were.

"Remember the **Maine"**

Our government sent the United States battleship *Maine* on a peaceful mission to Cuba to protect Americans living there. All went well until a great explosion sank the *Maine.* Most of her sailors were killed or drowned.

Who blew up the *Maine?* Even today, no one knows the answer to that question. At the time, people of the United States blamed the Spanish. Even though the Spanish said they did not do it, "Remember the *Maine*" became the slogan of many Americans who thought we should go to war with Spain. On April 25, 1898, our government declared war on Spain. The purpose of the Spanish-American War was to set Cuba free from Spain.

Since the only way to get to Cuba from either the United States or Spain was by water, the navies of both countries became very important. When the war began, **Admiral George Dewey** of the United States Navy was sent to the **Philippine Islands.** Although these islands are in the Pacific Ocean, near China, they also belonged to Spain. Admiral Dewey sailed into a bay of the Philippine Islands where a fleet of Spanish ships was docked. There the United States Navy destroyed the Spanish ships without receiving harm to our own ships.

The Rough Riders

Meanwhile, Americans were fighting the Spanish in Cuba and in the seas nearby. **Theodore Roosevelt,** who would one day become President of the United States, led a group of American soldiers known as the **Rough Riders.** The Rough Riders played an important part in winning the most important land battle fought in the Spanish-American War, the Battle of **San Juan Hill.** The entire war lasted only three months. It was the shortest war the United States had ever fought until that time.

The destruction of the battleship *Maine* angered Americans and led to the Spanish-American War.

Teddy Roosevelt and a group of his Rough Riders are shown here with their mascot Josephine (a mountain lion).

Commanding Officers Roosevelt's Rough Riders

Results of the Spanish-American War

As a result of the Spanish-American War, Spain gave Cuba her freedom and the United States received several islands that had previously belonged to Spain: the **Philippines** and **Guam** in the Pacific Ocean and **Puerto Rico,** an island near Cuba. In return, the United States paid Spain twenty million dollars.

During the years after the war, the United States tried to help the people of these islands by building hospitals and schools. Many missionaries from the United States went to the Philippine Islands. Americans helped the people of the Philippines to learn how to govern themselves.

Since then the Philippine Islands have become independent. The people of Puerto Rico and Guam are considered citizens of the United States but also have their own government.

Spain, which once owned a great wealth in American possessions, now owned none. Perhaps the most important result of the war to our country is that other countries now saw us as a "world power," because of our possessions around the globe.

Comprehension Check 16B

1. Which American admiral defeated the Spanish fleet in the Philippines?

2. What was the name of the group of American soldiers led by Theodore Roosevelt?

3. What battle did they fight in?

4. Who won the Spanish-American War?

The Panama Canal

The North American continent is connected to the South American continent by a narrow strip of land called the **Isthmus of Panama.** This thin strip of land is about 480 miles long and from about 30 to 120 miles wide. On one side of Panama is the Pacific Ocean. On the other side is the Atlantic.

Centuries ago when Balboa first discovered the Pacific Ocean, he thought how wonderful it would be if only there were a place for ships to sail through this narrow strip of land from one ocean to another. Instead, ships had to travel thousands of extra miles around South America to cross from one ocean to the other.

As time passed, men talked about building across the narrow strip of land a **canal** or man-made waterway that would connect the two oceans. However, no work was ever begun, because the problems would be too great. Even in the late 1800s, it would have taken millions of dollars to build a canal. Very few countries were willing to risk such a large amount of money, but every country agreed that such a canal would save ships going from ocean to ocean thousands of miles of travel.

In 1878, the French were the first to attempt to build a canal, but they ran into problems and had to stop.

The Spanish-American War made the United States realize how important a canal would be to our country's safety. During the war, a United States battleship was ordered to sail from California to Cuba. The ship began the long trip around the South American continent and finally reached Cuba sixty-eight days later. By then, the war was nearly over. The ship could have arrived in less than half the time if a canal had been built.

Fortunately, the United States won the war anyway. But what if a battleship were urgently needed to go from one ocean to the other in the future? In 1902 the French sold their rights to build a canal to the United States.

Building the canal kept 40,000 people busy. When the Panama Canal opened in 1914, all nations not at war with the United States were allowed to use the canal. Since the United States had bought the right to build this canal, since the United States first had the approval of the people of Panama to build this canal, and since the United States had paid over three hundred million dollars to build this Panama Canal, the United States now had the right to control and protect the canal.

Although the United States controlled the canal, the people of Panama have always regarded the ten-mile piece of land on which the canal is built as part of their country. With the passing of years, the people of Panama grew restless. They began to demand that the United States give the country of Panama more control over the canal. Even though the United States broke no law by building the canal in Panama and had every legal right to keep the canal, the United States graciously agreed to give the canal to Panama.

In 1978, the United States government voted on a treaty. By this treaty or promise, the United States gave the ownership of the Panama Canal to the country of Panama in the year 2000. According to the treaty, the United States will always have the right to defend the canal in case of war or trouble. However, the fact that this important canal was being placed in the hands of a small, weak country might tempt an enemy to take over Panama

Building the Panama Canal was a monumental task.

A large, modern ship is seen here traveling through the Panama Canal.

and thereby gain control of the canal. Many Americans believe that we should have kept the canal to make sure that it remained in safe hands.

Over 13,000 ships use the Panama Canal each year. Each ship, whether it is American or foreign, has to pay a toll to pass through the canal. This toll, figured by the size of the ship, usually amounts to $5,000 or more. If this price sounds high, you must consider not only the cost of building the canal, but also the enormous cost of keeping it repaired and operating. For the country that owns the ship, the toll is much cheaper than the price of sailing a large ship an extra 8,000 miles around the tip of South America.

A ship usually takes about eight hours to travel through the Panama Canal. Compare that with the weeks it would take to sail around South America. The Panama Canal is quite a shortcut! The Panama Canal is truly one of the greatest American building achievements of the 20th century.

★ People Worth Knowing More About ★

Colonel William Gorgas

Colonel William Gorgas

During the Spanish-American War, more men died from malaria and yellow fever than were killed in battle. Panama had the same problems as Cuba—its warm, moist air was an excellent place for mosquitoes carrying malaria and yellow fever to grow.

Colonel William Gorgas, who had been successful in Cuba in <u>destroying the mosquitoes that carried the two diseases</u>, was now sent to Panama, where he was successful again. Gorgas helped to save the lives of both the canal builders and the people who lived in Panama.

Answer the questions on notebook paper.

1. What was Alaska called before the United States purchased it from Russia?
2. Who arranged for the purchase of Alaska by the United States?
3. How much did the United States pay for Alaska?
4. What did those who thought Alaska was a frozen wasteland call the new territory?
5. What happened in 1896 that convinced everyone that Alaska was a valuable territory?
6. How does a territory differ from a state?
7. Why did it take so many years for Alaska to become a state?
8. How far is it from California to Hawaii?
9. Who discovered Hawaii?
10. In what year did both Alaska and Hawaii become states?
11. What island near Florida was fighting to gain its independence from Spain?
12. What happened in 1898 which made Americans angry and which led to the Spanish-American War?
13. Who destroyed the Spanish fleet in the Pacific?
    Where did his great victory take place?
14. Who were the Rough Riders?
    What important battle did they fight in?
15. Who won the Spanish-American War?
    How long did the war last?
16. Which territories did the United States receive as a result of the Spanish-American War?
17. What is a canal?
18. What country was the first to try to build a canal across the Isthmus of Panama?
19. When did the Panama Canal open?
20. In 1978, what did the United States agree to do with the Panama Canal?
21. How did William Gorgas help the men who built the Panama Canal?

Marines raising
the U.S. flag
(World War II)

TIME LINE OF IMPORTANT DATES

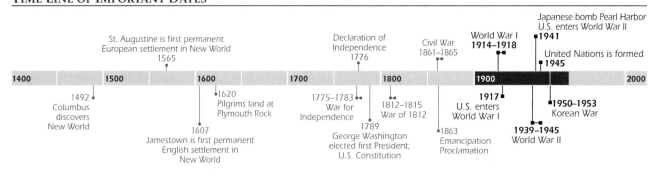

St. Augustine is first permanent
European settlement in New World
1565

Declaration of
Independence
1776

Civil War
1861–1865

World War I
1914–1918

Japanese bomb Pearl Harbor
U.S. enters World War II
1941

United Nations is formed
1945

| 1400 | 1500 | 1600 | 1700 | 1800 | 1900 | 2000 |

1492
Columbus
discovers
New World

1620
Pilgrims land at
Plymouth Rock

1775–1783
War for
Independence

1812–1815
War of 1812

1917
U.S. enters
World War I

1950–1953
Korean War

1607
Jamestown is first permanent
English settlement in
New World

1789
George Washington
elected first President;
U.S. Constitution

1863
Emancipation
Proclamation

1939–1945
World War II

204   *The History of Our United States*

The World Wars

World War I

Civilization had progressed so far by 1900 that many people thought the world could only get better and better. Little did they realize that in Europe the stage was being set for the two greatest wars the world had ever known—**World War I** (1914–1918) and **World War II** (1939–1945).

Both wars began with events in Germany. Many German people had rejected the Bible and embraced the teachings of modernist preachers, who said that Jesus is not God, that the Bible is not always true, and that a person's conscience should be his only guide. Without the true guide of the Bible, the Germans were in great danger of making unwise decisions.

The World Prepares for War

Kaiser Wilhelm II, the ruler of Germany in 1914, wanted Germany to control more land. Although England had the greatest navy in the world, the German ruler wanted to gain control of the seas. With this in mind, he began building up Germany's army and navy.

Other countries became fearful and decided to form alliances against Germany. An **alliance** is a promise between two or more countries to fight together against their enemies in time of war.

The countries that sided against Germany were called the Allied Powers or the **Allies.** Countries that sided with Germany were called the **Central Powers.** The few countries that decided not to take either side were called **neutral nations.**

European countries were preparing themselves for war. The only thing they lacked was an excuse to begin a war. The excuse came on June 28, 1914.

Archduke Francis Ferdinand would one day rule over the country of Austria-Hungary. One day he and his wife were visiting the small country of Bosnia that Austria-Hungary controlled. The control of Bosnia was causing much ill-will between Austria-Hungary and the small country of Serbia, which also wanted to influence Bosnia. As the archduke and his wife rode in an open car, a Serbian teenager shot them to death.

Austria-Hungary blamed Serbia, not just the teenager, for the assassination. Kaiser

The angry youth who murdered Francis Ferdinand and his wife did not know that his actions would plunge the world into war.

Wilhelm II of Germany, eager for an excuse to begin war, promised to help if Austria-Hungary went to war against Serbia. Soon Austria-Hungary did declare war.

Meanwhile, Russia promised to help Serbia. This act angered the Germans, who then declared war on Russia. Because France had promised to help Russia, Germany declared war on France, too.

One by one, the countries of Europe declared war on one another. Soon England declared war on Germany. One English-

Woodrow Wilson was President of the United States during World War I.

man said, "The lamps are going out all over Europe." Indeed, gloomy days were ahead.

For the first three years of the war, **President Woodrow Wilson** kept America neutral. Most Americans agreed that the United States should stay out of the war.

German U-Boats

Germany's powerful army marched into and defeated several European countries. Because England is an island, Germany could not use its army to defeat her. Instead, Kaiser Wilhelm II planned to

New Words

1. **alliance**—a promise between two or more countries to fight together against their enemies in time of war
2. **neutral nations**—countries that decide not to take sides during a war
3. **U-boats**—submarines used by the Germans in World War I
4. **dictator**—person who rules by force and allows his people little or no freedom
5. **Communism**—form of government that takes over a country and claims to own her businesses, homes, and land
6. **Fascist Party**—form of government that controlled Italy after World War I; allowed people to own their own property, but took away their freedoms
7. **National Socialist Party (Nazi Party)**—form of government led by Adolf Hitler in Germany after World War I
8. **atomic bomb**—powerful and destructive bomb used at the end of World War II to bring the war in Japan to a quick end
9. **concentration camps**—German prison camps found at the close of World War II where millions of men, women, and children had been penned up with very little food or had been cruelly massacred
10. **truce**—an agreement to stop fighting

New Names

11. **World War I**—one of the two greatest wars the world has ever known; fought from 1914 to 1918
12. **Kaiser Wilhelm II**—ruler of Germany during World War I
13. **Allies**—countries that sided against Germany in World War I; countries that sided against the Axis Powers in World War II; the most powerful Allies during World War II: Great Britain, Russia, and the United States
14. **Central Powers**—countries that sided with Germany in World War I
15. **Archduke Francis Ferdinand**—man who was shot to death with his wife while visiting Bosnia; their deaths triggered the beginning of World War I
16. **President Woodrow Wilson**—President of the United States during World War I
17. *Lusitania*—English passenger liner sunk by the Germans near the beginning of World War I
18. **Zimmermann Note**—German letter asking Mexico to enter World War I on Germany's side
19. **Veterans Day**—celebrated each year on November 11, the day on which World War I ended; honors all those who have served in the armed forces of our country
20. **League of Nations**—organization that was formed after World War I to try to preserve world peace
21. **"Roaring Twenties"**—name given to the prosperous years in America just before the Great Depression

During World War I, the Germans used U-boats to destroy any ships that might be carrying food or supplies to England.

destroy ships bringing food and supplies to England in order to starve the people of England into giving up.

With this plan in mind, the Germans began to use **U-boats.** These underwater boats or submarines moved unseen through the water and fired torpedoes at enemy ships that could be carrying food or supplies to England.

The Sinking of the Lusitania

In May 1915, an English passenger liner, the *Lusitania*, left New York. As it neared England, a German U-boat fired a torpedo into the side of the *Lusitania* without any

22. **Calvin Coolidge**—first American President to give his inaugural address over the radio
23. **Great Depression**—a hard time in America when banks closed and many people did not have jobs
24. **Joseph Stalin**—Communist dictator of Russia after Lenin; one of the cruelest dictators the world has ever known
25. **Benito Mussolini**—Fascist dictator of Italy
26. **Adolf Hitler**—Nazi dictator of Germany
27. **Emperor Hirohito**—emperor of Japan
28. **Tojo**—military leader of Japan who became more powerful than Hirohito
29. **World War II**—one of the two greatest wars the world has ever known; fought from 1939 to 1945
30. **Franklin D. Roosevelt**—President of the United States during World War II
31. **Axis powers**—Germany, Italy, Japan
32. **V-E Day**—Victory in Europe Day; May 7, 1945—the day Germany surrendered
33. **United Nations**—world organization established after World War II so that the nations of the world could work together to solve their problems
34. **President Harry S. Truman**—man who became President when Franklin D. Roosevelt died
35. **Berlin Wall**—"Wall of Shame" built by the Communists between Communist East Berlin and free West Berlin
36. **Korean War**—war that began when Communist North Korea invaded South Korea

New Places

37. **Geneva, Switzerland**—city where the headquarters for the League of Nations were set up
38. **Soviet Union**—cruel empire formed by the Communist Party near the end of World War I under the leadership of Lenin; threatened to control other countries
39. **Poland**—country where World War II started
40. **Pearl Harbor**—location of an important United States navy base in the Hawaiian Islands; a Japanese air raid on this navy base brought the United States into World War II
41. **Hiroshima** and **Nagasaki**—two Japanese cities on which the atomic bombs were dropped at the close of World War II
42. **Berlin**—German city which was divided after World War II

New Dates

43. **1914–1918**—World War I
44. **1915**—*Lusitania* is sunk
45. **1917**—United States enters World War I
46. **1939–1945**—World War II
47. **December 7, 1941**—Japanese bomb Pearl Harbor
48. **1941**—United States enters World War II
49. **1945**—United States drops two atomic bombs on Japan; Japan surrenders
50. **1950–1953**—Korean War

During the Great Depression, people were thankful for the food they received in soup kitchens and bread lines.

In 1925, **Calvin Coolidge** became the first President to give his inaugural address over the radio. Families gathered around the radio heard the new President talk about America's history and America's future. "Because of what America is and what America has done," President Coolidge said, "a firmer courage, a higher hope, aspires the heart of all humanity." Then he gave Americans a challenge to learn from their history. "We cannot continue these brilliant successes in the future," he said, "unless we continue to learn from the past."

In the 1920s, many Americans could afford to own an **automobile** because of the lower prices made possible by Henry Ford's assembly lines. Families began to go for Sunday afternoon drives and found it easier to visit grandparents and other relatives who lived in different parts of the country. Special highways built for automobile traffic amazed people. How surprised they would have been if they could have looked ahead to see modern highways filled with millions of cars in every size, shape, and color!

Business thrived as factories made many different products. Workers were hired to make even more products. For many Americans, the **"Roaring Twenties"** was a prosperous decade.

The Great Depression

In 1929, hard times came to America. Banks ran out of money. People did not have money to buy things. Factories closed down. Many people lost their jobs.

As weeks turned into months, people began to go hungry. Even though prices had dropped very low, many people still could not afford to buy food, clothing, or factory goods. Some families lost their homes because they could not pay their bills.

These difficult years from 1929 to 1940 became known as the **Great Depression.** Although millions of United States citizens suffered, their spirits were good, and families and individuals worked together to make the best of what they had. Many people who went through these years remember times when all else seemed to fail and God helped in special ways.

Our government under President Franklin Roosevelt worked to end the Great Depression by creating jobs such as building highways, dams, and bridges. Men who worked on these projects were paid by the government, but the government was just as poor as everyone else. Where did the money come from to pay these men? In a risky move, the government began to print and spend more money than it had.

If you were to go into a store and try to spend more money than you had, you'd eventually get into trouble! The government got into trouble, too. Printing too much money was causing the value of the dollar to go down. Though the government helped people temporarily during the Depression, some of the policies caused serious problems that are still with us today.

Sometimes it seemed as though the Great Depression would never end. By the late 1930s, however, things had begun to improve. Men found jobs and earned money to buy food, clothes, and other products. However, only when America went to war again did the last traces of the Great Depression disappear.

Plans for Peace That Failed

Peace-loving countries remembered World War I with horror. The United States, Great Britain, France, Italy, and Japan decided on a plan to reduce or cut back the number of weapons and the size of the armed forces that a country has. They agreed not to build any new battleships for ten years.

After the ten years were over, many countries began to build up their armed forces again. The United States concentrated on being strong enough to defend our country if the need arose. Japan built a huge navy capable of invading her neighbors. Germany also made her army, navy, and air force very strong.

Comprehension Check 17B

1. What are the years of the 1920s called?

2. What did the government do to try to end the Depression?

3. Why was Calvin Coolidge's inaugural address so special?

The World between the Wars

The United States was not the only country to suffer from the Great Depression. The war torn countries of Europe also knew much hunger and poverty as they worked to rebuild their cities.

Having forgotten God, many people of Russia, Germany, and Italy began listening to men who wanted to become more powerful, even if by war. Eager to see better times, many people believed the promises of prosperity that these men made. New forms of government came to power. **Dictators,** people who rule by force and allow their subjects little if any freedom, took control in Russia, Germany, and Italy. In Japan, which had been ruled by an emperor for years, military leaders became increasingly powerful.

By studying the changes in Russia, Italy, Germany, and Japan we can begin to understand why there was another world war.

Russia: Communism. Just before the end of World War I, the Communist Party took control of Russia. Under the leadership of Vladimir [vlăd′ə·mĭr] (Nikolai) Lenin, they built a cruel empire, the **Soviet Union,** that threatened to take control of other countries, too. In a free country such as ours, people can own their own businesses, homes, and land. When **Communism** takes over a country, the government claims to own these things. The people must work for the Communist government or suffer great losses. Although the people in the Soviet Union were allowed to vote, they usually had only one candidate to vote for—the Communist candidate! The Communist Party allowed no freedom of speech, press, or religion.

By 1929, **Joseph Stalin** had become the Communist dictator of the Soviet Union. Stalin was one of the cruelest dictators the world has ever known, eliminating by force and terror anyone who opposed him. He had millions of his own people either

Germany Conquers

By 1939, Hitler's army had taken over Austria and Czechoslovakia. When Hitler demanded that **Poland** give a piece of her land to Germany, Poland refused. Troubled by Hitler's desire to conquer, both England and France warned that if Germany attacked Poland, they would help Poland.

Franklin D. Roosevelt was President during the Great Depression and World War II.

Meanwhile, Hitler and Stalin made a secret agreement to divide Poland once the Germans had conquered it. The Germans then invaded Poland. First, France and Great Britain kept their word and declared war on Germany. Then Canada and other nations did the same. World War II had begun. Soon the Russian army marched into Poland. With two powerful armies attacking Poland, there was little that England and France could do. In less than three weeks, Poland was defeated and divided between her enemies, Germany and the Soviet Union. Another light had been snuffed out in Europe.

In April 1940, Germany attacked and defeated Norway and Denmark. In May, Germany defeated the three small countries of Belgium, The Netherlands, and Luxembourg. Then Germany invaded France and defeated her.

The free countries of the world were alarmed when France fell under German rule. Now, Great Britain was one of the few free countries left in Europe that was not occupied by Germany. Great Britain begged the United States for help.

This airplane factory—producing hundreds of bombers for the war—shows why Roosevelt called America the "great arsenal of democracy."

The United States Builds Its Armed Forces

At that time, **Franklin D. Roosevelt** was President of the United States. The defeat of France shocked the American people, and the country's factories began to make war supplies. The armed forces, though not yet at war, began to strengthen the army, navy, air force, and marines. Many guns and war supplies were sold or loaned to Great Britain and other countries struggling against their enemies. President Roosevelt called the United States "the great arsenal of democracy."

Germany Attacks England

Because England is an island nation, Hitler's armies could not invade the country by land. Instead, the Battle of Britain began. Month after month, German planes dropped bombs on England. Each day, Hitler expected England to give up, but the English people fought hard. England's air force was finally able to beat back the Germans. Though the war was far from over, the United States was relieved. Great Britain had not been conquered.

World War II

Country	Leader	Government	Axis or Allies
United States	Franklin D. Roosevelt	Republic	Allies
Great Britain	Winston Churchill	Constitutional Monarchy	Allies
Italy	Benito Mussolini	Fascism	Axis
Russia	Joseph Stalin	Communism	Axis/Allies
Germany	Adolf Hitler	National Socialism (Nazism)	Axis
Japan	Hirohito / Tojo	Militarism	Axis

Hitler Surprises the Russians

Since both Hitler and Mussolini hated Communism, perhaps you have wondered why Russia was siding with Germany. Do you suppose Communist Russia could trust a dictator who hated Communism?

Even though Germany and the Soviet Union had recently agreed not to invade each other for ten years, Hitler had been planning a surprise attack on the Russians. If Hitler defeated the Soviet Union, he could force the Russians to provide Germany with food and war supplies. England warned the Soviet Union that Germany would turn on her, but the Russians did not listen.

In June 1941, Germany attacked the Soviet Union. Joseph Stalin, Russia's dictator, now turned and asked for help from England and the United States. To keep the Germans from gathering Russian supplies, England agreed to help.

However, it was the cold Russian winter that helped Russia most. It was now December. The German soldiers had no warm winter clothing. Their food froze. Their trucks and tanks froze. Slowly but surely, the Russian army drove the Germans from the Soviet Union.

Three Wars in One

World War II involved more of the world than World War I had. <u>Fighting took place on three continents—Europe, Africa, and Asia.</u> Hitler led the war to conquer Europe; Hitler and Mussolini led the war to conquer and control the riches of Africa; and Japan's military leaders set out to conquer Asia and the islands in the Pacific. Together, <u>Germany, Italy, and Japan</u> became known as the **Axis powers.**

Those countries who struggled against them were called the Allied powers, or **Allies.** At that time, the most powerful Allies were <u>Great Britain and the Soviet Union.</u> <u>The United States</u> would soon join the Allies, and General Dwight D. Eisenhower would become the commander of Allied forces. It soon became clear that all three Axis powers would have to be defeated if World War II was to end.

Comprehension Check 17D

1. The invasion of what country started World War II?

2. Who was President of the United States during World War II?

3. On what three continents was World War II fought?

4. Who made up the Axis powers?

5. Who were the Allies?

The United States Enters the War

An important United States navy base called **Pearl Harbor** is on one of the beautiful Hawaiian islands. Because airplanes had been improved and were used for war as well as peace, it was important that the Hawaiian Islands be protected. If an enemy took control of Hawaii, it would not be long before the West Coast of the United States would be in danger of enemy air attacks.

You will remember that Japan wanted to control Asia and the islands in the Pacific. "The power of the United States Navy must be destroyed," the Japanese military leaders told each other. "If Pearl Harbor is destroyed it would be too hard for the Americans to bring other ships to the Pacific Ocean. Besides," the Japanese boasted, "Americans would rather give up than fight."

To trick the Americans, Japan sent men to Washington, D.C., to talk about making peace. Meanwhile, the Japanese secretly prepared a gigantic air raid on Pearl Harbor.

On Sunday morning, December 7, 1941, nearly 200 Japanese planes took off from aircraft carriers and flew over Pearl Harbor. Taking the Americans by surprise, they quickly destroyed the planes sitting on the airfields and then attacked the eight battleships that made up our Pacific navy. Seven battleships were either sunk or badly damaged. Over 2,000 American men were killed.

Later that day, Americans who were listening to their radios were shocked to hear their programs interrupted by an emergency news report—"Pearl Harbor has been bombed." On December 8, 1941, the

A World War II bombing mission

The United States was totally unprepared for the bombing of Pearl Harbor.

The atomic bomb brought a quick end to World War II.

United States and Canada declared war on Japan. Soon afterward, Germany and Italy declared war on the United States.

Victory Comes at Last

The Allies had before them a gigantic job of defeating three powerful enemies—Italy, Germany, and Japan. Different battles were fought in different places of the world at the same time. American men fought in the Pacific Ocean, China, the Mediterranean Sea, Africa, Europe, and the Atlantic Ocean.

In 1943, after fighting in North Africa, Italy was the first to surrender to the Allies. Next, the Allies focused on Europe. First, they fought to free France. Soon, the Allies began attacking Germany. Germany was finally forced to surrender on May 7, 1945, or V-E Day (Victory in Europe Day).

Japan remained the only enemy for the Allies to defeat. She had learned since Pearl Harbor that Americans were hard, courageous fighters. Although the attack on Pearl Harbor had almost completely destroyed the United States Navy in the Pacific, within a year the navy was ready to do battle again.

The Japanese had suffered much loss during the war, but they refused to surrender. Japan's military leaders seemed to care little about the thousands of Japanese citizens who were being killed in each battle and air raid upon their cities as well as the thousands of soldiers who died fighting for their country. Yet the Allies knew that Japan must surrender if the countries of Asia were to remain free.

The United States had to make a difficult decision. Should the powerful and very destructive **atomic bomb** be used to bring the war in Japan to a quick end? On August 6, 1945, an American bomber dropped an atomic bomb on the Japanese city of Hiroshima. A few days later, another bomb was dropped on Nagasaki. Both cities were destroyed. **Japan quickly surrendered,** and World War II, the largest war in history, ended.

After the war, Allied soldiers found German prison camps (called **concentration camps**) where men, women, and children had been penned up with very little food. In Germany and other lands held by Hitler, millions of Jews as well as many Germans and people of other nationalities had been cruelly massacred.

Again, America had been blessed. No enemies had fought in or destroyed our cities as had happened in other parts of the world. The soldiers of other countries had to return to poor, war-torn countries. American soldiers returned to peaceful homes. Once again, the United States left a war as the most powerful nation in the world.

The war had done much to help unite the American people. Many Americans had fought and died overseas. Women had gone to work in factories to produce weapons and supplies for the soldiers. Everyone wanted to do his part because America was fighting for a good, just cause. Throughout the war years Americans had a spirit of unity and patriotism.

Comprehension Check 17E

1. What event caused the United States to enter World War II?
2. On which continent did the fighting stop first?
3. What do we call the day that the fighting stopped in Europe?
4. What event caused the Japanese to surrender?

The UN meets in these headquarters in New York City.

Continuing World Problems
Dreams of Peace

As World War II was coming to an end, many Americans hoped for a lasting peace. Yet many had hoped for a lasting peace at the close of World War I. What could prevent a third world war?

At the closing of World War I, President Woodrow Wilson had planned a League of Nations where the countries of the world could talk out their problems peaceably. When the League of Nations was formed, however, the people of the United States had not wanted to become a part of it. Many realized that not every country in the world can be trusted, even if it promises to be friendly.

Now President Franklin Roosevelt and other world leaders began to dream of another world organization in which the nations of the world could work together to settle their problems. This organization would be called the **United Nations,** or the UN.

Franklin Roosevelt died before World War II ended. If the President of the United States dies while he is still in office, the Vice President takes his place. Vice President **Harry S. Truman** became our country's next President.

Before President Roosevelt died, he wrote a speech saying that the United Nations could help people by using "scientific" methods. "We must cultivate the science of human relations," he wrote, "the ability of all people, of all kinds, to live together and work together, in the same world, at peace." Science can bring us wonderful things, but peace comes from a kind of understanding that science can never bring. Roosevelt did not understand this, and neither did many people around the world.

In 1945, <u>representatives from fifty nations met in San Francisco, California, and formed the United Nations</u>. Later a building was built for the UN in New York City. Unfortunately <u>the United Nations failed to end wars and bring about world peace</u>. Between 1945 and 1990, over seventy-five wars were fought around the world. Over one billion people became slaves under Communism, and more than forty million people were executed by the Communists. The United Nations was not able to preserve the rights of these people. Many people think it actually helped to spread Communism.

Communism Becomes a Greater Problem

Although World War II defeated Nazism in Germany, Fascism in Italy, and militarism in Japan, it did not defeat Communism in the Soviet Union.

You will remember that Stalin agreed to fight on Germany's side if Germany went to war. Only after the Germans attacked the Soviet Union did the Russians decide to join the Allies. Although the Soviet Union supposedly fought with us to free Europe from Nazi rule, it soon became clear that she meant to control the small, helpless countries in which the Nazis were just defeated, as well as many other countries throughout the world.

The Communists spread their influence from Europe into Asia. Communists took control of China. Once again, the people of freedom-loving countries became fearful.

Berlin Is Divided

<u>After World War II, the German city of Berlin</u> <u>was divided</u>. West Berlin became free and independent, but East Berlin fell under the Communist rule of the Soviet Union. Robbed of their freedom, many people of East Berlin tried to escape to West Berlin. Finally in 1961, <u>the Communists built a wall between the two parts of the city</u>. People who tried to escape over the wall to freedom in West Berlin were shot and killed by Communist soldiers. The **Berlin Wall,** called the "Wall of Shame," became a dark and frightening symbol of Communism. By 1990, the Soviet Union had become so desperate for money and technology from free West Germany that it permitted the "Wall of Shame" to be torn down and allowed East Germany to unite with the rest of Germany.

The Korean War

At the end of World War II, the small Asian country of **Korea** was divided into two parts—the northern half under the Soviet Union's control, and the southern half under the United States' control.

The people of South Korea were allowed to hold elections, and they set up a free republic. In North Korea, the Russians set

The Berlin Wall was a symbol of Communism.

Marines fighting a battle against North Koreans

tries. In 1950, <u>Communist North Korea invaded South Korea</u>. The UN ordered North Korea to stop fighting, but the Communists would not obey. <u>The United Nations sent an army to South Korea</u>. Although <u>men from the United States made up most of this army</u>, fifteen other nations also sent troops to help South Korea. This struggle became known as the **Korean War.**

up a Communist government. The United Nations again failed to protect the rights of these people against Communist invaders.

The Communists had made it clear that they desired to gain control of other coun-

After three years of fighting, a **truce** or <u>agreement to stop fighting</u> was signed. In this agreement, North Korea was to remain under Communist control and South Korea was to be free.

★ ★ ★ ★ **Chapter 17 Checkup** ★ ★ ★ ★

Answer the questions on notebook paper.

1. Who was Germany's leader in 1914?

2. What is an alliance?

3. What happened on June 28, 1914, that caused World War I to begin?

4. Who was the President of the United States during World War I?

5. What is a U-boat?

6. What ship did the Germans sink in 1915, making the American people very angry?

7. What note caused America to enter World War I?
   Why did the note make Americans so angry?

8. Did the Allies or the Central Powers win World War I?
   On what day did World War I end?

9. What was the League of Nations?

10. Name two products that changed the lives and habits of millions of Americans during the 1920s.

11. What is the nickname for the 1920s?

12. When did the Great Depression begin?
    Why did the government create jobs through such projects as building highways, dams, and bridges?
    Was this a wise policy?

13. What is a dictator?

14. What happens when Communism takes over a country?

15. Who was the Communist dictator of Russia?

16. Who was the Fascist dictator of Italy?

17. How are people treated under Fascism?

18. Who was the Nazi dictator of Germany?

19. What three things did Nazism teach?

20. What general built up a powerful military dicatorship in Japan?

21. What country did Germany invade, resulting in the beginning of World War II?

22. What countries did Germany defeat during the first years of the war?

23. Who was the President of the United States during World War II?

24. Name the three continents on which World War II was fought.

25. Name the Axis powers.

26. Name the Allies in World War II.

27. What happened on December 7, 1941?

28. When did the fighting in Europe stop?

29. What did the United States do that caused Japan to surrender?

30. What was formed after World War II to preserve world peace?
    Has it succeeded in that task?

31. What city was divided when the Communists built a wall there?

32. What event in 1950 started the Korean War?

33. Who fought the North Koreans in the Korean War?
    Where did most of the soldiers fighting the North Koreans come from?

34. What is a truce?

35. How long did the Korean War last?

TIME LINE OF IMPORTANT DATES

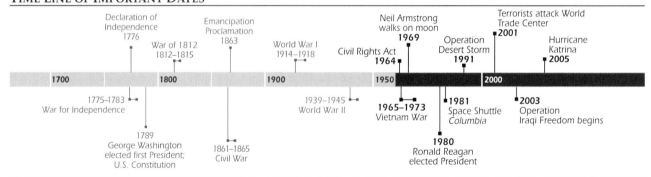

Declaration of
Independence
1776

War of 1812
1812–1815

Emancipation
Proclamation
1863

World War I
1914–1918

Civil Rights Act
1964

Neil Armstrong
walks on moon
1969

Operation
Desert Storm
1991

Terrorists attack World
Trade Center
2001

Hurricane
Katrina
2005

| 1700 | 1800 | 1900 | 1950 | 2000 |

1775–1783
War for Independence

1789
George Washington
elected first President;
U.S. Constitution

1861–1865
Civil War

1939–1945
World War II

1965–1973
Vietnam War

1980
Ronald Reagan
elected President

1981
Space Shuttle
Columbia

2003
Operation
Iraqi Freedom begins

222   *The History of Our United States*

Time for Freedom and Responsibility

By the end of World War II, the United States was the most powerful and prosperous nation in the world. In spite of the difficulties of the war, Americans had continued to work hard. They had improved their lives with new technology, both in the workplace and at home. Using new machines and methods, factories began producing televisions, automatic washers and dryers, dishwashers, and, eventually, microwave ovens and computers. Most Americans could afford the new conveniences. Jet airplanes replaced slower, propeller-driven aircraft. Atomic energy provided cheap and plentiful power. Americans enjoyed more wealth and freedom than any other nation in the world. Yet with this freedom came responsibility.

Freedom and Opportunity for All Americans

But the Lord said unto Samuel, Look not on his countenance, or on the height of his stature…for the Lord seeth not as man seeth; for man looketh on the outward appearance, but the Lord looketh on the heart. – 1 Samuel 16:7

For there is no respect of persons with God.
– Romans 2:11

Many Americans felt responsible to ensure equal freedoms to people of all races. Some minority groups had been treated unjustly because of their skin color or national background. But the years after World War II witnessed the increased participation of people of Asian, African, Latin American, and Native American descent in all aspects of American life. These minority peoples had served their country well during the war by working and fighting for freedom, and now was the time to overcome racial prejudice.

The first group to achieve more opportunities was black Americans who wanted to guarantee a better life for their children under the legal protection of the established government. In the court case known as **Brown v. Board of Education,** the Supreme Court ruled that schools should no longer be segregated—black students should be allowed to attend the same schools as white students.

In 1963, about 200,000 people who wanted civil rights for all Americans met in Washington, D.C. From the steps of the

Lincoln Memorial, **Dr. Martin Luther King, Jr.,** addressed the crowd:

I have a dream that one day this nation will rise up and live out the true meaning of its creed, "We hold these truths to be self-evident, that all men are created equal." . . . I have a dream that my four little children will not be judged by the color of their skin, but by the content of their character.

He believed that all people should live together in freedom, regardless of their skin color. Some Americans continued to show racial prejudice, but Dr. King said, "Don't let anyone pull you so low as to hate them." Sadly, Dr. King was shot and killed in 1968.

Dr. Martin Luther King, Jr., organized a civil rights campaign that spread nationwide.

Because of the efforts of Dr. King and many others, Congress passed the **Civil Rights Act of 1964.** This law <u>promised that *all* races would be able to vote, live, and work wherever they chose</u>.

Black Americans have been successful in every area of American life, including government. **Robert Weaver** became the first black American to be an adviser to the President when Lyndon Johnson appointed him as a cabinet member. President Johnson also nominated **Thurgood Marshall,** who became <u>the first black Supreme Court justice</u>.

New Words

1. **terrorism**—acts of violence intended to terrify people

New Names

2. *Brown v. Board of Education*—case in which the Supreme Court ended segregation in public schools
3. **Dr. Martin Luther King, Jr.**—young black minister who organized a civil rights campaign
4. **Civil Rights Act of 1964**—law that guaranteed voting, housing, and job rights for ethnic minorities
5. **Robert Weaver**—America's first black cabinet member
6. **Thurgood Marshall**—first black-American Supreme Court justice
7. **Senator Daniel Ken Inouye**—first Japanese American to serve in the U.S. Congress
8. **Representative Patsy Takemoto Mink**—first Japanese-American woman to serve in the U.S. Congress
9. **Interstate Highway System**—a project begun by President Eisenhower to build major highways to connect the entire country
10. **Alan B. Shepard, Jr.**—first American to fly in space
11. **John Glenn**—first American to orbit the earth
12. **Neil Armstrong**—first man to walk on the moon
13. **Cold War**—40 year period in which the U.S. and Soviet Union threatened to use atomic weapons against each other
14. **John F. Kennedy**—President of the U.S. during Cuban Missile Crisis; assassinated in Dallas, Texas, in 1963
15. **Fidel Castro**—Communist dictator of Cuba
16. **Cuban Missile Crisis**—a time when the Soviet Union shipped missiles to Cuba; ended when President Kennedy ordered a naval blockade of Cuba
17. **Lyndon B. Johnson**—became President after Kennedy's death; sent American troops to Vietnam
18. **Richard Nixon**—President who withdrew American troops from Vietnam; first President to resign from office
19. **Ronald Reagan**—President who sought to return America to traditional Christian values; known as the Great Communicator
20. **Reagan Doctrine**—belief that Communism should be stopped before it can attack and enslave a country

Americans of other national backgrounds have also held important government positions. Large numbers of Asian Americans came to the United States to escape Communist oppression in their homelands. These Americans have been noted for their willingness to work and to make great sacrifices to give their children a good education. The <u>first Japanese American to serve in the U.S. Congress</u>, **Senator Daniel Ken Inouye,** became one of the most influential senators in Washington, D.C. **Representative Patsy Takemoto Mink** was the <u>first Japanese-American woman to serve in the U.S. Congress</u>. Both she and Senator Inouye represented the state of Hawaii.

Many Spanish-speaking, or Hispanic, Americans have come from Mexico, Puerto Rico, and Cuba. They have achieved much success in American life. Both New Mexico and Florida have had Hispanic governors, and many Hispanic Americans have served in Congress.

Native Americans have also influenced American government. In 1992, Ben Nighthorse Campbell, a Native American from Colorado, won a seat in the U.S. Senate. He voted against harsh environmental laws and for job growth in the mining industry of his state.

Bob Martinez, Hispanic former governor of Florida

21. **Mikhail Gorbachev**—Soviet president who agreed to reduce Soviet weapons strength, to free the enslaved nations of Eastern Europe, and to stop encouraging Communist revolutions throughout the world

22. **Sandra Day O'Connor**—first woman justice appointed to the Supreme Court

23. **John G. Roberts, Jr.**—Chief Justice of the Supreme Court after William Rehnquist

24. **George Bush**—President during Operation Desert Storm

25. **George W. Bush**—President during the September 11 terrorist attacks and Operation Iraqi Freedom

26. **Saddam Hussein**—dictator of Iraq who invaded Kuwait and was suspected of hiding chemical weapons; removed from power during Operation Iraqi Freedom

27. **Operation Desert Storm**—the move to free Kuwait from Saddam Hussein; the shortest war our nation has ever fought

28. **Bill Clinton**—President when acts of terrorism against the United States began to increase

29. **Osama bin Laden**—leader of al Qaeda, the radical Islamic terrorist network responsible for the September 11, 2001, terrorist attacks

30. **"war on terror"**—term used for America's war against terrorists

31. **Operation Iraqi Freedom**—war fought to remove Saddam Hussein from power and to help the Iraqi people build a stable and free government

32. **Hurricane Katrina**—hurricane which hit Alabama, Mississippi, and Louisiana in 2005; devastated the city of New Orleans

New Places

33. **Cuba**—island country 90 miles south of Florida; ruled for years by Communist dictator Fidel Castro

34. **Grenada**—small island that President Reagan helped to free from Communism

35. **Iraq**—country once controlled by dictator Saddam Hussein

36. **Kuwait**—tiny country invaded by Iraq before Operation Desert Storm

New Dates

37. **September 11, 2001**—date of the worst terrorist attack in the United States; known as "9-11"

Some Famous Black Americans

Marian Anderson (1897–1993). Opera singer who became the first black American to sing at the Metropolitan Opera in New York City. In 1961, she was recognized as one of the world's ten most admired women.

Mary McLeod Bethune (1875–1955). Graduate of Moody Bible Institute and an educator who dedicated her life to improving the quality of education for blacks. She was the first black woman to head a federal agency.

Benjamin Oliver Davis, Sr. (c. 1877–1970). First black American to achieve the rank of brigadier general in the army.

Daniel "Chappie" James (1920–1978). Four-star general who, as a combat pilot, played important roles in World War II, the Korean War, and the war in Vietnam. He said he would be glad to fight in three more wars to defend his country.

James Weldon Johnson (1871–1938). Poet and statesman best known for "The Creation" from *God's Trombones,* a collection of black-American sermons in verse.

Jackie Robinson (1919–1972). First black major-league baseball player. He played for the Brooklyn Dodgers from 1947 through 1956, helping his team win six National League pennants.

Ethel Waters (1900–1977). Actress who was very successful on the stage and in films. She was also popular for her performances of gospel songs such as "His Eye Is on the Sparrow."

Phillis Wheatley (c. 1753–1784). Christian poet who became famous in America and England for her *Poems on Various Subjects.*

Daniel Hale Williams (1856–1931). Physician who pioneered in the field of heart surgery. He also established the first interracial hospital in the United States, Providence Hospital in Chicago.

Comprehension Check 18A

1. Give two examples of the new technology Americans enjoyed after World War II.

2. Who gave a famous speech about civil rights and influenced political leaders to pass the 1964 Civil Rights Act?

3. Who was the first black American to become an adviser to a President?

4. Who was the first Japanese American to serve in the U.S. Congress?

Enjoying America's Freedoms

In this time of new inventions and new ideas, America enjoyed faster and more efficient travel. **President Dwight D. Eisenhower** began a project called the **Interstate Highway System.** Major highways, called interstates, would connect all parts of America. To allow people to travel quickly, interstate highways would be wide, straight, and level. They were so wide that an airplane could land on them!

While interstate highways allowed Americans to travel faster on land, the National Aeronautics and Space Administration (NASA) helped American explorers travel

President Dwight D. Eisenhower

first moon landing

the International Space Station

to outer space. In 1958, the year NASA was founded, the United States witnessed the launching of the *Explorer I* satellite. Three years later, NASA <u>sent the first American</u>, **Alan B. Shepard, Jr.,** <u>into space</u>. In 1962, **John Glenn** became the <u>first American to orbit the earth</u>. After much careful planning, NASA succeeded in sending men to the moon in 1969. **Neil Armstrong** was the <u>first man to walk on the surface of the moon</u>.

The United States continued to send men into space. Soon people began talking about building a space station so that astronauts could live for several months in space. Was such a plan possible? When NASA developed the first space shuttle in 1981, it seemed that space travel would become more common. The space shuttle *Columbia* looked like a very large jet airplane and could be used again and again. Space shuttle launches became an exciting part of American life.

In 1986, school children and adults watched the launch of the space shuttle *Challenger* on television. One of the astro-nauts on the crew was <u>Christa McAuliffe, a schoolteacher</u>. Americans were shocked and saddened when the shuttle exploded shortly after takeoff. All seven crew members died in the explosion.

Despite the *Challenger* tragedy, NASA successfully launched many other space shuttle flights. Soon, the space station that was once a dream became a reality. However, Americans were again reminded of the dangers of space travel in 2003. The space shuttle *Columbia* had completed its mission at the space station. Upon reentering the earth's atmosphere, however, the shuttle broke up and burned. All seven crew members on board were killed.

Comprehension Check 18B

1. What project was begun by President Eisenhower to enable Americans to travel more quickly?

2. Who was the first American to travel in space?

3. Who was the first American to orbit the earth?

4. What schoolteacher died in the explosion of the *Challenger?*

5. Which space shuttle tragically broke up and burned when it reentered earth's atmosphere?

Preserving Freedom

In the last half of the 20th century, the United States was committed to helping other nations preserve their freedom. However, the Communist leaders of the <u>Soviet Union wanted to control the world by taking away freedom and spreading Communism</u>. The <u>conflict between the United States and the Soviet Union</u> became known as the **Cold War.** Although their armies did not fight each other, each country threatened to use atomic weapons against the other.

To prevent the spread of Communism to the West, President Eisenhower strengthened the North Atlantic Treaty Organization (NATO), an alliance of several Western European nations, Canada, and the United States. The purpose of NATO was to keep the Soviet Union from conquering free countries.

However, Communism did affect many parts of the world. Like a roaring fire that makes small but dangerous sparks, the Soviet Union sparked Communist "fires" around the world. One "fire" began with the <u>Communist takeover of Cuba in 1959</u>. Because Cuba is so close to Florida, Ameri-

President John F. Kennedy

cans were concerned. **President John F. Kennedy** promised to help Cuban freedom fighters defeat Communism in their country. The freedom fighters planned to invade Cuba at the Bay of Pigs and overthrow <u>Communist dictator</u> **Fidel Castro.** However, President Kennedy changed his mind at the last moment and did not keep his promise to help the Cubans. The failure of the invasion made the United States appear weak to the Communists.

Americans became more fearful when the <u>Soviet Union shipped missiles to Cuba</u>. Since Cuba is <u>only 90 miles from Florida</u>,

these missiles were dangerously close! This time, <u>President Kennedy</u> took a firm stand. He <u>ordered the United States Navy to form a blockade around the island of Cuba</u>, and the **Cuban Missile Crisis** came to an end.

In 1963, about one year after the Cuban Missile Crisis ended, President Kennedy and his wife Jackie visited Dallas, Texas. There, while traveling in a motorcade through downtown Dallas, <u>President Kennedy was shot and killed</u>. The tragedy of President Kennedy's assassination grieved Americans greatly. His Vice President, **Lyndon B. Johnson,** became President.

President Johnson made a major commitment to putting out the "fires" of Communism in the Southeast Asian country of South Vietnam. The <u>United States sent 500,000 troops to protect South Vietnam from the North Vietnamese Communists</u>. The conflict came to be known as the **Vietnam War.** Military leaders urged Congress to allow American forces to invade North Vietnam, but the government would not allow the military to do what was necessary to win. Eventually, **President Richard Nixon** <u>withdrew American troops from South Vietnam</u>.

the Vietnam Memorial in Washington, D.C.

Other troubling events added to the distress of our nation while Nixon was President. Several of his closest advisers were found guilty of criminal charges involving an illegal break-in called the Watergate affair. It became evident that the President had tried to keep the American people from knowing about the incident. When Congress threatened to remove President Nixon from office, he decided to resign. <u>Richard Nixon was the first President ever to resign from office</u>. His Vice President, **Gerald Ford,** became President.

Soon after American troops were removed from South Vietnam, the Communists gained control over all of Vietnam and its neighboring countries, Laos and Cambodia.

President Lyndon B. Johnson

President Richard Nixon

President Gerald Ford

By the end of the 1970s, Communists controlled parts of Asia, Europe, Africa, South America, and Central America. The United States seemed to be losing the Cold War.

Comprehension Check 18C

1. What was the long conflict between the United States and the Soviet Union called?
2. What Communist dictator took control of Cuba in 1959?
3. Which President was shot and killed while traveling in a motorcade in downtown Dallas?
4. Which President withdrew troops from Vietnam?
5. What incident forced President Nixon to resign from office?

A Return to Patriotism and Family Values

As the 1980 Presidential election drew near, Americans felt that something had to be done to strengthen our country. **Ronald Reagan** ran against **President Jimmy Carter,** who was seeking reelection. Reagan told the people that he wanted the country to return to traditional Christian values and end the killing of unborn children. He emphasized the need for America to rebuild its defenses and to take a strong stand against Communism. Because he seemed to say what many Americans felt in their hearts, <u>Reagan became known as the Great Communicator</u>. He easily won the election.

President Reagan restored the strength and confidence of the American military, enabling the nation to exercise peace through

President Jimmy Carter

strength. He believed in <u>stopping Communism before it could attack and enslave a country</u>—an idea that became known as the **Reagan Doctrine.**

In 1983, President Reagan proved that he would take military action to stand up against Communism. He learned that Cuba's Communist dictator Fidel Castro was making plans to spread Communism to Central and South America. Castro first planned to conquer the tiny island of **Grenada** and use it for a military base. When the people of Grenada and other Caribbean islands asked the United States for help, President Reagan agreed to help them. Aided by troops from several neighboring islands, <u>American forces quickly defeated the Cubans and liberated Grenada from Communism</u>.

The Communists' power was weakening. The Soviet Union had spent so much money building weapons and promoting Communism around the world that it had little left to provide basic food, shelter, and clothing for its people. Many people in the Soviet Union became displeased with the Communist system.

In 1987, President Reagan visited <u>Soviet President</u> **Mikhail Gorbachev.** Gorbachev was alarmed by the progress the United States was making in the development of weapons. The American military had invented weapons that the Soviet military could not defeat. In an attempt to save the Soviet Union from complete collapse, Mikhail <u>Gorbachev promised to reduce Soviet weapons strength, to free the enslaved nations of Eastern</u>

President Ronald Reagan with Soviet President Mikhail Gorbachev

Most of the former Soviet republics joined together to form the Commonwealth of Independent States (CIS). Christians in the United States and Europe rushed to get the gospel to the new nations and to help the Christians, who had been persecuted for so long, reach more people for Christ.

Europe, and to stop encouraging Communist revolutions throughout the world. In return, the United States promised to help the Soviet Union rebuild its economy and establish a government with more freedoms.

The Soviet Union continued to collapse. In fact, by the end of 1991, it no longer existed as a nation. Many of the Eastern European republics, which had once been controlled by Communism, had declared their independence from the Soviet Union. The President of the Russian Republic, Boris Yeltsin, declared the Republic of Russia to be an independent nation and took over all Communist Party property. He proclaimed a system of government much like that of the United States and even allowed religious freedom. After more than four decades, the Cold War between the United States and the Soviet Union had finally ended! To some people, it appeared that the war against Communism in the world had been won. Others realized, however, that Communism was still strong in other parts of the world, such as China.

Comprehension Check 18D

1. Which President believed in stopping Communism before it could attack and enslave a country? What was this policy called?

2. What island nation did American forces rescue from a Communist invasion in 1983?

The Supreme Court's Influence

America was founded as a Christian nation. Our Founding Fathers had great respect for God's Word and prayer. Therefore, most American public schools had included Bible reading and prayer in their daily routines. School children also recited the Pledge of Allegiance each day. In 1954, the words "under God" were added to the pledge to show that no nation can remain

The Supreme Court, including Clarence Thomas, John Roberts, Jr., and Samuel Alito.

great without God's blessing. However, in the <u>1960s, the Supreme Court ruled that Bible reading and prayer were illegal in public schools</u>. Many Americans who believed that the Bible should still hold an important place in education started Christian schools around the country.

Since the 1960s, decisions of the Supreme Court and other judges have contributed to the moral decline of America. <u>Justices on the Supreme Court make very important decisions for our country, and they serve for life</u>. When Presidents select poor judges, <u>their decisions bring consequences for years to come</u>. Yet when good judges are selected, Americans can be confident that the principles of justice and freedom with responsibility will bring peace and prosperity. Therefore, when a President has an opportunity to select a new Supreme Court justice, his choice is very important.

When President Reagan was elected in 1980, he told Americans that he wanted courts to honor the principles of the Consti-

tution. After he appointed several justices, the Supreme Court began to interpret the United States Constitution more in agreement with the traditional values of the Founding Fathers. Among the justices President Reagan appointed was **Sandra Day O'Connor,** the <u>first female justice to serve on the high court</u>.

In 1991, Justice Thurgood Marshall announced that he was retiring from the Supreme Court. President George Bush looked for a justice who would abide by the traditional principles of the Constitution. After a difficult process, **Clarence Thomas** was approved by the Senate to replace Justice Marshall. When he was confirmed a justice, Thomas said:

> . . . I'd like to thank America. I'd like to thank this country for the things it stands for and the people for the things that we stand for—our ideals.
>
> . . . I give God thanks for our being able to stand here today, and I give God thanks

for our ability to feel safe, to feel secure, to feel loved.

President George W. Bush (son of President George Bush) appointed two new Supreme Court justices. In 2005, Chief Justice William Rehnquist died, leaving open the highest position on the Supreme Court. President Bush selected **John G. Roberts, Jr.,** to become the new Chief Justice. In the same year, Justice Sandra Day O'Connor resigned. President Bush chose Samuel Alito to fill her seat.

Comprehension Check 18E

1. What words were added to the Pledge of Allegiance in 1954?
2. When did the Supreme Court remove Bible reading and prayer from public schools?
3. Who was the first woman justice ever to serve on the Supreme Court?
4. Whom did President George Bush choose to replace Justice Thurgood Marshall?

Times of Testing

As the 20th century ended and the new millennium began, the courage and patriotism of the American people and the strength of our nation were tested many times.

In the fall of 1990, **Saddam Hussein,** the dictator of **Iraq, invaded the tiny country of Kuwait.** He knew that Kuwait had an abundance of oil, and he wanted it for Iraq. Saddam Hussein was a cruel and evil man, intent on conquering innocent people and stealing their wealth. Early in 1991, **President George Bush** sent the United States military to force Hussein's troops out of Kuwait in compliance with UN resolutions. Under the brilliant direction of General Colin Powell and General Norman Schwarzkopf, Kuwait was liberated in just a few days. **Operation Desert Storm** was a great triumph for the American military and the cause of freedom. The whole conflict lasted only 2½ months, making it the shortest war our nation has ever fought. However, it proved to be only the beginning of a long struggle against the tyrant Saddam Hussein.

President George Bush

Colin Powell and Norman Schwarzkopf

Even after his troops were pushed out of Kuwait, most of the world suspected that he was building weapons of mass destruction. Since he was bitter about being forced out of Kuwait, many were concerned that Saddam Hussein might supply Muslim terrorists with chemical or nuclear weapons to use against America.

During the eight years that **Bill Clinton** was President, several acts of **terrorism** were committed within the United States. In 1993, a bomb exploded at the World Trade Center in New York City killing 6 people and injuring over 1,000. Five Muslim terrorists were found guilty of the crime. In 1995, a bomb exploded outside the federal building in downtown Oklahoma City. The bomb, planted by American terrorist Timothy McVeigh, killed 168 people, including 19 children. Later, Muslim terrorists who wanted to see America weakened attacked the American embassies in Tanzania and Kenya.

The worst terrorist attack the United States has ever experienced occurred during **George W. Bush's** first year as President. On **September 11, 2001,** or **"9-11"** as it is remembered, terrorists hijacked several passenger airliners. They used two of the hijacked airplanes to attack the World Trade Center in New York and another to hit the Pentagon in Washington, D.C. A fourth airplane crashed in a field in Pennsylvania. Approximately 3,000 people died in the attacks. Millions of heartbroken Americans felt a renewed sense of patriotism as President Bush addressed the nation on that fateful day:

> Freedom itself was attacked this morning by a faceless coward, and freedom will be defended.

It soon became known that **Osama bin Laden** and his radical Islamic terrorist network, al Qaeda, were responsible for the hijackings.

President Bush declared that America was at war against the terrorists and against any nation that helped them. The first target of the **"war on terror"** was the Taliban, a strict Islamic group that ruled in Afghani-

After September 11, Americans had a renewed sense of patriotism.

President Bill Clinton

President George W. Bush

stan. The Taliban had been known to work with al Qaeda. Therefore, President Bush ordered an invasion of parts of Afghanistan, where hundreds of al Qaeda terrorists were captured and killed. Unfortunately, Osama bin Laden remained in hiding.

Next, America turned her attention to Iraq. Still governed by dictator Saddam Hussein, Iraq was suspected of hiding powerful chemical weapons that could be given to terrorists. President Bush gave Saddam Hussein a deadline to allow proper international authorities to inspect his weapons. Because Hussein did not cooperate, the United States began **Operation Iraqi Freedom** in March 2003. The purpose of Operation Iraqi Freedom was to remove Saddam Hussein from power and to help the Iraqi people build a stable and free government.

In less than a year, Saddam Hussein's government was overthrown and he was

Iraqis voting in a free election

taken prisoner. However, there were many terrorists who did not want Iraq to be a free country. These "insurgents" attacked both American soldiers and the Iraqi people. In spite of the violence, the Iraqi people continued trying to establish a new government. In 2005, they enjoyed their *first free election in 50 years*. After the election, the new Iraqi government held a trial for Saddam Hussein. He was found guilty of the murders of many Iraqi people and was executed. Even after Hussein's execution, American troops remained in Iraq to help the Iraqi people build a democratic republic. President Bush realized that a stable, free government in Iraq would not only benefit the Iraqi people, but would also promote the security of the United States.

Terrorism was not the only test our nation faced during this time. Natural disasters also challenged the courage of the American people. In the late summer of 2004, four hurricanes hit Florida and the Gulf Coast. It was the first time in 118 years that four hurricanes had hit the same state in a single season. Then in 2005, **Hurricane Katrina** hit the shores of Alabama, Mississippi, and Louisiana. The city of <u>New</u>

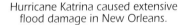
Hurricane Katrina caused extensive flood damage in New Orleans.

Orleans was especially devastated by the hurricane because it lies below sea level. Levees that held back the water gave way, and the city was flooded with up to 20 feet of water in some places. Other cities along the Gulf Coast also experienced terrible damage from winds and flooding. More than 1,300 people died because of Hurricane Katrina, and thousands lost their homes. People from all over the country volunteered time and money to help their fellow Americans recover from this terrible storm.

Comprehension Check 18F

1. What dictator of Iraq invaded Kuwait in 1990?
2. What war was fought to liberate Kuwait?
3. On what day did the worst terrorist attack in American history occur?
4. Who was responsible for the September 11 attacks?
5. What President declared a "war on terror"?
6. What hurricane devastated New Orleans in 2005?

Thankful to Be Americans

As we study American history, we see that we have many things for which to thank God.

We have a land rich in natural resources and a free society in which people can work to earn their own living and to produce food, minerals, timber, and sources of energy for others.

We have people who are constantly inventing better tools, machines, and labor-saving devices. Others are creating new books, music, and art for us to enjoy.

Most importantly, we have a country based on the dream of liberty and justice for all, the belief that all men are created equal and given the rights to life, liberty, and the pursuit of happiness.

We have a representative form of government based on the consent of the governed.

We have free churches that are granted their God-given right to conduct worship services without interference from the government.

America has been greatly blessed by God throughout our history. We have much to be thankful for, yet we know that no country can continue to be great without God's blessing.

We should pray daily that God will continue to bless our country. We should pray for revival and for a return to biblical principles in American families, churches, and government. As Christians, we should do our part to live right lives according to the Bible and to share with other people in America and throughout the world the message of the Bible.

As students in school, we can learn more and more about our country's founding and growth. We can learn about America's great men and women and try to be like them. We can learn to love our country and to do our part to keep America great.

When our country first began, the Pilgrims were thankful, although they had very little by today's standards. How much more thankful we should be for the way God has blessed America! Let us always be thankful and prayerful and willing to do our part to keep America a land abounding with liberty and justice for all.

Answer the questions on notebook paper.

1. What Supreme Court case ended segregation in American public schools?
2. What did the Civil Rights Act of 1964 promise?
3. Who was the first black Supreme Court justice?
4. Which President began the Interstate Highway System?
5. Who was the first man to walk on the moon?
6. What country sought to spread Communism around the world?
7. Why were Americans so concerned when the Soviet Union placed missiles in Cuba?
8. Who became President after President Kennedy was assassinated?
9. Why did President Johnson send American troops to South Vietnam?
10. How did the Vietnam War end?
11. Who was the first U.S. President to resign from office?
12. Which President is remembered as the "Great Communicator"?
13. What is the Reagan Doctrine?
14. Why are Supreme Court justices so influential?
15. Which war is the shortest war the United States has ever fought?
16. What is terrorism?
17. Which buildings were attacked by terrorists on September 11, 2001?
18. What military operation removed Saddam Hussein from power?

A globe is a very accurate way to study the earth because the earth is round. However, a globe is not very easy to keep in your desk or take with you on a long trip. Also, it wouldn't help you at all if you were trying to find where a particular street is in your city or town, or the right road to take to get to another state.

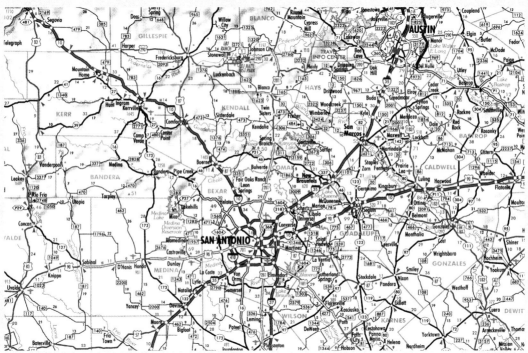

Maps are flat and can be used to show very large areas, or very small detailed areas. Maps can be very large or quite small; they can be folded up and tucked away until needed. We can study different kinds of maps to learn many things.

Maps of the world are not as accurate as globes because maps are flat. The globe is a round ball. Have you ever tried to flatten a round ball? It is impossible to do without badly distorting the ball. And so it is with a map of the world. No matter how we do it, the world is distorted in some way.

Maps of smaller places, like cities, towns, state parks, zoos, etc., *can* be shown accurately.

If you were in an airplane, you would see places from above. Maps are made in much the same way. When you look at a map, you are studying a place as it would be seen from above.

Maps often have small pictures or **symbols** that stand for real things. A **map key** tells you what the symbols on a map mean. *What symbols are used with this map?*

Study the picture and the map below. Can you tell that the map shows the highway interchange from above?

A **compass rose** helps you tell directions. The four main or **cardinal directions** are north (N), south (S), east (E), and west (W). **Intermediate directions** fall halfway between the cardinal directions. The intermediate directions are northeast (NE), northwest (NW), southeast (SE), and southwest (SW). *Use your finger to trace the road that runs east and west.*

Map Key

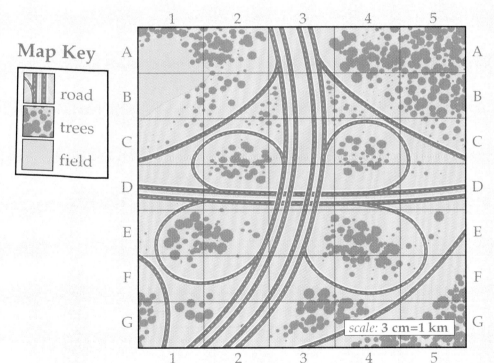

road

trees

field

scale: 3 cm=1 km

A **distance scale** helps us find out how far away from each other things are. We use a small distance to represent a much larger distance. *On the road that runs east and west, about how many kilometers of highway are shown on the map?*

A **grid** has lines that go up and down, and from side to side, forming squares or boxes. We can use these lines and boxes to help us locate places and things on a map. *Are there any roads in grid box A-1?*

1 World Facts

A. World Map Study

Learn to find the locations on the map below.

B. Important Terms

Learn the meanings of the following terms.

★ **Western Hemisphere:**
the half of the world that includes North and South America

★ **Eastern Hemisphere:**
the half of the world that includes Europe, Asia, Africa, and Australia

★ **geography:**
the study of the earth's surface

★ **equator:**
an imaginary line that encircles the earth halfway between the North Pole and the South Pole

C. Important Facts

Learn this information. *See answers below.*

1. The smallest continent
2. The largest continent
3. The second largest continent
4. The continent with only one country
5. The smallest ocean
6. The largest ocean
7. The coldest ocean
8. The warmest ocean
9. The ocean that separates Europe and North America
10. The most heavily traveled ocean

1. Australia 2. Asia 3. Africa 4. Australia 5. Arctic Ocean
6. Pacific Ocean 7. Arctic Ocean 8. Indian Ocean 9. Atlantic Ocean
10. Atlantic Ocean

Continents / Oceans / Equator / Hemispheres

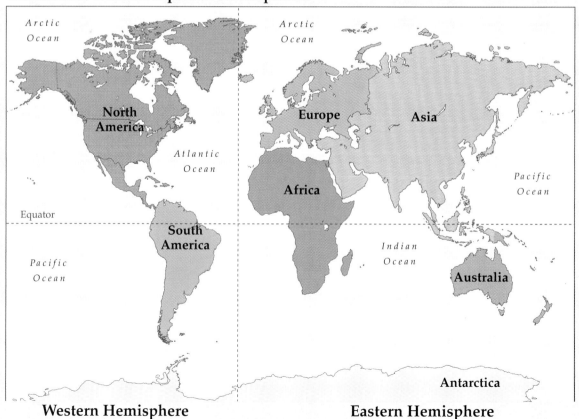

Western Hemisphere   **Eastern Hemisphere**

2 Water & Mountain Ranges

A. Western Hemisphere
Learn to find the locations on the map below.

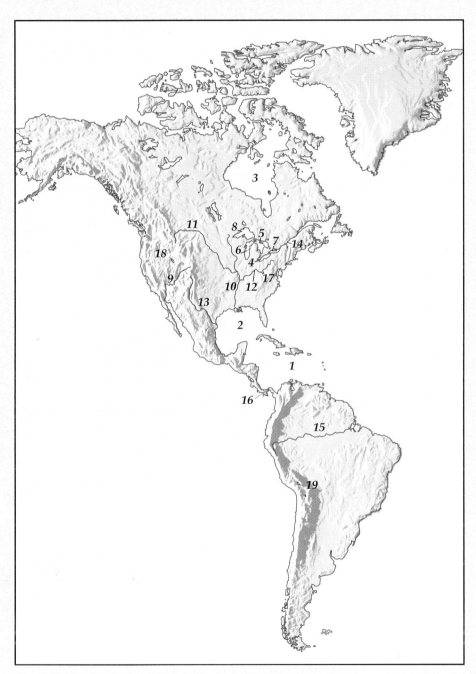

Seas, Bays, Gulfs

North America
1. Caribbean Sea
2. Gulf of Mexico
3. Hudson Bay

Lakes

North America
Great Lakes
4. Lake Erie
5. Lake Huron
6. Lake Michigan
7. Lake Ontario
8. Lake Superior

Rivers

North America
9. *Colorado River*
10. Mississippi River
11. Missouri River
12. Ohio River
13. *Rio Grande*
14. *St. Lawrence River*

South America
15. *Amazon River*

Canal

North America
16. *Panama Canal*

Mountain Ranges

North America
17. Appalachian Mountains
18. Rocky Mountains

South America
19. *Andes Mountains*

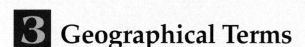

3 Geographical Terms

Learn the meanings of the following geographical terms.

A. ★ **sea:**
a large area of saltwater smaller than an ocean and partly or completely enclosed by land

★ **bay:**
a part of a body of water smaller than a sea and reaching into the land, generally with a wide opening

★ **gulf:**
a part of an ocean or sea which reaches into the land, generally with a narrower opening than a bay

★ **lake:**
an inland body of water (usually fresh)

★ **river:**
a natural flow of water emptying into another body of water

★ **source** (of a river):
the place where a river begins

★ **mouth** (of a river):
the place where the river flows into a larger body of water

★ **delta:**
the land deposited at the mouth of a river

★ **upstream:**
the direction from which a river flows

★ **downstream:**
the direction toward which a river flows

★ **channel:**
a deep, narrow body of water connecting two larger bodies of water; also, the deepest part of a river or harbor

★ **canal:**
a narrow, man-made channel of water that joins other bodies of water

B. ★ **desert:**
a land too dry or too cold to grow many plants

★ **oasis:**
a desert area made fertile by the presence of water

★ **mountain:**
a raised area of the earth's surface that rises somewhat abruptly and is larger than a hill

★ **mountain range:**
a long row of mountains

★ **valley:**
a lowland between hills or mountains

★ **sea level:**
the level of the ocean waters; used as a starting point to measure the height or depth of a location on earth

★ **altitude:**
elevation; height above sea level

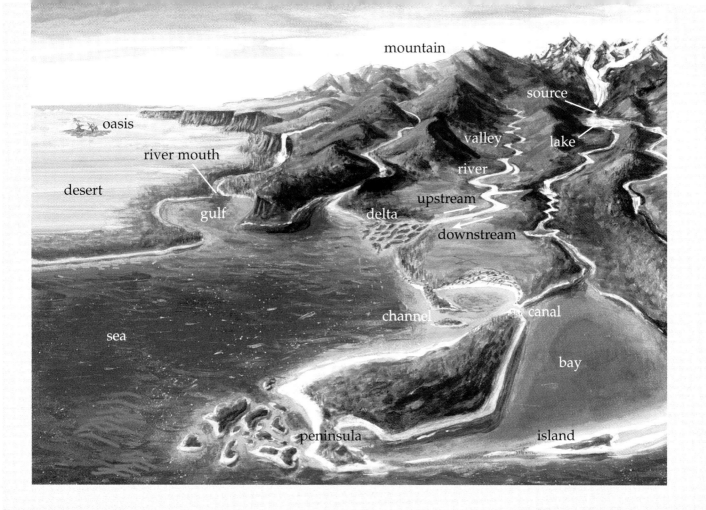

mountain

source

oasis

valley

lake

river mouth

river

desert

upstream

gulf

delta

downstream

sea

channel

canal

bay

peninsula

island

★ ★ ★ ★ ★ ★ Atlas ★ ★ ★ ★ ★ ★ ★

An **atlas** is a book of maps. The maps on the next 6 pages are like a book within a book. As you read and study *The History of Our United States,* you will want to turn to this atlas many times to find out more about the places you are studying. The **index** to the right will help you to find the maps you need. The numbers after the map names tell the pages where the maps can be found.

A **physical map** is a map that shows the land and water areas of the earth and gives their names. A **political map** shows nations, cities, and states as well as some rivers, lakes, and other bodies of water.

Atlas Index

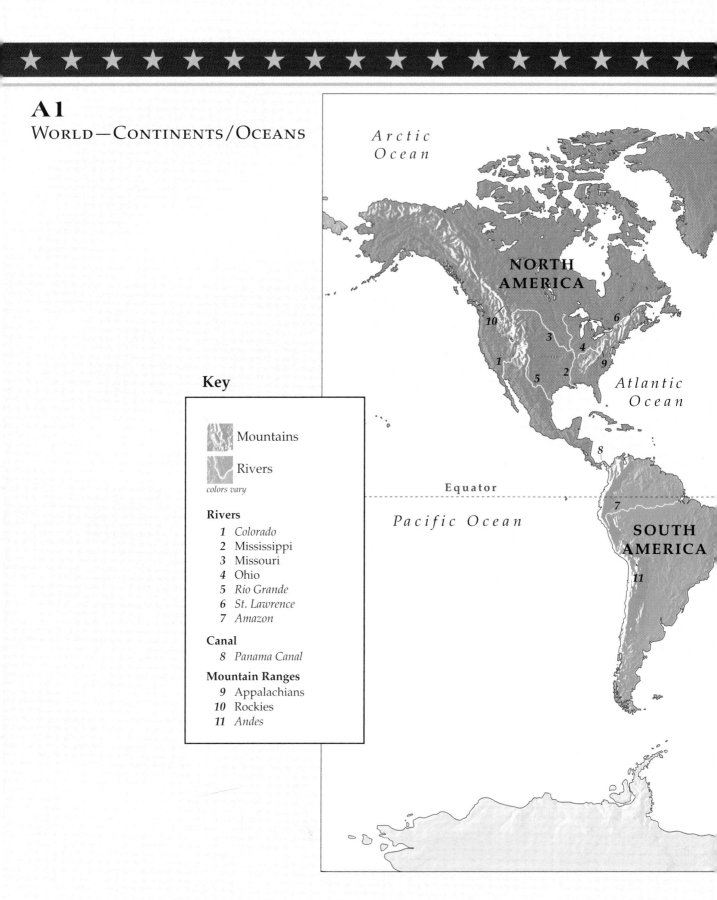

A1
WORLD—CONTINENTS/OCEANS

Arctic Ocean

NORTH AMERICA

Atlantic Ocean

Equator

Pacific Ocean

SOUTH AMERICA

Key

Mountains

Rivers

colors vary

Rivers
1 *Colorado*
2 Mississippi
3 Missouri
4 Ohio
5 *Rio Grande*
6 *St. Lawrence*
7 *Amazon*

Canal
8 *Panama Canal*

Mountain Ranges
9 Appalachians
10 Rockies
11 *Andes*

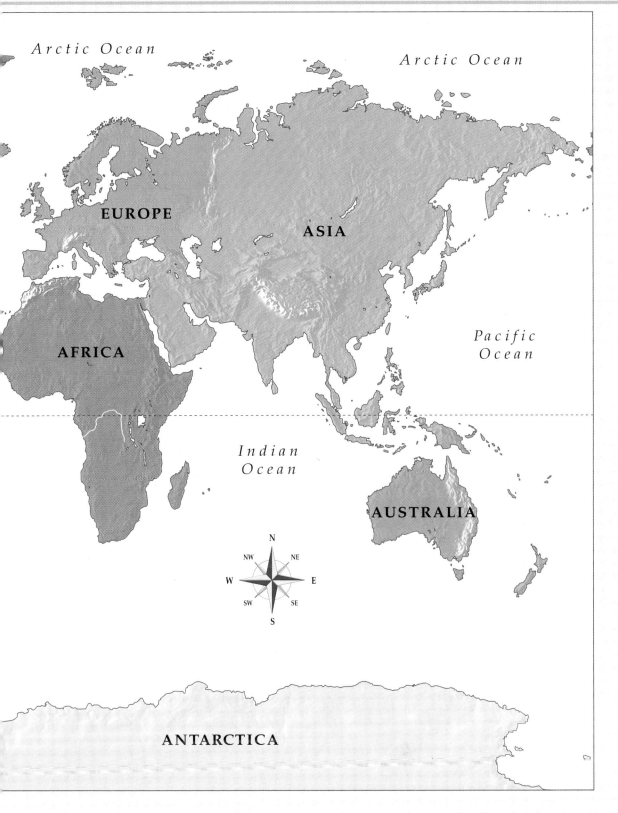

Arctic Ocean

Arctic Ocean

EUROPE

ASIA

Pacific Ocean

AFRICA

Indian Ocean

AUSTRALIA

N
NW NE
W E
SW SE
S

ANTARCTICA

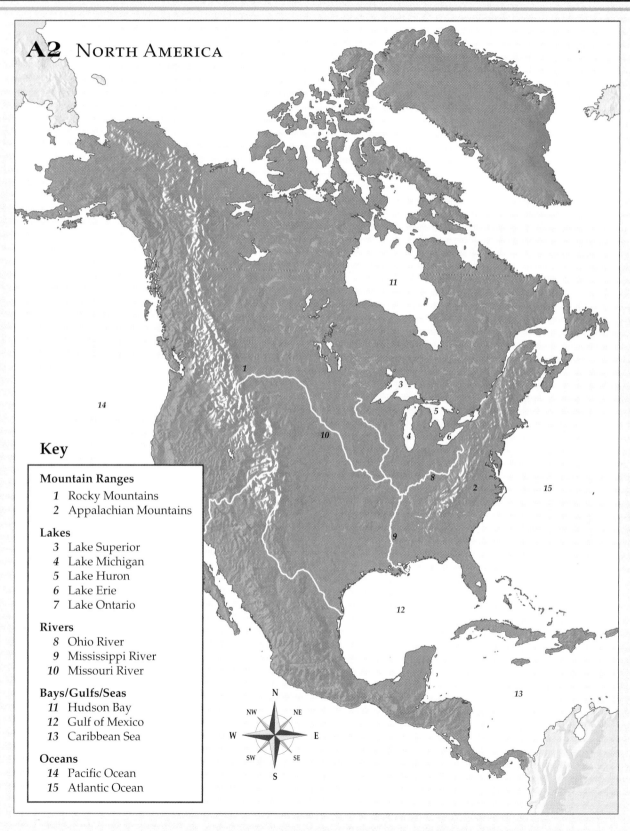

A2 NORTH AMERICA

Key

Mountain Ranges
1 Rocky Mountains
2 Appalachian Mountains

Lakes
3 Lake Superior
4 Lake Michigan
5 Lake Huron
6 Lake Erie
7 Lake Ontario

Rivers
8 Ohio River
9 Mississippi River
10 Missouri River

Bays/Gulfs/Seas
11 Hudson Bay
12 Gulf of Mexico
13 Caribbean Sea

Oceans
14 Pacific Ocean
15 Atlantic Ocean

A3 NORTH AMERICA
COUNTRIES

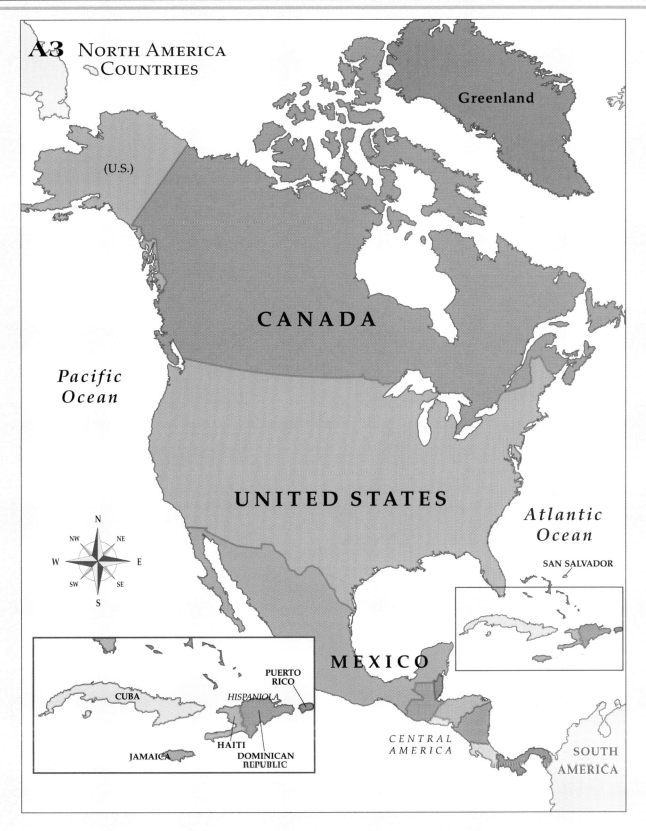

Greenland

(U.S.)

CANADA

Pacific
Ocean

UNITED STATES

Atlantic
Ocean

SAN SALVADOR

N
NW   NE
W   E
SW   SE
S

MEXICO

CENTRAL
AMERICA

SOUTH
AMERICA

CUBA

HISPANIOLA

PUERTO
RICO

HAITI

JAMAICA

DOMINICAN
REPUBLIC

Olympia

Washington

Missouri R

Montana

Helena

Salem

Oregon

Boise

Idaho

Wyoming

Sacramento

Carson City

Nevada

Salt Lake City

Utah

Cheyenne

Denver

Colorado

Colorado River

California

Arizona

Santa Fe

New Mexico

Phoenix

Rio Grande

*Pacific
Ocean*

RUSSIA

CANADA

Honolulu

Hawaii

Alaska

*Pacific
Ocean*

Juneau

Pacific Ocean

M E

Distance Scale

1 inch = about 250 miles

CANADA

Maine
Augusta ◉

North
Dakota
◉ Bismarck

Minnesota

Great Lakes

Michigan

Vermont
◉
Montpelier
New Hampshire
◉ Concord
Massachusetts
Boston ◉

St. Paul ◉
Wisconsin
Lansing
◉

Albany ◉
New York
◉
Rhode Island
Providence
Hartford
Connecticut

◉ Pierre

**South
Dakota**

Madison
◉

Pennsylvania
Harrisburg ◉
◉ Trenton
New Jersey

Iowa
◉
Des Moines

Indiana

Ohio
Columbus
◉

Washington
D.C. ✪
◉ Dover
Delaware
Annapolis
Maryland

◉

Nebraska
Lincoln ◉

Illinois
◉
Springfield

Indianapolis
◉

**West
Virginia**
Charleston
◉

Richmond
◉

Jefferson City
◉
Ohio River
◉ Frankfort

Virginia

Topeka
◉

Kansas

Missouri

Kentucky

**North
Carolina**
◉ Raleigh

Nashville
◉

Oklahoma
◉ Oklahoma
City

Arkansas
◉
Little
Rock

Tennessee

Columbia
◉ **South
Carolina**

Alabama
◉ Atlanta

Georgia

Montgomery
◉

Mississippi River

Texas
Austin ◉

Louisiana
◉ Jackson
Mississippi

Baton Rouge ◉

◉ Tallahassee

*Atlantic
Ocean*

Florida

Gulf of Mexico

BAHAMAS

CUBA

Documents are an important part of the history of our United States. Memorizing these historical documents will help you understand why America has become such a great nation. As you learn each document, you will get a glimpse of the thoughts and ideas of our Founding Fathers and of other patriotic Americans throughout history. You will also learn our fifty states and capitals and the names of our Presidents.

The American's Creed (4 weeks)

I believe in the United States of America as a government of the people, by the people, for the people, whose just powers are derived from the consent of the governed; a democracy in a republic; a sovereign Nation of many sovereign States; a perfect Union, one and inseparable; established upon those principles of freedom, equality, justice, and humanity for which American patriots sacrificed their lives and fortunes.

I therefore believe it is my duty to my country to love it, to support its Constitution, to obey its laws, to respect its flag, and to defend it against all enemies.

from The Declaration of Independence (6 weeks)

In Congress, July 4, 1776

When, in the course of human events, it becomes necessary for one people to dissolve the political bands which have connected them with another, and to assume, among the powers of the earth, the separate and equal station to which the laws of nature and of nature's God entitle them, a decent respect to the opinions of mankind requires that they should declare the causes which impel them to the separation.

We hold these truths to be self-evident:—That all men are created equal; that they are endowed by their Creator with certain unalienable rights; that among these are life, liberty, and the pursuit of happiness. That, to secure these rights, governments are instituted among men, deriving their just powers from the consent of the governed; that, whenever any form of government becomes destructive of these ends, it is the right of the people to alter or to abolish it, and to institute a new government, laying its foundation on such principles, and organizing its powers in such form, as to them shall seem most likely to effect their safety and happiness. Prudence, indeed, will
dictate that governments long established should not be changed for light and transient causes; and, accordingly, all experience hath shown that mankind are more disposed to suffer, while evils are sufferable, than to right themselves by abolishing the forms to which they are accustomed. But, when a long train of abuses and usurpations, pursuing invariably the same object, evinces a design to reduce them under absolute despotism, it is their right, it is their duty, to throw off such government, and to provide new guards for their future security. . . .

Preamble to the Constitution (2 weeks)

We the people of the United States, in order to form a more perfect Union, establish justice, insure domestic tranquillity, provide for the common defense, promote the general welfare, and secure the blessings of liberty to ourselves and our posterity, do ordain and establish this Constitution for the United States of America.

First Amendment to the Constitution *(2 weeks)*
(Article One to the Bill of Rights)

Congress shall make no law respecting an establishment of religion, or prohibiting the free exercise thereof; or abridging the freedom of speech, or of the press; or the right of the people peaceably to assemble, and to petition the government for a redress of grievances.

The Rights of Americans *(2 weeks)*

1. The right to worship God in one's own way
2. The right to free speech and press
3. The right to petition for grievances—in fair and honest judgment
4. The right to privacy in our homes
5. The right to own private property
6. The right to own, keep, and bear arms
7. The right to move about freely at home or abroad
8. The right to habeas corpus—without excessive bail
9. The right to trial by jury—innocent until proven guilty
10. The right to free elections and personal secret ballots
11. The right to the service of government as a protector and referee
12. The right to freedom from arbitrary government regulation and control
13. The right to work in callings and localities of our choice
14. The right to bargain for goods and services in a free market
15. The right to contract about our affairs
16. The right to go into business, compete, and make a profit

Lincoln's Gettysburg Address *(6 weeks)*

Fourscore and seven years ago our fathers brought forth upon this continent a new nation, conceived in liberty, and dedicated to the proposition that all men are created equal.

Now we are engaged in a great civil war, testing whether that nation, or any nation so conceived and so dedicated, can long endure. We are met on a great battlefield of that war. We have come to dedicate a portion of that field as a final resting place for those who here gave their lives that that nation might live. It is altogether fitting and proper that we should do this.

But, in a larger sense, we cannot dedicate—we cannot consecrate—we cannot hallow this ground. The brave men, living and dead, who struggled here, have consecrated it far above our poor power to add or detract. The world will little note nor long remember what we say here, but it can never forget what they did here. It is for us, the living, rather, to be dedicated here to the unfinished work which they who fought here have thus far so nobly advanced. It is rather for us to be here dedicated to the great task remaining before us—that from these honored dead we take increased devotion to that cause for which they gave the last full measure of devotion; that we here highly resolve that these dead shall not have died in vain; that this nation, under God, shall have a new birth of freedom; and that government of the people, by the people, for the people, shall not perish from the earth.

Facts about the States *(6 weeks)*

(Memorize States and Capitals)

State	Capital	Abbreviations*	Date of Admission	Order of Admission
Alabama	Montgomery	Ala., AL	1819	22
Alaska	Juneau	Alaska, AK	1959	49
Arizona	Phoenix	Ariz., AZ	1912	48
Arkansas	Little Rock	Ark., AR	1836	25
California	Sacramento	Calif., CA	1850	31
Colorado	Denver	Colo., CO	1876	38
Connecticut	Hartford	Conn., CT	1788	5
Delaware	Dover	Del., DE	1787	1
Florida	Tallahassee	Fla., FL	1845	27
Georgia	Atlanta	Ga., GA	1788	4
Hawaii	Honolulu	Hawaii, HI	1959	50
Idaho	Boise	Idaho, ID	1890	43
Illinois	Springfield	Ill., IL	1818	21
Indiana	Indianapolis	Ind., IN	1816	19
Iowa	Des Moines	Iowa, IA	1846	29
Kansas	Topeka	Kans., KS	1861	34
Kentucky	Frankfort	Ky., KY	1792	15
Louisiana	Baton Rouge	La., LA	1812	18
Maine	Augusta	Maine, ME	1820	23
Maryland	Annapolis	Md., MD	1788	7
Massachusetts	Boston	Mass., MA	1788	6
Michigan	Lansing	Mich., MI	1837	26
Minnesota	St. Paul	Minn., MN	1858	32
Mississippi	Jackson	Miss., MS	1817	20
Missouri	Jefferson City	Mo., MO	1821	24

*The standard abbreviation is given first. The second abbreviation should be used with ZIP code.

State	Capital	Abbreviations*	Date of Admission	Order of Admission
Montana	Helena	Mont., MT	1889	41
Nebraska	Lincoln	Nebr., NE	1867	37
Nevada	Carson City	Nev., NV	1864	36
New Hampshire	Concord	N.H., NH	1788	9
New Jersey	Trenton	N.J., NJ	1787	3
New Mexico	Santa Fe	N.Mex., NM	1912	47
New York	Albany	N.Y., NY	1788	11
North Carolina	Raleigh	N.C., NC	1789	12
North Dakota	Bismarck	N.Dak., ND	1889	39
Ohio	Columbus	Ohio, OH	1803	17
Oklahoma	Oklahoma City	Okla., OK	1907	46
Oregon	Salem	Oreg., OR	1859	33
Pennsylvania	Harrisburg	Pa., PA	1787	2
Rhode Island	Providence	R.I., RI	1790	13
South Carolina	Columbia	S.C., SC	1788	8
South Dakota	Pierre (pîr)	S.Dak., SD	1889	40
Tennessee	Nashville	Tenn., TN	1796	16
Texas	Austin	Tex., TX	1845	28
Utah	Salt Lake City	Utah, UT	1896	45
Vermont	Montpelier	Vt., VT	1791	14
Virginia	Richmond	Va., VA	1788	10
Washington	Olympia	Wash., WA	1889	42
West Virginia	Charleston	W.Va., WV	1863	35
Wisconsin	Madison	Wis., WI	1848	30
Wyoming	Cheyenne	Wyo., WY	1890	44

*The standard abbreviation is given first. The
 second abbreviation should be used with ZIP code.

Facts about the Presidents *(6 weeks)*
(Memorize Presidents in Order)

No.	Name	Born/ Died	Years in Office	State of Birth	State of Residence When Elected
1	George Washington	1732–1799	1789–1797	Va.	Va.
2	John Adams	1735–1826	1797–1801	Mass.	Mass.
3	Thomas Jefferson	1743–1826	1801–1809	Va.	Va.
4	James Madison	1751–1836	1809–1817	Va.	Va.
5	James Monroe	1758–1831	1817–1825	Va.	Va.
6	John Quincy Adams	1767–1848	1825–1829	Mass.	Mass.
7	Andrew Jackson	1767–1845	1829–1837	S.C.	Tenn.
8	Martin Van Buren	1782–1862	1837–1841	N.Y.	N.Y.
9	William Henry Harrison	1773–1841	1841	Va.	Ohio
10	John Tyler	1790–1862	1841–1845	Va.	Va.
11	James K. Polk	1795–1849	1845–1849	N.C.	Tenn.
12	Zachary Taylor	1784–1850	1849–1850	Va.	La.
13	Millard Fillmore	1800–1874	1850–1853	N.Y.	N.Y.
14	Franklin Pierce	1804–1869	1853–1857	N.H.	N.H.
15	James Buchanan	1791–1868	1857–1861	Pa.	Pa.
16	Abraham Lincoln	1809–1865	1861–1865	Ky.	Ill.
17	Andrew Johnson	1808–1875	1865–1869	N.C.	Tenn.
18	Ulysses S. Grant	1822–1885	1869–1877	Ohio	Ill.
19	Rutherford B. Hayes	1822–1893	1877–1881	Ohio	Ohio
20	James A. Garfield	1831–1881	1881	Ohio	Ohio
21	Chester A. Arthur	1830–1886	1881–1885	Vt.	N.Y.
22	Grover Cleveland	1837–1908	1885–1889	N.J.	N.Y.
23	Benjamin Harrison	1833–1901	1889–1893	Ohio	Ind.
24	Grover Cleveland	1837–1908	1893–1897	N.J.	N.Y.
25	William McKinley	1843–1901	1897–1901	Ohio	Ohio

No.	Name	Born/ Died	Years in Office	State of Birth	State of Residence When Elected
26	**Theodore Roosevelt**	1858–1919	1901–1909	N.Y.	N.Y.
27	**William Howard Taft**	1857–1930	1909–1913	Ohio	Ohio
28	**Woodrow Wilson**	1856–1924	1913–1921	Va.	N.J.
29	**Warren G. Harding**	1865–1923	1921–1923	Ohio	Ohio
30	**Calvin Coolidge**	1872–1933	1923–1929	Vt.	Mass.
31	**Herbert Hoover**	1874–1964	1929–1933	Iowa	Calif.
32	**Franklin D. Roosevelt**	1882–1945	1933–1945	N.Y.	N.Y.
33	**Harry S. Truman**	1884–1972	1945–1953	Mo.	Mo.
34	**Dwight D. Eisenhower**	1890–1969	1953–1961	Tex.	N.Y.
35	**John F. Kennedy**	1917–1963	1961–1963	Mass.	Mass.
36	**Lyndon B. Johnson**	1908–1973	1963–1969	Tex.	Tex.
37	**Richard M. Nixon**	1913–1994	1969–1974	Calif.	N.Y.
38	**Gerald R. Ford**	1913–2006	1974–1977	Nebr.	Mich.
39	**James E. Carter**	1924	1977–1981	Ga.	Ga.
40	**Ronald Reagan**	1911–2004	1981–1989	Ill.	Calif.
41	**George H. W. Bush**	1924	1989–1993	Mass.	Tex.
42	**William J. Clinton**	1946	1993–2001	Ark.	Ark.
43	**George W. Bush**	1946	2001–	Conn.	Tex.

Note: Pictures are indicated by
  p and maps by *m*.

Coronado, Francisco de, 18, 19–20
Cortés, Hernando, 17–18, 17p
Cotton gin, 147–148, 147p
Croatoan, 35, 35p
Crockett, Davy, 132, 139–140
Cuba, 7, 225, 228–229, 228m
Cuban Missile Crisis, 224, 228–229

★ ★ D ★ ★

Da Gama, Vasco, 7, 12, 12p
Dame school, 72, 75–76, 75p
Dare, Virginia, 34–35
Davis, Benjamin Oliver, Sr., 226
Davis, Jefferson, 149–150
Dawes, William, 102, 107
De Soto, Hernando, 18, 20–21, 21p
Declaration of Independence, 102, 109–111, 120, 123, 110p, 111p, 120p
Dewey, Admiral George, 196, 199
Dictator, 132, 139
Discovery, 34, 36
Dock, Christopher, 73, 80, 80p
Dove, 63
Drake, Sir Francis, 18, 21, 21p

★ ★ E ★ ★

Edison, Thomas Alva, 177, 185–187, 185p, 186p
Edwards, Jonathan, 83–85, 83p
Eisenhower, President Dwight D., 226, 226p
Eliot, John, 26, 28
Elizabeth I, Queen of England, 21, 33–34, 21p, 34p
Emancipate, 148, 153
Emancipation Proclamation, 149, 153–154, 153p
Ericson, Leif, 7, 9

★ ★ F ★ ★

Fascism, 212
Ferdinand, King of Spain, 6
Ferdinand, Archduke Francis, 205–206, 205p

Finney, Charles, 176–177
Flag Day, 103, 114
Flatboat, 132, 134
Ford, President Gerald, 229, 229p
Ford, Henry, 177, 187–188, 187p, 188p
Fort Christina, 59
Fort Le Boeuf, 94, 95, 95m
Fort McHenry, 133, 136–137
Fort Sumter, 149, 151, 151p
Fort Ticonderoga, 103, 108–109, 109p
"Forty-niners," 133, 141–142, 141p
Franklin, Benjamin, 87, 110, 122–123, 125–126, 122p
Free states, 148–149
French and Indian War, 93–99, 92p, 95m
Frontier, 132
Fulton, Robert, 176, 181, 181p
Fundamental Orders of Connecticut, 48, 54

★ ★ G ★ ★

Gadsden Purchase, 133, 141, 130m
Geneva, Switzerland, 207, 209
George III, King of England, 101–109
Gettysburg Address, 155, 155p
Gettysburg, Battle of, 149, 154, 156
Ghost towns, 142
Glenn, John, 224, 227
Goddard, Robert, 177, 191, 191p
Godspeed, 34, 36
Gold Rush, 133, 141–142
Gorbachev, Mikhail, 225, 230–231, 231p
Gorgas, William, 197, 202, 202p
Grand Canyon, 19–20, 20p
Grant, General Ulysses S., 149, 154, 156–157, 154p, 157p
Great Awakening, 83–90
Great Depression, 207, 210–211
Greene, General Nathanael, 103, 117
"Green Mountain Boys," 108–109
Grenada, 225, 230
Guam, 197, 200

★ ★ H ★ ★

Hale, Nathan, 102, 113, 113p
Hancock, John, 102, 110
Hartford, CT, 49, 54
Harvard, 73, 76–77, 76p
Haynes, Lemuel, 106
Henry, Patrick, 102, 106, 106p
Hessians, 102, 109
Hirohito, Emperor, 207, 213
Hiroshima, 207, 217
Hitler, Adolf, 207, 212–215, 212p
Holmes, Obadiah, 48, 50
Homespun, 72, 78
Homestead Act, 165, 170–171
Hooker, Thomas, 48, 54, 54p
Hornbook, 72, 75–76, 75p
House-raising, 71–72
Houston, General Sam, 133, 140
Hudson, Henry, 57–58, 57p
Hurricane Katrina, 225, 235–236, 235p
Hussein, Saddam, 225, 233

★ ★ I ★ ★

Immigrants, 175–176, 175p
Inauguration Day, 122, 127
Independence Hall, 121p, 122
Indians (see Native Americans)
Indigo, 58, 65
Industry, 176, 179
Inouye, Daniel Ken, 224–225
Interstate Highway Systems, 224, 226
Iraq, 225, 233–235
Ironclad ships, 148, 152–153
Isabella, Queen of Spain, 6
Isthmus of Panama, 197, 200–202, 201m

★ ★ J ★ ★

James I, King of England, 34, 36, 39
James, General Daniel "Chappie," 226
Jamestown, 35–38, 37p
Jefferson, President Thomas, 110, 135

Johnson, President Andrew, 149, 158
Johnson, James Weldon, 226
Johnson, President Lyndon B., 224, 229, 229p
Jonathon, 48, 53
Jones, John Paul, 103, 116–117, 117p
Judson, Adoniram, 176, 178

★ ★ K ★ ★

Kennedy, President John F., 224, 228–229, 228p
Key, Francis Scott, 132, 136–137, 136p
Khan, 5
King, Dr. Martin Luther, Jr., 223–224, 224p
Kitty Hawk, NC, 177, 189–190, 190p
Korean War, 207, 219–220, 220p
Kuwait, 225, 233–234

★ ★ L ★ ★

Land Ordinance of 1785, 132–133
League of Nations, 206, 209
Lee, General Robert E., 149, 154, 156–157, 154p, 157p
Lenin, Vladimir (Nikolai), 211
Lewis, Captain Meriwether, 132, 135
Lexington and Concord, 103, 107
Liberty Bell, 110, 111p
Liele, George, 176, 178
Lincoln, President Abraham, 148, 150–160, 150p, 153p, 155p, 158p, 159p
London Company, 34, 36
Lord Baltimore (see Calvert, George)
Louisiana Purchase, 132, 135–136, 130m
Loyalists, 102, 106
Lusitania, 206, 207–208

★ ★ M ★ ★

Madison, President James, 122
Maine, 196, 199, 199p
Marshall, Thurgood, 224
Martinez, Bob, 225p
Mason, John, 48, 53
Massachusetts, 35, 40
Massachusetts Bay Colony, 48, 49
Massacre, 102
Massasoit, Chief (see Chief Massasoit)

Matzeliger, Jan Ernst, 177, 192
Mayflower, 34, 40–43, 40p
Mayflower Compact, 35, 41–42, 41p
McAuliffe, Christa, 227
McCormick, Cyrus, 164, 172, 172p
McGuffey, William H., 133, 144
Menlo Park, NJ, 177, 185
Merchant, 34, 36
Merrimac, 149, 152–153
Mexican Cession, 141, 130m
Mexican War, 140–141
Middle Colonies, 57–62, 56m
Militarism, 213
Mink, Patsy Takemoto, 224–225
Minutemen, 102, 106
Mississippi River, 20, 21p
Missouri Compromise, 148, 149–150
Model T Ford, 187–189, 187p, 188p
Monitor, 149, 152–153, 152p
Monroe, President James, 132, 137
Montezuma, 17–18, 17p
Moody, Dwight L., 176–177, 176p
Morgan, Garrett A., 177, 192
Morse code, 176, 183
Morse, Samuel, 177, 182–183, 182p
Mount Vernon, 123, 127, 78p
Mussolini, Benito, 207, 212, 212p

★ ★ N ★ ★

Nagasaki, 207, 217
NASA, 226–227
National Socialist Party (see Nazism)
Native Americans, 7, 17, 25–31, 24–30p, 43–44, 43p, 44p, 88–89, 93–99, 94p, 166–167, 166p, 225
Nazism, 206, 212–213
Neutral nations, 205, 206
New Amsterdam, 57–60
New England Colonies, 47–54, 46m
New England Primer, 73, 76
"New France," 19, 22, 93, 94
New Netherland, 57–60
New Sweden, 58–59
New World, 6, 11, 11m
New York, 57–58, 123
Niña, 6, 7p
Nixon, President Richard M., 224, 229, 229p

Northwest Ordinance of 1787, 132–134
Northwest Territory, 103, 116, 118, 132–133, 130m

★ ★ O ★ ★

O'Connor, Sandra Day, 225, 232
Of Plymouth Plantation, 35, 43
Oglethorpe, James, 58, 66–68, 66p
Oklahoma City bombing, 234
Oklahoma Land Rush, 165, 171, 171p
Old World, 6, 11
Old-field school, 73, 77
Operation Desert Storm, 225, 233–234
Operation Iraqi Freedom, 225, 235
Oregon Territory, 133, 142–143, 130m, 142p
Oxford University, 85

★ ★ P ★ ★

Panama Canal, 200–202, 201p, 201m, 202p
Patriots, 102, 106
Pearl Harbor, Hawaii, 207, 216, 216p
Penn, William, 58, 61, 62, 62p
Philadelphia, 59, 62, 122–123, 62p
Philippines, 197, 200
Pilgrims, 35, 38–44, 33p, 39p, 41p, 44p
Pinta, 6, 7p
Plantations, 58, 65, 65p, 78p
Plymouth, 35, 42
Pocahontas, 37
Poland, 207, 214
Polk, President James K., 133, 140–141
Polo, Marco, 5–6
Ponce de León, 7, 13, 14
Pony Express, 176, 182, 182p
Powell, General Colin, 233, 233p
Proclamation, 148
Promontory Point, UT, 165, 167
Providence, RI, 49, 51
Puerto Rico, 197, 200
Puritans, 48–50

★ ★ Q ★ ★

Quakers, 58, 60–62, 74, 60p
Quebec, 19, 22, 93–94, 98, 32m
Quinnehtukqut, 49, 54

★ ★ Credits ★ ★

Credits are listed left to right, top to bottom on a page; if all pictures on page are from the same source, the credit is listed only once. Any images provided by the publisher are not listed. Map images throughout are from Mountain High Maps®, copyright © 1997 Digital Wisdom, Inc.; they are not listed in the credits below. The following abbreviations are used· CB—Corbis; CC—Corel Corporation; GR—The Granger Collection, New York; PR—Photo Researchers, Inc.

Cover—plane GR, *The First Thanksgiving at Plymouth* by Jennie A. Brownscombe from the collections of the Pilgrim Society; i—GR; iii—CB; iv—CB; 1—flag Jupiterimages; 2—CC; 6-7—GR; 9—bottom GR; 11-13—GR; 17—GR; 20—CB; 21—Bettmann/CB, GR; 22—bottom Photri; 24—Tom McHugh/PR, Jay Pasachoff/Bettmann/CB, Jim Steinberg/PR, GR; 25—Alan G. Nelson/Earth Scenes, Arnold J. Kaplan/Photri; 26—Bettmann/CB; 27-28—GR; 29—Bettmann/CB; 30—GR, UPI/Bettmann/CB; 33-35—GR; 37—Bettmann/CB, GR; 39-40—GR; 41—Photri; 43—Bettmann/CB; 44—*The First Thanksgiving at Plymouth* by Jennie A. Brownscombe from the collections of the Pilgrim Society; 47—Michael Gadomiski/Earth Scenes; 48—Bettmann/CB, Photo courtesy of Consultwebs.com; 49—GR; 51—Bettmann/CB; 52—GR; 54—GR; 57-58—GR; 59—Chromosohm-Joe Sohm/PR; 60—GR; 62—GR; 64—Stock Montage; 65—Bettmann/CB; 66-67—GR; 70—Photri, top right Tetra Images/Robertstock; 71—GR, Photri; 72—Jeff Greenberg/PR; 73—GR; 74—Bettmann/CB, Jim Mayhew/Bettmann/CB; 75—Van Bucher/PR, Bettmann/CB except bottom; 76—Bettmann/CB; 78—Photri, Nancy Rotenberg/Earth Scenes; 79—John Singleton Copley, American, 1738-1815, *Paul Revere,* 1768, Oil on canvas, 89.22 x 72.39 cm (35 ⅛ x 28 ½ in.), Museum of Fine Arts, Boston, Gift of Joseph W. Revere, William B. Revere, and Edward H. R. Revere, 30.781, bottom Photri; 80—courtesy Christopher Dock Mennonite High School; 82-83—GR; 85—Bettmann/CB; 86—GR; 88—GR; 90—GR; 92-93—GR; 94—Culver Pictures; 96-97—GR; 100—courtesy Board of Selectmen/Abbot Hall, Marblehead, Massachusetts; 102—GR; 104—Bettmann/CB; 106—GR; 107—Charles Hoffbauer/courtesy of New England Financial A MetLife Company, GR; 108-109—GR; 110—*Signing of the Declaration of Independence* is located in the Rotunda

of the United States Capitol/courtesy Architect of the Capitol; 111—GR, Photri; 112—GR; 113—Bettmann/CB; 114—GR, Bettmann/CB; 115—*Surrender of the General Burgoyne* is located in the Rotunda of the United States Capitol/courtesy Architect of the Capitol, GR; 116—GR; 117—Bettmann/CB; 120-121—CC; 122—GR; 124—GR; 126-127—GR; 128—GR, NASA; 131—George Caleb Bingham, *Daniel Boone Escorting Settlers through the Cumberland Gap,* 1851-52. Oil on canvas, 36 ½ x 50 ¼". Mildred Lane Kemper Art Museum, Washington University in St. Louis. Gift of Nathaniel Phillips, 1890.; 134—GR; 136—Photri; 138—GR; 139—Photri; 140—GR, Garry McMichael/PR; 141—Photri; 142—GR; 144—GR; 146—CC; 147—GR; 149—GR; 150—bottom CB; 151—Photri; 152—courtesy Chicago History Museum; 153—GR; 154—CB, GR; 155—Photri; 157—Tom Lovell/National Geographic Image Collection; 158—GR; 162-163—GR; 164—Tommy Thompson/Two Tree, Inc.; 165—Photri; 166-167—GR; 168—GR, Bettmann/CB; 169—GR; 170—Bettmann/CB; 171-172—GR; 174—GR; 175—Unocal, GR; 176—Moody Bible Institute; 177—Brown Brothers; 179—GR; 180—Photri; 181—GR; 182—Bettmann/CB, GR; 184-186—GR; 187—Brown Brothers; 188—Bettmann/CB; 189-190—GR; 191—Photri; 195—John Buitenkant/PR; 197—top CC; 198—GR, CC; 199—Photri; 200—Culver Pictures; 201—bottom Photri; 202—Will & Deni McIntyre/PR, Brown Brothers; 204—CB; 205—Bettmann/CB; 206—GR; 207—CB; 208—Photri; 209—Bettmann/CB; 210—SuperStock; 212—GR, CB; 214—GR, CB; 216—Photri, GR; 217-218—CB; 219—UPI/Bettmann/CB; 220—Photri; 222—NASA; 224—Photri; 225—courtesy Bob Martinez; 226—Bettmann/CB; 227—NASA; 228—top courtesy John F. Kennedy Presidential Library and Museum; 229—Photri, Yoichi R. Okamoto/LBJ Library, Getty Images, courtesy Gerald R. Ford Library; 330—Jimmy Carter Library; 231—UPI/Bettmann/CB, Steven Chenn/CB; 232—Steve Petteway/Collection, The Supreme Court Historical Society; 233—George H. W. Bush Presidential Library, SSgt. C. Regner/DOD/Photri; 234—Ira Wyman/CB, Eric Draper/White House/Handout/CNP/CB, Reuters/CB; 235—Francoise DeMulder/CB, Photri; 246—Aaron Haupt/PR, ©Texas Department of Transportation; 247—CC.